Women and Minorities
in American Professions

SUNY Series, The New Inequalities
Edited by A. Gary Dworkin

Women and Minorities
in American Professions

Edited by
Joyce Tang
and
Earl Smith

To my friend & colleague, best wishes — and good luck in your new position.

Love,
Earl

STATE UNIVERSITY OF NEW YORK PRESS

Published by
State University of New York Press, Albany

For information, address State University of New York Press,
State University Plaza, Albany, N.Y., 12246

Production by Cathleen Collins
Marketing by Theresa Abad Swierzowski

The following publishers have generously given permission to reprint the following
quotations from copyrighted works. From "Keeping Comparisons Comparable" by
Joan Norman Scott, which first appeared in *California Lawyer*, January 1992, © 1992
California Lawyer. From "A Woman's Chance for Law Partnership," by Joan N.
Scott in *Sociology and Social Research*, January 1987, *71*, 2, © 1987 University of
Southern California.

Library of Congress Cataloging in Publication Data

Women and minorities in American professions / edited by Joyce Tang
  and Earl Smith.
    p.   cm. — (SUNY series, the new inequalities)
  Includes bibliographical references and index.
    ISBN 0–7914–3105–3 (hc : alk. paper). — ISBN 0–7914–3106–1 (pb :
alk. paper)
    1. Women in the professions—United States. 2. Minorities in the
professions—United States.   I. Tang, Joyce, 1962–   II. Smith,
Earl, 1946–   .   III. Series.
  HD6054.2.U6W65   1966
  331.4′81—dc20   95–49538
                                                            CIP

10 9 8 7 6 5 4 3 2 1

Contents

Foreword

Is the glass half full or half empty? Is the doughnut best described by the size of the hole or the thickness of the pastry? These and similar cliched questions force themselves into one's mind while reading the far-from-cliched chapters in *Women and Minorities in American Professions.* Chief among the many virtues of this book is the authors' and editors' insistence that the world is complicated, that what looks like progress or success from one perspective is stasis or even regression from another. On the one hand, this book could not have been written a generation, or even a decade, ago—there simply were not enough women and minorities in American professions to be worth serious aggregate analysis. On the other hand, white women, African Americans or Asians of both genders, and Latinos and Latinas still face barriers to professional success that range from annoying to daunting.

Let us first celebrate progress. As Joyce Tang and Earl Smith point out, between 1983 and 1993, the proportion of women in the labor force hardly changed, whereas the female proportion of lawyers increased from 15 percent to 23 percent, the female proportion of executives rose from 32 percent to 42 percent, and the female proportion of professors rose from 36 percent to 43 percent. These are huge gains by historical standards. Even during that decade of—to put it mildly—stasis in racial and ethnic civil rights, the proportions of black and Latino/a executives rose substantially.

Sheer numbers are not the only grounds for celebration. Rosemary Wright shows a narrowing of the gendered salary gap in computer work; women earned 83 percent as much as men in 1982 and 90 percent as much in 1989. This too is a gain that may be historically unprecedented. Female social workers are steadily gaining on male social workers in the attainment of administrative positions (see chapter 6), and 11 percent of army officers are now African American—perhaps the only position of high status in

American society in which blacks are represented roughly in proportion to their share of the population (see chapter 7).

One cannot overestimate the importance of these changes. For the first time in American history, one-third of African Americans can be described as middle class by conventional criteria, and increasing professional attainment has spearheaded their extraordinary change in circumstances since the 1960s. Also for the first time in American history, a substantial proportion of women (of any race or ethnicity) can be called members of the middle class on the strength of their own accomplishments rather than as a consequence of who they chose as fathers or husbands. Their changed status is similarly both explained and demonstrated by their growing presence in the professions. What the consequences of these upheavals in ascriptive relations will be for the nation's politics, economics, family life, and culture are, at this point, anybody's guess.

Women and Minorities in American Professions provides grounds for discouragement or even anger as well as cause for celebration. The proportion of African American computer workers and dentists decreased during the decade after 1983, as did the proportion of Hispanic computer workers and social workers. Only 6 percent of African American women in the armed services are officers, compared with 19 percent of white women, and the former begin the effort to climb the officer ranks at a disadvantage because they start in Reserve Officer Training Corps rather than in Officer Candidate School. Female dentists work just as many hours a week as do their male colleagues, but see only two-thirds as many patients and earn only two-thirds as much money, according to Dennis Kaldenberg and his colleagues (see chapter 4). Female lawyers find they need to eschew marriage and children more than do their male counterparts. Unlike their male colleagues, almost no married female lawyers have spouses who contribute to their career by working as homemakers.

We know no more about what the implications of these continued failures will be than we know about the implications of the amazing success stories described above. Middle-class African Americans, for example, are now less convinced of the desirability and attainability of "the American dream" than were their much poorer counterparts thirty years ago. That surprising disjunction between objective improvements in life circumstances and subjective discouragement and embitterment is largely accounted for by the fact that well-off blacks see so much more room for change, and so many remaining barriers to attaining levels of success that they really warrant. (See Hochschild, *Facing Up to the American Dream: Race, Class, and the Soul of the Nation* [Princeton University Press, 1995] for more on this point.) Which will carry the day politically—gratification in light of comparisons with the past, or fury in light of comparisons with white counterparts or with America's broken promises of equal opportunity for all? We cannot say, but this book at least sets the stage for serious social scientific examination of the failure as well as the redemption of the American dream.

One of the great virtues of *Women and Minorities in American Professions* is that it provides us with a rich array of theoretical structures for understanding this complex mix of progress, stasis, and regression. The theories proffered include the numerical phenomenon of sex ratios, the psychological process of socialization, the mismatch between institutional expectations and biological necessities, historical patterns of path dependency, and plain old-fashioned racism or sexism. All are plausible; most find support in one or another professional context; some are refuted by the new data collected and analyzed by the authors of *Women and Minorities in American Professions*. Along the way the authors propose some wonderful new concepts, such as the distinction between minders and grinders on the one hand and finders and keepers on the other, or the "hybrid theory of controlled progress for women in feminizing occupations," or the addition of concrete walls and sticky floors to the well-known architectural feature of glass ceilings.

In short, *Women and Minorities in American Professions* opens intellectual and political doors in the course of showing us which professional doors have and have not been opened to white women and minorities of both sexes. It leaves us, as do all good books, with as many questions as answers. Does any one, or some small subset, of the theories used in various chapters explain all kinds of changes across many professions and various ascriptive groups? That aggregative book remains to be written and perhaps now can be, given new research reported here. Will change in the future resemble trajectories from the past—and if so, which trajectories, the positive or the negative? Or is the main lesson of the past decade that "the future will not be like the past" because the phenomena that changed the status of women and minorities in the 1980s have disappeared or have been transformed by the 1990s? (See chapter 5 for a consideration of this point.) Perhaps most importantly, how can we—politically as well as emotionally—simultaneously celebrate progress and castigate stasis at the same time for the same people in the same situations? Humans seek resolution of ambiguity; the greatest difficulty posed by and the greatest virtue of *Women and Minorities in American Professions* is that it does not allow us either the comfort of self-congratulation or the purity of righteous anger alone.

Jennifer L. Hochschild

1

Introduction

JOYCE TANG AND EARL SMITH

Women and minorities[1] have made significant inroads in traditionally white male-dominated professions in America. But have educated women and minorities been successful in professional occupations? This is the first book to address this question. Drawing on case studies from eight professions, ranging from management to military service, this book asks how, and with what measure of success, women and minorities fare in comparison to men and whites. This collection of interpretative essays reveals a paradox of gender and/or racial convergence in some labor market indicators and divergence in other measures.

Demographic trends suggest that the U.S. workforce will become more diverse in terms of gender and racial composition. Women and minorities have increased their relative and absolute numbers in the U.S. population. Women are already a force to be reckoned with in U.S. labor markets. In 1993, women constituted 51.2 percent of the U.S. population and 45.8 percent of the civilian labor force. Additionally, their strong participation in higher education reflects their increasingly important role in the professional labor force. The proportion of women enrolled for undergraduate and graduate training in the early 1990s was higher than that for men (National Science Foundation [NSF] 1994:2). Compared to women, minorities represented a smaller but significant proportion of the population (20 percent) and workforce (22 percent). Minority enrollment in college (23.1 percent) and advanced education (19.2 percent) is comparable to their proportion in the population (NSF 1994:4). How do educated

Table 1.1. Percent Female, Blacks, and Hispanics in Selected Civilian Professional Occupations, 1983 and 1993

	1983			*1993*		
Total Population	233,792,000			257,927,000*		
Total Employed	100,834,000			119,306,000		
	Female	*Black*	*Hispanic*	*Female*	*Black*	*Hispanic*
Population	51.4*	11.6	7.2	51.2*	11.9*	9.7*
Labor Force	43.7	9.3	5.3	45.8	10.2	7.8
Lawyers	15.3	2.6	0.9	22.9	2.7	2.1
Computer Systems Analysts and Scientists	27.8	6.2	2.7	29.9	5.8	2.4
Dentists	6.7	2.4	1.0	10.5	1.9	3.0
Administrative and Managerial Executives	32.4	4.7	2.8	42.0	6.2	4.5
Social Workers	64.3	18.2	6.3	68.9	21.4	6.0
College and University Teachers	36.3	4.4	1.8	42.5	4.8	3.1

Sources: U.S. Bureau of the Census, *Statistical Abstracts of the United States 1985*, Table No. 29, and *Statistical Abstracts of the United States 1994*, Table No. 637.

Notes: Because of the relatively small proportions of Native Americans and Asians in the labor force, their percentages in each professional occupation are not reported here. All the selected occupations are listed under the "Managerial and Professional Specialty" (U.S. Bureau of the Census 1994). Executive, administrative, and managerial specialties includes public officials and administrators; financial managers; personnel and labor relations managers; purchasing managers; marketing, advertising, and public relations managers; administrators in education and related fields; medical and health managers; property and real estate managers; and management-related occupations.

* Estimated or projected (middle series) figures.

women and minorities fare in the labor market and what does the future hold for these workers? Do professional women and minorities enjoy career opportunities similar to their male and white counterparts? How does gender and/or race affect career processes in different professional settings? The following eight chapters offer answers to these questions by examining gender and/or racial differences in entry, earnings, and access to career advancement opportunities. Taken together, they provide an up-to-date and dynamic account of the fame and fortunes of newcomers—women and minorities—in American professions.

Most research shows that women and minorities have made significant gains in professional training and employment (Coates, Jarratt, and Mahaffie 1990; Jacobs 1995; Pavalko 1988). Because of the growing presence of women and minorities in professional occupations, some scholars have suggested that the progress they have made reflects a decline in the significance of gender and/or race in career advancement in both the private and public sectors (Farley and Allen 1989; Wilson 1978). However, others have contended that the achievements of women and minorities in both academic and business settings have been grossly exaggerated (Bergmann 1986; Collins 1993; Kanter 1973; Reskin and Roos 1990; Sokoloff 1992). One of the principal objectives of this book is to examine the validity of these opposing arguments through the use of case studies. Case studies of specific professions, although in no way representative of the standing or experience of all women and minority professionals, offer us the opportunity (1) to assess the level of progress women and minorities have made in recent decades and (2) to speculate what lies ahead for them in the twenty-first century. Most contributors in this volume rely on quantitative or qualitative data to examine the careers of women and minorities, although some have incorporated both kinds of data in their analyses. Using cross-sectional or trend data gathered from personal interviews and surveys, authors unravel complexities in the process of career advancement for women and minority professionals.

Another goal is to provide an account of the progress of women and minorities in selected white-collar professions. Instead of paying attention to the status of women and minorities relative to men and whites in general or in a particular profession, which has been the focus of other studies,[2] we document their experience in selected professions with varying degrees of representation and success. Because the forces affecting the representation and achievements of women and minorities in one profession might be quite different from those in others, we have selected a number of professions showing a disproportionate concentration or a steady increase of women and/or minorities (U.S. Bureau of the Census 1994). We study the careers of women in several male-dominated professions—law, computer work, and dentistry. We also examine how women and minorities fare in certain female-dominated (e.g., social work) or white male-dominated professions (e.g., management, military service, higher education, and academic medicine).

Additionally, we explore possible explanations for career (in)equities within and across professions, which have received growing attention from sociologists and others who are studying the women and minority experience. By employing comparative and case study approaches, we hope to be able to identify patterns of gender and racial differences *within* and *across* well-paying professions in (1) segregation and discrimination, (2) career paths, and (3) labor market outcomes. As will be seen later, differences in their career experiences and outcomes observed across these selected professions reflect a host of social and institutional factors at work. The 1990s and the coming years will present opportunities as well as obstacles to women and minorities who have professional skills and training. In our view, identifying the forces which exclude women and minorities in professional occupations would have important policy making and theoretical implications. First, social scientists, policy makers, and business leaders would have a clearer idea of what can and should be done to facilitate the entry, retention, and promotion of women and minority workers. Second, the experiences of these workers would tell us the extent to which education and training can improve their career attainment. Third, the empirical findings of women and minorities in selected professions would generate issues for research on work and occupations.

This introductory chapter sets the context for exploring gender and racial differences in American professions. We first briefly define what a profession is. Then we review changes in gender and racial compositions in these professions in the last decade, followed by a summarization of the chapters in this volume. Finally, we discuss the theoretical significance of these findings relative to research on work and occupations.

Although social scientists have used different approaches in understanding professions (Abbott 1988; Wilensky 1964), most would agree a profession has several major elements. These features help set "professionals" apart from "non-professionals," in terms of status, autonomy, and compensation (Freidson 1986; Trice 1993). First, the requirement of an extended period of formal training for a body of knowledge or skills facilitates a monopoly of control. Only those who have acquired this specialized knowledge or skills from established institutions may provide services in the labor market. In addition to formal training, workers in these occupations would form their own associations to promote solidarity and serve members' interests. This is a vital means to secure professional autonomy via collegial control over practice standards. However, a monopoly of control over the claims of exclusive knowledge and entry to the profession is incomplete unless these associations are able to obtain official state recognition. Workers with state licensure, certification, or union status have the exclusive legal right to provide services or perform certain tasks in the labor market. This legal protection helps eliminate potential competitors. Finally, it is not uncommon to find professional associations which have developed a code of ethics for practitioners. Its adoption signifies a strong dedication to their profession and commitment to putting social interests above their own self-interests. All of these help define what professionals ought to be. They are workers with formal knowledge and expertise in an occupation in which peer evaluation is the norm rather than the exception. Unlike other workers, they enjoy the exclusive right to serve their clients. Nonetheless, there is a formal code of conduct to set boundaries on acceptable professional behavior and practice.

Not all the professions featured in this book are truly "free" professions. Law and dentistry may come close to having all the main elements of a professional occupation. Over the years, lawyers have been able to maintain control over their jurisdiction. Dentists also enjoy a high degree of professional autonomy compared to their counterparts in medicine. Entry to law and dentistry is regulated by academic and non-academic requirements. Only licensed lawyers and dentists can practice in the United States. These gatekeeping techniques are so effective that even foreign nationals with similar credentials or experience from abroad cannot practice in the United States unless they satisfy the U.S. licensing requirements.

In contrast, there are fewer restrictions to move into other professions. Experience can substitute for formal education in computer work. Employers can promote an experienced worker without an advanced degree in management[3] to head a division of young, college-educated workers. Degrees in social work are required for some but not all social workers. The military is quite different from other professions in that extensive training is required for all participants. Compared to their counterparts in civilian employment, workers in this "total institution" do not have a high degree of professional independence. On the other hand, the rites of passage into the military may induce a relatively strong sense of professional commitment. Advanced degrees in one's field are usually required for teaching in higher education. Yet, a medical degree is not required for teaching in medical schools. None of these professions in the civilian sector has a monopoly of jurisdiction control. If this is the case, women and minorities should have greater access to these professions than to the legal or dental professions. On the other hand, women and minorities may be more attracted to professions with tighter gatekeeping for social status, autonomy, and earnings.

Two questions are relevant to these discussions: How has women and minority representation in these professions changed since the 1980s, and are there any trends toward gender and/or racial equality in their representation? To answer these questions, we draw from census data. The last

ten years was a decade of change for women and minorities in certain professional occupations. Table 1.1 summarizes the representation of women,
blacks, and Hispanics among lawyers, computer systems analysts and scientists, dentists, administrative and managerial executives, social workers, and
college and university teachers. An optimistic reading of the data in Table
1.1 is that women have improved their participation in all the professions,
especially in law and management. In 1993, women represented 22.9 percent of the "legal eagles," as opposed to 15.3 percent in 1983. During the
same period, the proportion of women in administrative and managerial
professions has increased from 32.4 percent to 42 percent. Also, women
had increased their level of representation in higher education between
1983 and 1993. However, the data mask the fact that women and minorities
in academe tend to concentrate in less prestigious four-year colleges, hold
non-tenure track positions, and are employed at lower ranks (Chamberlain
1988; Jackson 1991). Women have strengthened their dominance in social
work, at least numerically. On the other hand, one can argue that social
work has become more sex-segregated than ever. In 1993, nearly seven out
of every ten social workers were women. Continuous high demand for
social services, due to the aging of our population, suggests that their influence in this profession will remain unabated. Although computer work has
become feminized in recent years, women have made little net gain in
higher-paying positions such as systems analysts. In 1993, less than one-
third of the computer systems analysts and scientists were women.

Of all the selected professions, dentistry has the lowest rate of female
participation, a stark contrast to women's relative representation in social
work, although both professions are highly sex-segregated. Only one out of
every ten dentists in the United States is a woman, although there are more
women than men in the total U.S. population. Given the low level of female
representation in dentistry, the profession is unlikely to see sex desegrega-
tion in the near future.

Compared to their female counterparts, blacks and Hispanics have
made only modest progress in some fields. Blacks remain overrepresented
in social work. They accounted for 21.4 percent of social workers in 1993,
compared to 18.2 percent in 1983. In contrast, the level of Hispanic representation in this field dropped slightly to 6 percent in 1993 from 6.3 percent in 1983. Hispanics' increase in participation in law, management, and
higher education in the last ten years was negligible. Regardless of the
degree of gatekeeping, both blacks and Hispanics are heavily underrepresented in these professions. The trend of economic restructuring and
merger in corporate America suggests shrinkage of the middle management levels. These structural changes may have a greater adverse impact on

minorities than on whites, because of minorities' recent entry into these professions. Meanwhile, the call for diversity in the workforce may lessen the negative impact of "rightsizing" on minorities. Given the current low levels of relative representation in management, it would take blacks and Hispanics some time to reach their parity in this profession, proportionate to their numbers in the U.S. population.

Interestingly, while computer work has become one of the fastest-growing fields, non-Asian minorities' level of participation in computer science and systems analysis has declined slightly. In 1993, blacks and Hispanics constituted 21.6 percent of the U.S. population, but accounted for only 8.2 percent of computer scientists and systems analysts. Their dismal rates of participation in these fields reveal the underlying "pipeline" problem in training rather than the result of gatekeeping.

Do women in private law practice mirror the images—successful, career-minded—portrayed in the television series *LA Law?* Joan Norman Scott's study of lawyers in private practice in Los Angeles reveals mixed results (chapter 2). Her analysis underscores the interplay of sociocultural processes with structural arrangements in shaping the careers of lawyers. Scott found that subjects in the cohort she interviewed have similar professional status. There are as many women as men in the most aggressive area of law practice—litigation. Yet women are not rewarded at the same level as are men. Scott attributes the gender gap in earnings and promotions to gender roles expectation and structural barriers. The roles and positions women occupy in private law practice reflect the influence of larger social forces on their careers. The feminine and supporting roles of women in the family and society spill over to the workplace. Female lawyers in private practice are locked into positions of "minders" or "grinders" with little or no prospect for external business contacts and advancement. This is because, argues Scott, male lawyers, as gatekeepers, still have difficulty seeing their female counterparts occupying such aggressive role as "finders" of business. In addition to family obligations, not being a part of the old boy's network and lack of mentors are the major obstacles to women's advancement in this prestigious male-dominated profession. Fortunately, Scott predicts some positive changes for women lawyers in private practice. For one, a larger proportion of women entering law would inevitably change the structure of the profession. Diversity in the workforce is the key to recruiting and keeping talents. Career tracks with different emphasis on family and career orientations would allow women lawyers to progress according to their needs. In addition to changes on the part of law firms, Scott observes that women are actively seeking changes themselves. To catch up

Table 1.2. Summary of Forces of Exclusion in Professional Occupations

Profession	Women/ Minorities	Forces of Exclusion	
		Socio-cultural	*Institutional/Occupational*
Lawyer (private practice)	Women	1) Gender role expectations • women not perceived as "finders" and "keepers" • men expect women to be more committed to family rather than to careers 2) Family demands • marriage • caring for the sick or the elderly • motherhood	1) Job-specific • long working hours • emphasis on "billable" hours 2) Weak networking 3) Lack of mentors
Computer Work	Women	1) Socialized away from mathematics and science 2) Lack of hardware tinkering experience	1) Male engineering culture
Dentist	Women	1) Gender stereotypes • provider selection • evaluation of competence 2) Family demands	1) Extended career path • begin as dental assistant or dental hygienist
Manager	White Women/ Minorities	1) Bias in performance evaluation • favoritism toward men and whites 2) Assignment to female- or ethnic-oriented markets	
Social worker (administration)	White and African American Women	1) Gender role stereotyping • women as caregivers • men as leaders	1) Patriarchal relations in society and workplace
Military	African American Women and Men	1) Perceived lower cognitive abilities	1) Use of the Armed Forces Qualification Test

Table 1.2. (*continued*)

| Profession | Women/ Minorities | Forces of Exclusion | |
		Socio-cultural	*Institutional/Occupational*
		2) Concentration in Reserve Officer Training Corps (ROTC)	
Higher Education	Native Americans	1) Cultural bias in curriculum	1) Lack of public financial support to tribal colleges
		2) Alienation on mainstream college campus	2) Lack of role models and mentors
			3) Trivialization of research by Native Americans
Medical School (Faculty)	Women and Minorities	1) Lack of mentor and role model	
		2) Inadequate financial and physical resources for research	
		3) Rigid tenure and promotion policies	

with their male counterparts, they have learned how to play the game better by developing and extending their networks.

The small increase in women's representation in computer systems analysis and science between 1983 and 1993, observed in Table 1.1, may reflect the high entry and high exit rates among women. How well do women perform in these male-dominated fields? Are there signs of similar changes in the structure of these professions to facilitate the integration of women? In her chapter on women in computer work (chapter 3), Rosemary Wright notes a narrowing gender gap in earnings among computer workers. Sex segregation in field specialization and work activities has also declined over the years. Wright attributes these developments to the rising numbers of women in computer work. Women have made collective progress in computer work because they gain "strength in numbers." On the other hand, her analysis reveals a disturbing finding—that of high rates of entry into and exit from computer work among women. Many women depart from the field because of growing dissatisfaction with their careers. Wright contends that while women are making progress as a group in this high-paying profession, there is a social control of individual advancement in computer work. Despite their large numbers in computer science fields, women do not fit into the male-oriented, engineering culture of computer work. Women's alienation in computer work is related to their lack of engineering background. Lack of hardware knowledge and tinkering socialization have relegated women to marginal positions in computer work. Wright's research suggests that gender roles socialization can have a lifelong impact on one's career prospects. Even in technical work, where one's gender is least expected to affect work performance, the male, antisocial culture has made female computer workers the outsiders. Instead of changing the engineering culture of computer work, many women in this field choose to change their occupations.

What do we know about women in the dental profession? In addition to offering a historical account on women's role in dentistry in Western cultures, Dennis Kaldenberg, Anisa Zvonkovic, and Boris Becker examine the professional experiences of male and female dentists (chapter 4). Based on the analysis of data provided by the American Dental Association and their own surveys, Kaldenberg et al. found the professional experiences of female dentists to be quite different from those of their male counterparts. Like their female counterparts in law and computer work, women dentists are disadvantaged in this male-dominated profession. For example, female dental school graduates are less likely than male graduates to move directly into private practice. Female dentists working in organizations are confronted with the "glass ceiling." They also remain in salaried or part-time positions for a longer period of time. Like their counterparts in other professions, female dentists experience more career interruptions due to family obligations. After controlling for age, ownership of private practice, and practice setting, female dentists still earn less than their male peers. Pricing differences and patients' preference for male care providers may explain a large part of the gender earnings gap. These gender differences suggest that women in professional occupations are confronted with similar types of problems experienced by women in other occupations. Arguing from the social constructionist perspective, Kaldenberg et al. maintain that gender role expectations affect how male and female dentists structure their careers. Similar to Scott's view of women lawyers, Kaldenberg et al. contend that when women gain a sizable presence in the dental profession, they will transform the male-oriented work culture. Instead of conforming to the typical—male—career pattern, female dentists may be charting new career paths. Dentistry may be one of the few high-paying professions where women would find least conflict between their traditional and professional roles.

After exploring the changing gender contours in law, computer work, and dentistry, the second part of this book considers the experiences of professional women and minorities in private, public, and educational settings. Nancy DiTomaso and Steven Smith chronicle the changes and challenges facing minorities and white women in management (chapter 5). Their chapter offers insights into the predicament of aspiring minorities and white women in corporate America. DiTomaso and Smith argue that although minorities and white women have entered management in great numbers, they are still underrepresented in managerial jobs. So why do these groups still lag behind whites and men in rising to the top? Where do minorities and white women belong in the corporate hierarchy? Have affirmative action policies made a dent in white male dominance in management? DiTomaso and Smith address these questions by first considering the traditional approaches to explaining racial and gender differences in career achievements. Then they discuss bias in performance appraisal as a reason for holding back minorities and white women. Oftentimes, informal practices are more important than formal practices in allocating rewards in bureaucratic structures. And informal practices tend to favor white men over minorities and white women in determining who will be hired and/or who will advance. DiTomaso's and Smith's discussions seriously challenge the notion of meritocracy in distributing rewards. On the issue of "glass ceiling," they state that the gains of minorities and white women in management are concentrated in lower-status positions or slots targeted to minority- or female-oriented-markets. Despite a growing concern over the negative impact of affirmative action on white males, most research shows minorities and women have not come close to challenging white male dominance in the upper echelons of the corporate world. However, implicit in their message is that only minorities and women with good education and skills will continue to thrive in a business culture that values diversity in the workforce.

How did social work evolve into a "female" profession? How do white and minority women measure up with men? Leslie Leighninger's chapter on social work explores these issues (chapter 6), as she underscores the role of white women in the historical development of social work. Ironically, women do not fare as well as men do in this traditionally female profession. Female social workers lag behind their male counterparts in earnings and access to authority positions. Men dominate the administrative positions in social services agencies and in higher education, while women are concentrated in counseling and clinical services jobs. Leighninger attributes male dominance in leadership positions in this "female" profession to gender role stereotyping and an extension of social control in a patriarchal society. Her argument is in line with the contention by Scott, Wright, and Kaldenberg et al. that the male ideology is the dominant occupational culture. The idea that men should be "in charge" and women in supportive positions is prevalent in male- and female-dominated professions. On the other hand, this pattern of sex segregation in social work may imply gender differences in work orientation. Consistent with their traditional roles, female social workers may derive more satisfaction from directly helping others, while their male counterparts are more concerned with reaching the top.

Earl Smith addresses similar issues facing African Americans in the U.S. military by focusing on two aspects of the career process—officer selection and advancement through rank (chapter 7). Smith maintains that African Americans, despite their large numbers in the military establishment, have not achieved equity with whites in rank, prestige, and power. His portrayal of the predicament of African Americans in one of the most integrated professions provides strong evidence for Gunnar Myrdal's (1944) notion of "An American Dilemma." He also points out that African American women in uniform have to overcome the hurdle of being minority females in a predominantly male profession. According to Smith, the use of the Armed Forces Qualification Test (AFQT) in recruitment or job assignment has severely limited the career opportunities for both African American women and men. Smith ends the chapter with a call for a heightened socio-political, economic, and humane approach to in-service promotions and civilian appointments for all African Americans who are either drafted or have volunteered to serve the nation.

Allan Liska's section on Native Americans in higher education (chapter 8) underscores the important linkage between an underrepresentation of Native Americans in college training and their invisibility in college teaching. High education costs and cultural barriers have contributed to low college admissions and graduation rates among Native Americans. Liska suggests that providing more support to tribal colleges may be an effective way to significantly increase their participation in higher education. Meanwhile, given the very small number of Native Americans who have completed doctoral training, Native American professors on mainstream college campuses may be the exception rather than the norm. Liska also tells us why Native Americans who are pursuing doctorates have a preference for certain fields. According to Liska, a lack of public funding to tribal colleges and collegial recognition to research by Native American professors would make reaching parity with whites in higher education a distant goal. Under these circumstances, Native Americans would have to resort to self-help strategies to improve their participation in higher education.

Joyce Tang considers the case of medical school faculty, which has received less attention from social scientists (chapter 9). Her analysis of the faculty roster data from the Association of American Medical Colleges shows that non-Asian minorities, especially black women, have made significant gains in terms of representation on medical school faculties. Generally, Asians and Hispanics have fared better than blacks in the areas of career status and advancement. Yet, minority medical faculty as a whole are still heavily underrepresented in authority positions. The "glass ceiling" phenomenon is prevalent across sectors (as in DiTomaso's and Smith's study of minorities and white women in business and industry) and across disciplines (as in Scott's study of lawyers and Leighninger's analysis of social workers). Similar to women in private law practice and social work, as well as Native Americans in higher education, women and minority medical faculty have few role models or mentors. Thus, mutual support and encouragement, argues Tang, is a way for women and minorities to gain solid ground in academic medicine. Institutions should also play an active role in implementing changes in policies and practices, according to Tang.

What do the experiences of women and minorities in these professions tell us about stratification in the labor market? What is the outlook for educated women and minorities in professional occupations? The chapters in this volume underscore the fact that despite formidable obstacles, women and minorities constitute a small but growing number in American professions. Whether they are in traditionally male-, female-, or white-dominated professions, women and minorities generally do not measure up with their male and white counterparts. Education is a ladder of mobility into well-paying, high-status professions, but it is not crucial in gaining access to high-profile or authority positions. Whether a capable woman or an aspiring minority would become a partner in a law firm, a manager, a dean of a medical school, or a military officer is beyond the influence of individual characteristics.

There is a clear consensus among the contributors of this book that gender and racial inequality in labor market outcomes is largely due to social control and the structure of the profession. As will be seen in the following chapters, women and minorities face similar problems in advancing their careers across professions. On the one hand, employers expect professional women to be as committed to their careers as are men. On the other hand, these women are expected to meet the obligations of their traditional gender roles. Women are more likely to be penalized in their career attainment if they put family above career. Additionally, the career prospects of women and minorities in professional occupations are handicapped by weak networking and the absence of mentors. To step outside their marginal statuses in the labor market requires a transformation of the socialization and labor market processes.

No matter how difficult it is to predict the future for professional women and minorities, these newcomers will slowly but surely gain ground. Changes in the global market, coupled with demographic shifts, have challenged U.S. employers to respond to the needs of increasingly diversified consumer and labor markets. Equally important, professional women and minorities would not be spectators in this process. The challenge for researchers of work and occupation is to monitor the trends and patterns of gender and racial changes in professional labor markets: Are there parallels in the changes we observe between professionals and other workers? Another issue that deserves our attention is the exploration of the relative influence of social control on career processes: Is there clear and convincing evidence of social control on professional women and minorities in comparable situations? How can professional women and minorities circumvent these social and institutional forces, with or without the backing of affirmative action? Social scientists should also examine changes in the structure of the profession when (1) more women and minorities are attracted to white- and male-dominated professions or (2) men take over positions from women in traditionally female professions.

NOTES

1. Throughout this book, we use the term *minorities* to refer to members of racial and ethnic groups in the United States: Native Americans, blacks, Hispanics, and Asians. They are considered minorities because of their proportional representation in the U.S. population. In 1995, racial and ethnic minorities constituted approximately 26 percent of the total population (U.S. Bureau of the Census 1994:18). If the present trend continues, the aforementioned might become, in numerical terms, the majority group after 2050. In recent years, blacks, Hispanics, and others increasingly have used the terms African Americans and Latinos, respectively. In this book, these terms are used interchangeably.

2. Most of these recent studies or anthologies deal with the (lack of) mobility of women and minorities relative to whites and especially white males (Blauner 1989; Essed 1990; Hill and Jones 1993; Jiobu 1990; Payne and Abbott 1990; Simpson and Yinger 1985). Others focus on the overall

career achievements of members of a minority group, such as African Americans (Benjamin 1991) or Asian Americans (Hsia 1988). Some have documented the barriers facing women and minorities in general terms (Amott 1993; Bergmann 1986; Jacobs 1989; Sokoloff 1992; Tomaskovic-Devey 1993) or in specific professions (Cole 1992; Epstein 1993; McIlwee and Robinson 1992; Smith 1992; Zuckerman, Cole, and Bruer 1991). The professions which have received the most attention from social scientists studying gender and race segregation are related to high-tech industries (Colclough and Tolbert 1992; Falk and Lyson 1988; Nash and Fernandez-Kelly 1983; Pearson and Bechtel 1989; Sawers and Tabb 1984; Ward 1990; Wright 1987) or lower-status, lower-paying jobs (Griffith 1993; Romero 1992). Only a few book-length studies have probed deeply into the career development process of women in the professions. Reskin and Roos's (1990) *Job Queues, Gender Queues* documents the process of desegregation-resegregation by sex, based on case studies of "feminizing" male occupations, ranging from book editors to bakers to bartenders. In *Gender Differences at Work*, Williams (1989) examines occupational sex segregation in the U.S. Marine Corps and nursing. The research annual, since 1980, *Current Research on Occupations and Professions*, edited by Helena Lopata and others, is a series featuring a wide range of occupations. However, none of these books examines the career progress of educated minorities and women across a wider spectrum of white-collar professions.

3. Administrative and managerial positions have been classified as "professional occupations" both in the U.S. Census and in scholarly research. Those who perform primarily administrative or managerial tasks may have received formal (e.g., a master's degree in business administration) and on-going professional or organizational training. Additionally, there are professional associations (e.g., the American Management Association) for managers to advance members' career interests. Administrators may not possess as much professional autonomy as do doctors or dentists. However, managers, like scientists or engineers, are "semi-professionals."

REFERENCES

Abbott, Andrew. 1988. *The System of Professions.* Chicago: University of Chicago Press.

Amott, Teresa. 1993. *Caught in the Crisis: Women and the U.S. Economy Today.* New York: Monthly Review Press.

Benjamin, Lois. 1991. *The Black Elite: Facing the Color Line in the Twilight of the Twentieth Century.* Chicago: Nelson-Hall.

Bergmann, Barbara R. 1986. *The Economic Emergence of Women.* New York: Basic Books.

Blauner, Bob. 1990. *Black Lives, White Lives: Three Decades of Race Relations in America.* Berkeley: University of California Press.

Chamberlain, Mariam K. Ed. 1991. *Women in Academe: Progress and Prospects.* New York: Russell Sage Foundation.

Coates, Joseph F., Jennifer Jarratt, and John B. Mahaffie. 1990. *Future Work: Seven Critical Forces Reshaping Work and the Work Force in North America.* San Francisco: Jossey-Bass.

Colclough, Glenna and Charles M. Tolbert II. 1992. *Work in the Fast Lane: Flexibility, Division of Labor, and Inequality in High-Tech Industries.* Albany: State University of New York Press.

Cole, Stephen. 1992. *Making Science: Between Nature and Society.* Cambridge, MA: Harvard University Press.

Collins, Sharon M. 1993. "Blacks on the Bubble: The Vulnerability of Black Executives in White Corporations." *The Sociological Quarterly* 34(3):429–447.

Epstein, Cynthia Fuchs. 1993. *Women in Law.* 2nd ed. Urbana: University of Illinois Press.

Essed, Philomena. 1990. *Everyday Racism: Reports from Women of Two Cultures.* Claremont, CA: Hunter House.

———. 1991. *Understanding Everyday Racism: An Interdisciplinary Theory.* Newbury Park, CA: Sage.

Falk, William W. and Thomas A. Lyson. 1988. *High Tech, Low Tech, No Tech: Recent Industrial and Occupational Change in the South.* Albany: State University of New York Press.

Farley, Reynolds and Walter R. Allen. 1989. *The Color Line and the Quality of Life in America.* New York: Oxford University Press.

Freidson, Eliot. 1986. *Professional Powers: A Study of the Institutionalization of Formal Knowledge.* Chicago: University of Chicago Press.

Griffith, David. 1993. *Jones's Minimal: Low-Wage Labor in the United States.* Albany: State University of New York Press.

Haas, Violet B. and Carolyn C. Perrucci. Eds. 1984. *Women in Scientific and Engineering Professions.* Ann Arbor: University of Michigan Press.

Hill, Herbert and James E. Jones, Jr. Eds. 1993. *Race in America: The Struggle for Equality.* Madison: University of Wisconsin Press.

Hsia, Jayjia. 1989. *Asian Americans in Higher Education and at Work.* Hillsdale, NJ: Lawrence Erlbaum Associates.

Jackson, Kenneth W. 1991. "Black Faculty in Academia." Pp. 135–148 in *The Racial Crisis in American Higher Education*, edited by Philip G. Altbach and Kofi Lomotey. Albany: State University of New York Press.

Jacobs, Jerry A. 1989. *Revolving Doors: Sex Segregation and Women's Career.* Stanford: Stanford University Press.

———. Ed. 1995. *Gender Inequality at Work.* Thousand Oaks, CA: Sage.

Jiobu, Robert Masao. 1990. *Ethnicity and Inequality.* Albany: State University of New York Press.

Kanter, Rosabeth Moss. 1973. *Men and Women of the Corporation.* New York: Basic Book.

McIlwee, Judith S. and J. Gregg Robinson. 1992. *Women in Engineering: Gender, Power, and Workplace Culture.* Albany: State University of New York Press.

Myrdal, Gunnar. 1944. *An American Dilemma: The Negro Problem and Modern Democracy.* New York: Harper.

Nash, June and Maria Patricia Fernandez-Kelly. Eds. 1983. *Women, Men, and the International Division of Labor.* Albany: State University of New York Press.

National Science Foundation. 1994. *Women, Minorities, and Persons with Disabilities in Science and Engineering: 1994.* Arlington, VA: National Science Foundation (NSF 94–333).

Pavalko, Ronald M. 1988. *Sociology of Occupations and Professions.* 2nd ed. Itasca, IL: F.E. Peacock.

Pearson, Willie, Jr. and Kenneth Bechtel. Eds. 1989. *Blacks, Science, and American Education.* New Brunswick, NJ: Rutgers University Press.

Reskin, Barbara F. and Patricia A. Roos. 1990. *Job Queues, Gender Queues: Explaining Women's Inroads into Male Occupations.* Philadelphia: Temple University Press.

Romero, Mary. 1992. *Maid in the U.S.A.* New York: Routledge.

Sawers, Larry and William K. Tabb. Eds. 1984. *Sunbelt/Snowbelt: Urban Development and Regional Restructuring.* New York: Oxford University Press.

Simpson, George Eaton and J. Milton Yinger. 1985. *Racial and Cultural Minorities: An Analysis of Prejudice and Discrimination.* 5th ed. New York: Plenum.

Smith, Earl. 1992. *A Comparative Study of Occupational Stress in African American and White University Faculty.* Lewiston, NY: Edwin Mellen.

Sokoloff, Natalie J. 1992. *Black Women and White Women in the Professions: Occupational Segregation by Race and Gender, 1960–1980.* New York: Routledge.

Tomaskovic-Devey, Donald. 1993. *Gender and Racial Inequality at Work: The Sources and Consequences of Job Segregation.* Ithaca, NY: ILR Press.

Trice, Harrison M. 1993. *Occupational Subcultures in the Workplace.* Ithaca, NY: ILR Press.

U.S. Bureau of the Census. 1994. *Statistical Abstracts of the United States 1994.* 114th edition. Washington, DC: U.S. Government Printing Office.

Ward, Kathryn. Ed. 1990. *Women Workers and Global Restructuring.* Ithaca, NY: ILR Press.

Wilensky, Harold J. 1964. "The Professionalization of Everyone." *American Journal of Sociology* 70:137–158.

Williams, Christine. 1989. *Gender Differences at Work: Women and Men in Nontraditional Occupations.* Berkeley: University of California Press.

Wilson, William J. 1978. *The Declining Significance of Race.* 2nd ed. Chicago: University of Chicago Press.

Wright, Barbara Drygulski. Ed. 1987. *Women, Work, and Technology: Transformations.* Ann Arbor: University of Michigan Press.

Zuckerman, Harriet, Jonathan Cole, and John T. Bruer. Eds. 1991. *The Outer Circle: Women in the Scientific Community.* New York: W.W. Norton.

Zussman, Robert. 1985. *Mechanics of the Middle Class: Work and Politics Among American Engineers.* Los Angeles: University of California Press.

2

Watching the Changes

Women in Law

JOAN NORMAN SCOTT

WATCHING THE CHANGES

Watching the numbers of women grow within the traditionally male-oriented law profession is witnessing historical change. Jean Allard (1990) noted the difference between then and now when she called to order a 1990 Mid-winter Section meeting of the Business Law Section of the American Bar Association (ABA). Jean Allard was the first woman chair of the prestigious group. The panel of speakers consisted of young women lawyers, who set forth their arguments for part-time employment arrangements and called upon law firms to recognize the value of their work:

> How different it is for you women today than it was for me thirty years ago. Just look how many women are here in the room as listeners . . . and look at how many women there are as members involved in the Section. And although I'm frequently asked, I contend that it doesn't really matter what it was like when I went to law school and was the only woman in the class that finished the three years, or when I first began practicing and was the only woman in the firm and was one of only a few practicing in Chicago. A lot has changed. It's kinda like imagining what it was like before TV—that world is completely irrelevant today. There

was awkwardness and a funny alienation in that world that was totally male. I have watched the changes, the changing environment. Life for women is more comfortable and nicer. But it hasn't been easy, and the job is not finished yet. But the big difference is in the numbers—there are just so many more women in the profession who can state the case. . . .

A mere handful in the early 1960s, women made up about 20 percent of the legal profession in 1990, according to the 1990 *Lawyers Almanac.* "That's a goodly number," declared Rosabeth Kanter (1977a, 1977b). From her investigation and from the research upon which much of this chapter is based, we learn that people with common interests are able to organize themselves into groups when there are enough of them. The magic proportion appears to be 20 to 30 percent of the whole. Thus, women have reached the lower boundary of the critical proportion where they may effect change. Even before they reached that point, the very structure of the legal profession felt the impact of their presence. For example, before women, who ever heard of a part-time lawyer?

This chapter examines the following questions: What is it like for women lawyers after twenty-five to thirty years of women's gradual encroachment into the law? What kind of success are women actually experiencing? The chapter focuses on private practice. The inherent demand and competition for business development within the private practice of law runs more counter to gender-related social expectations for the behavior of women described by Gilligan (1982) than those which might be imposed by a corporate or government employer. This notion is further implied by the on-going trend of more men than women choosing first-time employment in private practice since 1982. For example, of the 1993 law school graduates choosing private practice, 60.6 percent of men chose private practice, as opposed to 53.2 percent of women (Collins 1995). Thus, private practice is seen by some to represent the greatest challenge.

Partnership is the mark of success in private practice. Partnership means increased compensation, broader responsibility, and longer hours. The onus of keeping clients satisfied with good and thorough work centers on partners. Generally, an attorney works as an associate for about seven years before being invited into the partnership. Those associates who are found acceptable are asked to be partners. Occasionally, an attorney is "passed over." That individual may join another firm or remain an associate with the original firm and potentially be invited to join the partnership at a later date. Alternatively, individuals may decide that the challenges of private practice are not suitable for them. The corporate or government environment provides them with a satisfying opportunity to practice law without the pressures of building and maintaining their own firm. For instance, when working for the government or a corporation, one is generally not mandated to bring in enough money to pay the rent each month, and hours tend to be relatively regular and predictable compared to those of private practices.

A contemporary picture of the constituents of the world of law comes from the participants of a study of lawyers in the city of Los Angeles. It is a comparative study of their professional standing, defined by the type of law school they attended, years of practice, level of practice, and specialty areas. Also compared were the number of weekly hours each participant worked, their marital status, and family obligations. The study investigated the effect of structure on how men and women viewed their achievement within the profession. Following Kanter's research, structure was defined as sex ratio. The research question asked, does the ratio of women to men affect the way men and women attribute their achievement? Information regarding the participants was gathered by way of a structured telephone interview. The attribution questionnaire was subsequently mailed to participants. Most anecdotes and quotes in this chapter come from those interviews. The study findings are complemented by the study findings with interviews and quotes from women lawyers I have met at the ABA meetings and law profession-related events. I use pseudo names where study participants are concerned and real names for subsequent interviewees.

The inquiry grew out of the overall findings that women tend to expend more effort than do men with the same qualifications on the same job (e.g., Bielby and Bielby 1988; Major, McFarlin, and Gagnon 1984). Weiner's model of achievement (Weiner 1974; Weiner, Frieze, Kukla, Reed, Rest, and Rosenbaum 1972), derived from the attribution theory, states that women attribute success to their effort, and men attribute success to their ability. Thus, I hypothesize that women working in offices, where the ratio of women to men is 20 to 30 percent, will rely on their effort more than men will in offices with a similar sex composition. Additionally, these women might rely on their effort more than other women working in offices with lesser, or greater proportions of women.

A HISTORICAL PERSPECTIVE

To place this comparison of men and women lawyers into a historical perspective, we turn to an earlier study which estimated the probability of women lawyers becoming partners in their law firms (Scott 1987). This study grouped lawyers into five-year cohorts in which they were admitted to the bar. The cohorts were divided further into groups of men and women, according to their status of "partner" or "associate." The study utilized the 1986 listing for the city of Los Angeles in the Martindale-Hubbell Directory of Law (Martindale) from which to obtain its sampling universe.[1]

Cohort Size

Historical events stand out in Table 2.1, not only for women, but for men. We see the momentum of the women's liberation movement of the 1960s embodied in the growth spurt of women into the profession (e.g., the women's 1976–1980 cohort). Military service claimed most men during the 1941–1945 World War II period. Hence, only five male attorneys who are still professionally active passed the bar during that period.

Cohort and Partnership Wait Time

The average time to reach partnership is seven years. Few partners, men or women, exist before the 1981 cohort. The ongoing concern expressed in a recent survey of women in law by the Women Lawyers Association of Los Angeles (Walters 1994) is clear in the 1976–1980 cohort. For these people, only 32 percent of the women are partners, in contrast to 69 percent of the men.

Women Attorneys Tend to Be in the Same Age Range

An age breakdown of the sample indicates the rolling tide of the women's liberation movement. Of all women in this sample, 71 percent are between twenty-five and thirty-nine years old, with only 16 percent above age forty. At the time of this research, women had not been in law long enough to have marked representation above age forty. By contrast, 55 percent of the men are between twenty-five and thirty-nine years old, and 39 percent of the men are age forty and over.

Women Sometimes Get a Later Start

The larger proportion of women associates (65 percent), compared to the men (43 percent) in the thirty-four to thirty-nine age group, suggests a cou-

Table 2.1. Trends in Admittance to the Bar by Admission Cohort, Sex, and Partnership Status: Los Angeles ($N=1,772$).

	Women				Men			
Cohort	Partners	Associates	Total	%Partners	Partners	Associates	Total	%Partners
1981–85	12	176	188	6.4	21	384	405	5.2
1976–80	36	78	114	31.6	155	226	381	68.6
1971–75	17	6	23	73.9	204	35	239	85.4
1966–70	4	1	5	80.0	142	8	150	94.7
1961–65	1	1	2	50.0	87	4	91	95.6
1956–60	2	1	3	66.7	57	0	57	100.0
1951–55	1	0	1	100.0	63	0	63	100.0
1946–50	1	0	1	100.0	24	1	25	96.0
1941–45	0	0	0	—	5	0	5	100.0
1940 and before	0	0	0	—	19	0	19	100.0
Totals	74	263	337		777	658	1435	

Source: Martindale Hubbell Law Directory,1986.

Figure 2.1.   Admission to Bar by Age Group

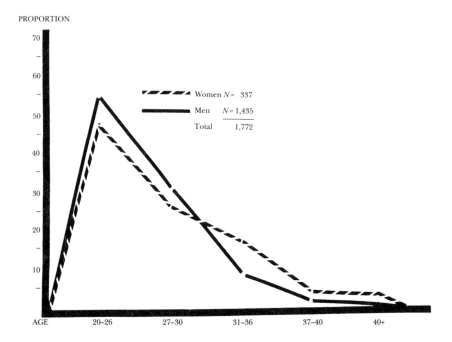

PROPORTION

Women *N* = 337
Men   *N* = 1,435
Total   1,772

AGE   20–26   27–30   31–36   37–40   40+

Note: Sample represents 25 percent of lawyers listed in the city of Los Angeles, section of Martindale-Hubbell Law director, 1986.

ple of things. First, there may be more women associates than men because they were "passed over." Another explanation could be the tendency for women to reenter the workforce after marriage or childbirth. Figure 2.1 illustrates that, for this sample, women over age thirty are more likely to embark on a law career than are men in the same age group. In other words, some of the women in the thirty-four to thirty-nine age group may be newly admitted to the bar, lacking sufficient tenure to become partner.

Women Are Launching Their Career with Timing Similar to Men

Figure 2.1 reflects what we shall see in the study described below. The tendency is for women, like men have always done, to progress from undergraduate training directly to law school, and to begin their law career prior to age twenty-six.

HOW FAR WOMEN HAVE COME:
PROFESSIONAL SIMILARITIES AND PERSONAL DIFFERENCES

Participating in the survey study were 113 women and 112 men, drawn in a randomized procedure from the 1988 Martindale. Like the partnership probability study, the lawyers were all in private practice in the city of Los Angeles. The sample included 11 Asians, 6 blacks, 203 Caucasians, 7 Latinos, and 4 "other," of which 54 percent were women. Because of the few ethnic and racial minorities in the sample, the research focused on women.

A Japanese American lawyer whom I interviewed for the study commented on the small numbers of minorities in law. He observed that law schools have widened their doors to accept women, but have not emphasized minority admissions. For example, he argued that Asians needed greater representation to gain more visibility within the private sector and cited the small numbers of minorities who are presently in law schools as an ongoing limitation to their organizational efforts. Whether law schools focus on women as admission candidates at the expense of minority individuals is not the subject of this research but it merits further investigation.

Similarities: Professional Standing

Professional standing was measured by the number of years of experience as a practicing lawyer, partnership or associate status, and the status of the law school attended. The status of the law schools in this research was defined by the Law Scholastic Aptitude Test means, achieved by the respective student bodies as reported in Barron's 1988 *Guide to Law Schools*. The highest scores designated schools of national standing, followed by regional and local standings, respectively.

Since women have entered law more recently than men, men would have a higher professional standing than women. Men would have practiced law for a longer period of time and would have a greater representation at the partnership level than women. Because the partnership probability study illustrated the scarcity of women in law who were over age forty (Scott 1987), comparison of the men and women in this study was limited to those who were between the ages of twenty-five and forty.

None of these expectations were realized. No statistical differences were found in the length of time they had been practicing law, nor in their partnership status. Moreover, there were no statistical differences in the status of the law schools attended by women and men. In addition, there were no differences in the kind of law that men or women were likely to practice. There were twenty-three different specialty areas represented within the sample, which could be classified into either litigation or transactional. Litigators are involved with legal disputes and the judicial process before a judge. Transactional attorneys are involved in disputes and arrive at agreements as representatives of a corporate or personal interest. Generally, the participants said their specialty area took them into either arena. The majority of lawyers in this Los Angeles sample were litigators.

These findings may, in part, be explained by the removal of obstacles to women's participation in the legal profession: entry to law schools and the increased willingness of law firms to hire women. Hillary Rodham Clinton (1988) included these facts in her report to the American Bar Association Commission on Women in the Profession ("the Commission"). Underscoring their achievement is, of course, the talent and dedication of these women toward their careers.

Finding as many women as men in litigation suggests that women are surmounting yet another obstacle. Litigation is commonly considered the most aggressive area of law. Litigation joins business development, or "rain-making," as one of the last frontiers for women in law (Africa 1990). Social anticipations for women are to be nurturing and caring and for men to be more aggressive (Gilligan 1982). The reports abound that women lawyers experience subtle discrimination when they adapt the aggressive and domineering style expected of their male counterparts (Goldberg 1988). The goal is for women to be accepted for their expertise as lawyers without reference to gender. For example, Marcia Clark, the District Attorney of Los Angeles and prosecutor in the O. J. Simpson trial, is recognized by many legal authorities with whom I have spoken as "a good lawyer," without the qualifier that she is a "good *woman* lawyer."

Differences: Marriage and Family

The women and men in this sample have similar professional status. In all but the youngest group of women, that is where the similarity stops. The findings demonstrate that a law career in private practice institutes a dichotomous impact on marriage and family life for men and women. Over twice as many women as men in the thirty-five to forty age category reported they were single. Moreover, married life for women lawyers is not the same as that for men. Of the sixty-five married women in the sample, the spouses of fifty-nine worked and three were students. By contrast, only thirty-five of the spouses of the sixty-nine men worked, and one was a student. The married women in this sample probably do not have the same level of personalized support system deemed desirable to maintain a home and family as do men ($p \leq .001$). Moreover, there were significantly fewer women than men with children ($p \leq .001$).

Economic Opportunities and Career Status

A widespread complaint of survey participants for the Women Lawyers Association of Los Angeles (Walters 1994) is that women are not compensated to the same degree as men. Associated with this complaint is that women do not have the same opportunities to be involved in endeavors that command increased compensation, namely, finding business. A common theme underlying this complaint was cited by the women participating in the present study. The theme resonates attitudinal and structural barriers that are ultimately traced to gender expectations for behavior. Two of these expectations are the kinds of work women are socially expected to do, and the number of hours demanded just to keep the job.

Minders and Grinders vs. Finders and Keepers

The Los Angeles survey reveals that men readily accept women into their practice to perform the routine tasks, to be the "minders" and "grinders" (i.e., tasks deemed to be feminine). The Commission found that the types of cases assigned to men and women differ with respect to their importance, visibility, and client contact. Moreover, women often find themselves in supporting roles such as document preparation, even on cases where they have been the lead lawyer in its preparation. The supportive role naturally fits women's traditional socialization, which stresses cooperating, putting the needs of others first, and following nurturing, passive careers. In contrast, men are expected to pursue tasks requiring high achievement and competition (Gilligan 1982). A well-used example is participation in sports, where men learn at an early age how to compete and to either win or lose. When women behave like men, their actions may be misconstrued as negative character attributes. For example, research on women managers finds that they must be assertive in order to compete with the male majority. If too assertive though women may risk being regarded as pushy or unfeminine, even by other women (Mathison 1987).

Men have difficulty thinking of women as "finders" and "keepers" of business. Society's understanding of how lawyers should act is based on men studying men. By virtue of their socialization, women have a different style of lawyering than do men (Menkel-Meadow 1985). Africa (1990) noted that few women lawyers viewed themselves, or were seen by others, as "finders," for reasons reflected in how they were socialized to act. Graham (1986) reported several quotes on the subject: "It's sort of like waiting to be asked out for a dance. If you can't ask a man out for a date, it's probably even harder to ask him for $500,000 worth of legal business." Another example women report is their concern over how their "rainmaking" overtures are perceived by male clients. Many women believe men continue to confuse women in their roles as professionals with women in their social or sexual roles. Graham also reported a practical explanation from a newer woman partner: Clients in matters involving high stakes are more likely to look to senior people in law firms. At this point, the senior people may not be men. This woman surmised that the problem was related more to the age than to the sex of the lawyer.

The upshot of men not viewing women as "finders" is that women are most often excluded from the formal and informal settings where business development takes place. The Los Angeles survey indicates that women are further hampered from the "finder" status since men do not readily mentor women and teach them how to bring in business. This is consistent with the literature: Men are reluctant to invest their time to teach women about lawyering because of perceived lack of lifetime career commitment (Epstein 1970, 1993).

A Lesson for Women: Working Hard Is Not Enough

Another way of stating this dilemma is that women are socialized to do things in ways that differ from men, which impacts on their economic advancement. Here we see remnants of traditional behavior and expectations. Women's notion for success seems to be, if you work hard, you will be rewarded (Bielby and Bielby 1988; Major et al. 1984). Men take a different approach. They may work hard, but they rely more on their perceived ability, especially when performing male-oriented tasks (e.g., Weiner 1974; Weiner et al. 1972). The findings from the survey by the Women Lawyers Association of Los Angeles described earlier suggest that women have a lot to learn. Some may not be sure of what they need to learn.

A woman lawyer in her mid-30s whom I interviewed in the study learned the hard way what it is all about. For four months, "Laura" commuted thirty miles daily, from her West Side office to a new East Side branch office. She had volunteered to open the new office fully expecting her effort to be rewarded with the position of managing partner. In addition to attending to the myriad details involving the opening of a new branch office, Laura maintained her general practice and supervised the care of her invalid mother. Because her hours were extraordinary, Laura missed those critical informal and formal settings where networking takes place, that is, the lunches and golf games with senior partners and potential clients in which her male counterpart participated. Her male counterpart became the managing partner of the branch office Laura built, without ever setting foot on the premises.

Laura remarked in her interview, "I sure learned my lesson!" She learned that for promotion, she had to get the job done by networking through the gatekeeper. Being with the senior partners and potential clients over lunch and dinner creates the opportunity for cementing business relationships.

THE STRUCTURE OF PRIVATE PRACTICE: BILLABLE HOURS!

". . . in what other occupation do you write down what you do every minute of the day . . . not most women's training. . . .!" M.

Private practice is structured on billable hours, which can severely impact on personal and family life. Women are especially affected because of the traditional ties to children and home. The amount of hours billed is directly linked to partnership and compensation, and women who choose to put in fewer hours and spend more time with their families are considered "less serious" by their male colleagues. Part-time work has never been a part of that structure. Kingson (1988) quoted Vicki M. Davis, then a sixth-year associate with two small children, who opted for a four-day week: "Much of what keeps people working hours, which potentially eliminates personal and family time, is the promise of partnership. Once you take that away, it gets to be demoralizing."

In truth, the term *part-time* has become a misnomer. The number of required billable hours has risen to the point that so-called part-time has become full-time, from 1,700 hours a few years ago to about 2,300 hours today in the top firms. Smaller firms, around thirty-five and under, have fewer time pressures. Kingson emphasized that regardless of the size of the law firm, the average number of annual hours billed does not reflect the total time actually devoted to carrying on the practice. This fact was expressed by virtually every participant in the study of Los Angeles lawyers described here. The point is that women make up an increasingly large proportion of the law profession, yet the rules of structure have not signifi-

cantly changed to accommodate what today comprises 20 percent of its
members.

CAREER ORIENTATION AND MISCONCEPTIONS

Primary career orientation is the key to the advancement and empower-
ment of women in the legal profession. However, misperceptions abound
over a woman's career orientation. Two matters of dispute are (1) the perception that women work fewer hours and are, therefore, less career committed than men, and (2) the diverse careers among women brought about
by gender-related expectations.

DO WOMEN REALLY WORK FEWER HOURS THAN MEN?

An offshoot of the so-called "mommy track" or part-time preference
through the child-rearing years is the stereotype that women work fewer
hours than men. The interpretation of "mommy track" is side-tracked or
derailed, since hours equal income for law firms and service to clients, and
working fewer hours is a death-knell to advancement and partnership. The
stereotype is backed by data. The 1990 *Lawyers Almanac* reported that,
annually, women lawyers work about 200 fewer hours than do men lawyers.
Similarly, for the full-time associates and partners, the men in the present
study reported working slightly more hours than the women (the average
per week was 56.8 hours by the men, and 54.3 hours by the women, which is
statistically nonsignificant). However, the general comparison fails to give
the whole picture. Such comparisons cannot show the wax and waning of
different levels of responsibility attached to raising children (see Allen
1992).

Figure 2.2 illustrates the complexity of comparing the number of
hours worked for men and women. The number of hours worked was
defined as being the number of hours per week that was devoted to prac-
tice-related matters. This was preferred to billable hours, to get an overall
picture of lawyers' work style. It was hypothesized that hours worked would
be dependent on the age of the child. The assumption was that the work-
hour availability of women with young children was not comparable to
women with older children or to single, childless women.

Note that none of the women reported working less than the standard
forty-hour work week. Three women who have children said they worked
about forty-five hours. The remainder said they worked at least fifty hours.

Figure 2.2. The Number of Reported Hours Worked Each Week, By Sex
and Age Group, Full-time Associates and Partners

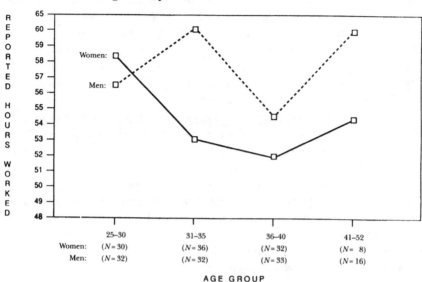

One woman who has a child reported working seventy hours "with little
time for anything else in my life."

As hypothesized, it was age group, not gender, that showed significant
differences in the number of hours worked when the 231 men and women
lawyers in the Los Angeles sample were divided accordingly ($p \leq .004$).
Women work long hours but fewer hours than men, except for the very
young and those over forty, perhaps due to family responsibilities.

Men over forty reported working the most hours. Women under thirty
work almost as many hours as men over forty. Both groups work grueling
hours, but the oldest groups of women and men apparently devote the
most time to their law practice. Comments from their interviews and also
from my observations and discussions with other senior lawyers reveal why
this might be true: the longer one practices, the more clients a lawyer is
likely to have, and the more clients one is likely to attract by virtue of being
well and favorably known. Providing good and prompt service is the time-
honored tradition of business development. As time progress, the more
work he or she must either do, or supervise. Note that time spent on active
business development, or "rainmaking," was not included in the measure-
ment of "hours worked."

In contrast, men and women in the thirty-six to forty age group worked fewer hours than any other group. We can understand why the hours of the women were reduced. Child care was most often cited as the reason. Moreover, these women had working spouses, and most added women's traditional role, that of caring for the children and home, to their legal careers. Their comments reflect cultural expectations, which continue to view women as being responsible for household and child care, whether the wife works or not (e.g., Stafford 1980).

What are the family responsibilities of the men in the thirty-six to forty age group? Their spouses pursued the traditional homemaker role, which means that these men had help with child care and the overall organization of home life, unlike attorney moms.

Lawyers in the thirty-one to thirty-five age group were in the scrambling years, building their reputations for partnership invitations. The slight drop in reported hours by women in the thirty-one to thirty-five age group is partially explained by the eleven women who have children. As with the other age groups, most of the men were married to women who chose the homemaker role. Less encumbered than some of the thirty-one to thirty-five age women, these men were able to put in impressive hours. Thus, men on the partnership track have an automatic lead over women who are raising children.

Reality: There Is More Career Diversity Among Women Than Men

Male gatekeepers have problems comprehending how to turn the varying degrees of career emphasis, typified by women, into a valuable asset. By not meeting the needs of women and their maternal responsibilities, they lose their recruiting and training investment, along with the brightest and the best (Schwartz 1989). For example, take the situation of a woman lawyer in my study. "Nancy" complained that she had just been invited into the partnership at the junior level, after a tenure of seven years with the firm. She was disappointed that a younger man who had not been with the firm as long as she had been invited into the senior level, with the added compensation that goes with that position. Nancy explained that she was probably kept from the higher level since she had been billing fewer hours the previous two years. She felt it was more important for her, a single mother, to care for her daughter, who was ten years old at the time we spoke. Nancy confided to me during our interview that she was looking for another position. Hence, this firm stood to lose its investment in time, talent, and experience.

From my interviews and observations I noted an associated difficulty, in that male gatekeepers have problems distinguishing between the strictly career-focused woman and the woman who prefers a better balance between career and family. The tendency is for male gatekeepers to assume that women will leave the practice permanently for their families.

The characteristics of career goals for men are relatively straightforward, as are their opportunities. Men graduate from law school and go to work. More than one male hiring partner commented to me that he can, at least theoretically, expect that the male lawyer will stay with the firm long after he has matured professionally, to where he has earned the cost of training him.

Women's goals are not as clear-cut as men's. Ten percent of the women, in contrast to .08 percent of the men, had some reduced hourly arrangement with their firm that would allow them to continue practicing without partnership potential. These were women with children, who did not desire any increase in workload. For the moment, these women were content to be "minders" and "grinders." All but one (who had a severe illness) planned on reentering the partnership track when their child-rearing responsibilities lightened. Their interview comments revealed they were enthusiastic about resuming their careers at a higher level, taking their place among the "finders."

Career goals for women are affected by their age, social role, and attitude toward motherhood. Marrying and having children jeopardizes their careers. The hiring partner wonders about the cost of training a woman: Will she reduce her hours while her children are young, bringing additional cost to the firm? Will she quit? If she marries, will she be likely to leave her position with her firm should her husband be transferred? It's easier for male managing partners to figure out what men are going to do with their lives, if only because they share their gender-based career paths.

Problem: Women Get Pigeonholed

It is sometimes hard for a male managing partner to perceive that a beautiful young woman holds the talent and authority of a lawyer. In other words, a male gatekeeper is likely to judge a woman according to his perception of the woman, and not as a professional. For example, Sharla Frost (her real name), an attractive and highly career-dedicated woman, remarked that she sometimes has difficulty being taken seriously. I met Frost at the 1994 ABA meeting in New Orleans. She said men seldom see beyond her soft voice and small stature to the strength and independence of her personality. At the time of our interview, Frost was an associate with a large and prestigious firm. She is a litigator and is heavily involved with an organized group of local women dedicated to teaching women how to be "finders." Frost wanted to come to the 1994 ABA annual meeting in New Orleans to meet other women lawyers and to network. She wanted to further her career goals to learn the ropes about being a lawyer and learn how to bring in business. The ABA is the most desirous informal or formal setting for strategic networking. Frost believed her senior partner would be pleased with her clear-cut career aspirations. To her chagrin, he said "no," explaining that traveling to the annual convention was not a necessary thing for her to do and implying that she was not worth the expense to the firm. A determined woman, Frost went anyway. She said to me she was "having a ball making so many connections all over the country." She added, "My firm is really lucky that I have absolutely no maternal instincts whatsoever. I love what I do, I love being a lawyer, and I am learning so much. I am so glad I came!" (Frost, 1994)

ABOUT MENTORING

The interviews with the women and men in the study bring up two issues about mentoring: (1) the lack of mentors as a function of large–sized firms, and (2) the lack of senior women to mentor younger lawyers (either women or men).

The Assigned Mentor

The women and men in the study each reported that they had a mentor. However, their responses revealed the emergence of a new form of mentoring, which affects both women and men. This is the "assigned mentor," which most lawyers in large firms reported having. The assigned mentor could be by specialty area, or by project, depending upon the procedures of a particular firm. The assigned mentor tends to be a man, since there are still more men than women in the senior positions. Sometimes the assigned mentor becomes the personal mentor, especially when the mentoring relationship is between two men. More often than not, the personal mentoring relationship seldom has time to develop because of the automatic rotation procedure, which exposes the new lawyer to different areas of law—and a new assigned mentor. Thus, the traditional mentoring institution, where the experienced individual extends his or her professional hand to the younger associate, may take on new characteristics as a product of the mega-firm.

Not Enough Senior Women

The real issue for women regarding mentoring and bringing in business may be the availability of women as mentors to women. Having a woman mentor was reported by only 17 percent of the participants, including men and women, which indicates the scarcity of women teaching other women how to be lawyers, or to demonstrate to younger men who and what women, who choose to practice law, are all about. One woman participant summed up the need for women mentors in this way: "He (her mentor) was a wonderful friend and taught me how to be a good lawyer, but he could not teach me how to act like a lawyer."

The problem with men mentoring women has been exacerbated in recent years with the onset of sexual harassment lawsuits. I asked several senior male partners about their feelings about mentoring women. They emphatically stated that they fear the consequences in today's litigious environment. Some women I spoke with presented another side of the argument. These women stated that they believed men used the sexual harassment threat as an excuse not to mentor women as a ploy in the perceived ongoing power struggle. There is obviously a great deal of work and communication to be done on this subject.

THE INFLUENCE OF THE PROPORTION OF WOMEN TO MEN

Kanter's Sex Ratio Theory and Attributions of Achievement

Are women in settings with a high proportion of men more likely to say they failed because of sources outside of their control, like men are expected to do? Results provide support for both the attribution theory and Kanter's theory of sex ratios. How people make attributions seems to change with the sex ratio structure that is associated with social expectations.

Kanter's Theory of Sex Ratio

Kanter's (1977a, 1977b) theory informs us how influences change according to the proportions of the minority group to the dominant group. Her model applies to the sex ratio partitioning of this sample. The "skewed" group lies in the percentage of women, 0 percent to 21 percent. Women practicing in these offices are the "token women." The percentage of women between 22 percent to 30 percent compare to Kanter's "tilted" group, where the numbers are sufficient to organize. It is here that most of the conflict occurs. Finally, the highest percentage of women, between 31 percent to 76 percent, includes the "balanced" group, where outcomes affecting individuals tend to be related to personal or other structural factors, not intergroup conflict.

The law offices with proportions of women between 21 percent and 30 percent could represent the law profession in the present and immediate future. Conflict between women and men is the highest here, since this is where the largest actual number of women are employed. The offices are torn between the demand by young women for a balanced lifestyle, the economic need of the firm for their lawyers to work extended hours, and the fear of losing training investment in good lawyers if their demands are not met. Under conflict, the sexes respectively stepped up their socially normed attribution: women tended to attribute their failures to sources outside of their control, when asked about their ability ($p \leq .06$). Men attributed their successes and failures to sources outside of their control, asked about how hard they tried under uncertain conditions ($p \leq .01$). Embodied within the conflict is men feel their boundaries threatened as women grow in numbers and strength (Astrachan 1986). The reluctance evidenced by men to adjust the structure of the law profession to the needs of women may be a response to this threat.

Women practicing in law offices of 0 percent to 20 percent attributed their achievements to effort and their failures to their ability, to about the same degree as men. This is pursuant to Kanter's sex ratio, which predicts that women working in male-dominated environments, the "token" women, tend to be more like the men than they might be if they worked in offices with larger proportions of women.

If the future of the law profession can be compared to law offices composed of 31 percent women, we get a glimpse of what it might be like when women reach more or less balanced proportions. Here, men were more similar to women in how they attributed their achievements. These offices incorporated values typical of the law, which are related to aggression and dominance, with the relational values of women.

CONCLUSION

Meeting the Challenges

The challenges facing women in law juxtaposition the socialization expectation and biological processes of women against the enormous time and competitive demands of the male-oriented law profession. Corinne Cooper

(1995), Professor of Law at the University of Missouri Law School in Kansas City, relates the two issues confronting women today. The first has to do with life concerns, which have been raised in this chapter: "Women still have primary responsibility for children and home. As a result, two-career families tend to place a disproportionate burden on women." Second, she observes that "although women are coming out of law schools in equal numbers, the hiring of women is no longer a priority within some firms. Some firms are saying that they 'have enough women.'"

Firms that have grown reluctant to hire women are likely burdened by the financial cost of employing them. The cost of employing women has been estimated in the business management world to be 2.5 times higher than the cost of employing men in management positions (Schwartz 1989). Contributing to their high cost, Schwartz reported, is that one-half of women who take maternity leave either return to their jobs after the agreed-upon time, or not at all.

Career-dedicated women are dissatisfied with the "mommy track" because of the derogatory implications inherent in being a part-time rather than a full-time lawyer. The mommy track concept, and more recently baby-sitting services (e.g., *Wall Street Journal* 1995), are laudable efforts by law firms to incorporate women into their firms. Unfortunately, when attorneys cut their hours in the private practice of law, they lose respect and the opportunities to be involved with more interesting cases (Kingson 1988).

Underlying the mommy track stigma is the misperception that all women wish to work part-time for all or most of their careers. While this is true for some women, career-dedicated women return to their careers when responsibilities for child care permit them to. Thus, the structure of the profession is challenged to understand the wide dispersion among women in their intent and availability.

Women are challenged to learn how to be the finders and keepers of business and to achieve in a male-oriented profession. Inroads to this challenge began when a group of women organized to teach interested women how to network and develop business (Africa 1990). Their efforts established the ABA Women Rainmakers Interest Group, an outgrowth of the ABA's Law Office Management Section. Through their numerous events and programs, Women Rainmakers train and provide advisers for women in marketing, networking, and other business development techniques. Ellisa Openbaum Habbart of Wilmington, Delaware, sums up the leadership dimension of their role: "Women Rainmakers offer excellent resources, such as training in client development and leadership, in addition to offering networking opportunities which may apply to all legal professionals" (1994). Women attorneys appear worldwide in the first

Rainmakers' directory. "We are providing professionals the opportunity to contact women attorneys from all over the world," stated Dixie Lee Laswell of Chicago (1994), who co-chairs the group.

A recent comprehensive investigation of all law students in the United States at the beginning of their second year of law school revealed that men were achieving significantly better than were women. Moreover, significant gender differences in self-concept were reported. Men rated their academic ability, competition, public speaking, and self-confidence significantly higher than did the women (Wightman 1995).[2] This implies that women are seeing themselves as less competent than men in areas critical to business development skills, before they even get to a law firm. This new information supports the observations of Africa (1990) and other founders of Rainmakers, that women as a group need to circumvent their socialization and learn the leadership skills necessary to be finders and keepers.

Structural changes are needed within the profession that anticipate and appreciate the various degrees of career dedication among women. Some women, like Sharla Frost and Ellisa Openbaum Habbart, are successful as finders and keepers. Others, like "Laura" (one of the study participants whose story was told earlier), work hard and want to learn how decisions are made in a male-oriented profession. Others are serious, competitive, and highly capable, but their work conflicts with family responsibilities. They are more like "Nancy," another study participant whose story also was told previously, feeling they must reduce their practice time during the child-rearing years. It is important to acknowledge that many law firms currently do work out their part-time arrangements on a case-by-case basis.[3] However, legitimizing the mommy track into a predictable and respectable course across the profession would bring stability to the law careers of women with families and take the surprise and uncertainty out of law firm management.

In sum, the private practice of law is challenged to build new definitions around the concept of primary career orientation, which incorporates balanced family living as well as accommodates diversity in career concentration. Meeting this challenge would greatly benefit men and women—and the profession as a whole.

ACKNOWLEDGMENTS

Special thanks and appreciation for her time and valued input is extended to Judith Treas, professor of sociology, and immediate past chair, University of California at Irvine. Many thanks for great support to Elaine Draper, assistant professor, University of Southern California. And to the many women and men of the law profession who participated in my research efforts, my personal thanks.

NOTES

1. "Martindale" is a directory produced nationally by a private firm, which invites all attorneys to fill out a form at the time of their admission to bars throughout the country. Lawyers who accept the invitation are undoubtedly those who feel that a national directory listing is important for business, and they tend to be lawyers in private practice. The listing specifies the capacity in which the lawyer practices, which made it possible to randomly draw a one-in-four systematic sample. The sample includes only those lawyers listed as "partner" or "associate," and excludes lawyers practicing as employees of the government or in private corporations. The sample ($N = 1,722$) represents 25 percent of lawyers in private practice, listed in the 1986 city of Los Angeles, section of Martindale.

2. Comparisons were between white men and white women, and between minority men and minority women.

3. Several study participants reported that their firm would work out part-time tracks for their women lawyers on a case-by-case basis.

REFERENCES

Africa, Martha F. 1990. *The Last Frontiers: Women Lawyers As Rainmakers and Litigators.* American Bar Association Section of Law Practice Management and Section of General Practice. Chicago, Illinois, August 4.

Allard, Jean. 1990. Mid–winter meeting of the American Bar Association, Boston, MA, April 7.

Allen, Peter. 1992. "Keeping Comparisons Comparable." *California Lawyer* (January):24.

Astrachan, Anthony. 1986. *How Men Feel.* Garden City, NY: Anchor Press/Doubleday.

Bielby, Denise and William T. Bielby. 1988. "She Works Hard for the Money: Household Responsibilities and the Allocation of Work Effort." *American Journal of Sociology* 93:1031–59.

Clinton, Hillary Rodham. 1988. "American Bar Association Commission in the Profession—Report to the House of Delegates." June.

Collins, Judy. 1995. National Association for Law Placement. Washington, DC. Personal communication. February 21.

Cooper, Corrine. 1995. Personal communication. February 14.

Epstein, Cynthia F. 1970a. *Woman's Place: Options and Limits in Professional Careers*. Berkeley: University of California Press.

———. 1993. *Women in Law*. 2nd ed. Urbana, IL: University of Illinois Press.

Feather, N.T. and J.G. Simon. 1975. "Reactions to Male and Female Success and Failure in Sex–linked Occupations: Impressions of Personality, Causal Attributions, and Perceived Likelihood of Different Consequences." *Journal of Personality and Social Psychology* 31:20–31.

Frost, Sharla. 1994. Annual Meeting of the American Bar Association, New Orleans, Louisiana, August 6.

Gilligan, Carol. 1982. *In a Different Voice*. Cambridge, MA: Harvard University Press.

Goldberg, Stephanie B. 1988. "Gender Bias." *American Bar Association Journal* (October) 1:144.

Graham, Deborah. 1986. "Rainmaking: The Next Major Hurdle for Women." *Legal Times* (May 19):9, 16–19.

Habbard, Ellisa O. 1994. Personal communication. November 2.

Jones, Landon. 1991. *Great Expectations*. New York: Ballentine Books.

Kanter, Rosabeth M. 1977a. *Men and Women of the Corporation*. New York: Basic Books.

———. 1977b. "Some Effects of Proportions on Group Life: Skewed Sex Ratios and Responses to Token Women." *American Journal of Sociology* 82:965–990.

Kingson, Jennifer A. 1988. "Women in the Law Say Path Is Limited by 'Mommy Track.'" *The New York Times* (May 8):A1, A15.

Laswell, Dixie L. 1994. Personal communication. November 2.

Major, Brenda, Dean B. McFarlin, and Diana Gagnon. 1984. "Overworked and Underpaid: On the Nature of Gender Differences in Personal Entitlement." *Journal of Personality and Social Psychology* 47:1399–1412.

Mathison, David L. 1987. "Assertiveness Breeds Contempt." *Journal of Social Psychology* 126:599–606.

Menkel-Meadow, Carrie. 1985. "Portia in a Different Voice: Speculations on a Women's Lawyering Process." *Berkeley Women's Law Journal* (Fall):39–63.

Russo, N.F., R.M. Kelly, and M. Deacon. 1991. "Gender and Success-related Attributions: Beyond Individualistic Conceptions of Achievement." *Sex Roles* 25:331–350.

Schwartz, Felice. 1989. "Management Women and the New Facts of Life." *Harvard Business Review* (January–February):65–76.

Scott, Joan N. 1987. "A Woman's Chance for a Law Partnership." *Sociology and Social Research* 71:119–122.

————. 1990. *Attributions of Causality of Achievement and Self-Evaluation: Men and Women Lawyers*. Ph.D. dissertation, Department of Sociology, University of Southern California, Los Angeles, CA.

Stafford, Frank P. 1980. "Women's Use of Time Converging with Men's." *Monthly Labor Review* 103:57–59.

Stephan, Walter G. and Dale W. Woolridge. 1977. "Sex Differences in Attributions for the Performance of Women on a Masculine Task." *Sex Roles* 3:321–328.

Wall Street Journal. 1995. "Working Weekends?" (January 24):1. Eastern Edition.

Walters, Donna K. H. 1994. "Barriers Still Persist, Women Lawyers Say." *Los Angeles Times* (March 10), Business Section D:1.

Weiner, Bernard. 1974. *Achievement Motivation and Attribution Theory*. Morristown, NJ: General Learning Press.

Weiner, Bernard, Irene Frieze, Andy Kukla, Linda Reed, Stanley Rest, and Robert M. Rosenbaum. 1972. "Perceiving the Causes of Success and Failure." Pp. 95–120 in *Attribution*, edited by E.E. Jones, D.E. Kanouse, H.H. Kelley, R.E. Nisbett, S. Valins, and B. Weiner. Morristown, NJ: General Learning Press.

Wightman, Linda. 1995. *Women in Legal Education: A Summary of Data Comparing the Law School Experiences of Men and Women*. Newtown, PA: Law School Admissions Council.

3

Women in Computer Work

Controlled Progress in a Technical Occupation

ROSEMARY WRIGHT

INTRODUCTION

Computer work has been widely touted in the last two decades as being one of the fastest growing and most highly paid occupations for women (Rytina 1982; Silvestri and Lukasiewicz 1992). Indeed, women have worked on and with computers since World War II, when the first programmers were called the "ENIAC girls" (Kraft 1979). While women were off to a great start, after the war computer work became the province of electrical engineers rather than mechanical wire carriers, and the gender composition shifted (Kraft 1979). Because early computers were designed by electrical engineers, the development of both computer hardware and software was driven by engineering values and norms (Hughes 1987; Tarallo 1987), creating an occupational culture closely aligned with and similar to that of electrical engineering (Trice 1993). More men than women were attracted by the culture, and computer work remained primarily male throughout the 1950s and 1960s (Kraft 1979).

Although the next two decades saw no real change in the occupational culture, women's share of computer work increased substantially during the 1970s and 1980s, accompanying women's greater participation in the general labor force: The female portion of computer systems analysts and other specialists, for example, rose from 9 percent in 1971 to 35 percent in

1990 (U.S. Bureau of Labor Statistics, 1976–1995). In the first part of the 1990s, however, women's representation began to fall, and as of 1993, fell to 30 percent (U.S. Bureau of Labor Statistics 1994). In a similar but earlier trend women's share of computer and information science bachelors degrees rose from 14 percent in 1971 to 37 percent in 1984 (Vetter 1992), but as of 1993 had fallen back to 28 percent (U.S. Department of Education, unpublished data).

These trends suggest women's progress in computer work has at least leveled off, if not reversed. Interestingly, independent of the time the research was performed, previous studies also present a mixed message about women's advancement. Two works suggest opposite conclusions— the first that there has been little progress, the second that there has been so much progress that gender usually does not warrant asking.

A non-management literature looks for gender inequality, finding it in the form of a gender gap in earnings, as well as gender segregation between specialties and industries (e.g., Donato 1990; Donato and Roos 1987; Glenn and Tolbert 1987; Kraft and Dubnoff 1986; Strober and Arnold 1987). A management literature, in contrast, appears to include gender almost as an afterthought, analyzing and finding few differences in salaries by occupational specialty, organizational and occupational turnover, career goals, and career progression (e.g., Cournoyer 1983; Freedland 1987; Igbaria and Siegel 1992; Wagner and Benham 1993). An in-depth review of these and other studies may be found in Wright (1994). All previous research is problematic in that each literature only examines part of the picture, and with exactly one exception (Strober and Arnold 1987)—both literatures exclude engineers from their purview and measure gender differences at single points in time, rather than how those differences change over time, or both.

Given the falloff in women's participation and this mixed reading of women's progress, I examine that progress here in terms of year-to-year trends in women's participation and women's separation from men—participation by comparing men's and women's rates of entry into and rates of exit from computer work, and separation within the field by computing both the gender gap in earnings and the amount of gender segregation across specialties and industries. I formulate and test hypotheses based on Jacobs's theory of social control (1989), Reskin and Roos's theory of male flight (1990), Kanter's tokenism theory (1977), and Blalock's minority-resistance theory (1967).

My results support Kanter's theory, by showing that women are making collective progress, and Jacobs's theory by showing high exit rates, which suggests women are treated as deviant and encouraged to leave their jobs. I argue that these messages of social control are delivered by the engineering culture of computer work. This culture appears to affect Asian and black women as well as white women, but not Asian or black men. Drawing upon Jacobs's and Kanter's theories, I propose a new model of progress for women in traditionally male occupations, one which incorporates and is based on a hybrid theory of *controlled progress*.

HYPOTHESES

Turning first to the issue of participation, Jacobs's (1989) theory of social control argues that women receive lifelong social control messages about male-dominated occupations: They do not belong and should not be in them. As a result, women decline to enter male-dominated majors and occupations, and choose to leave male-dominated majors and occupations at surprisingly high rates. This suggests my first hypothesis:

> *Social Control Hypothesis:* Independent of the proportion of women, as long as computer work is male-dominated, women should be less likely than men to enter and more likely than men to leave both computer-related majors and computer work itself.

In contrast to Jacobs's theory, Reskin and Roos's (1990) theory of male flight argues that as women increasingly enter previously male occupations, men will leave (more than women will leave) because they fear the declining status and lower salaries which frequently coincide with women's entry (see Wright and Jacobs 1994). Male flight thus suggests a second hypothesis, opposed to part of the first:

> *Male Flight Hypothesis:* As the proportion of women increases in computer work, men should be more likely than women to leave that work.

Turning from participation to separation, there are two ways by which we may compare how well women are doing compared to men in an occupation over time—by how men's and women's earnings compare and by the degree to which men and women are segregated within the occupation. If women's lot is improving, both the earnings gap and the degree of segregation should be narrowing. If women's lot is *not* improving, then both measures should be widening.

Kanter's tokenism theory (1977) is usually known for its proposition that women do poorly in male-dominated organizations because they are few in number, or tokens. Extending the argument from organizations to occupations and from absolute to relative terms, a logical corollary is that women should do better in male-dominated occupations as their proportions increase. There will be "strength in numbers" (Jacobs 1992). My third hypothesis is therefore:

> *Kanter Hypothesis:* As the proportion of women increases over time in computer work, the gender gap in earnings will narrow and the degree of gender segregation across specialties, industries, and work activities will decline.

In contrast to Kanter's theory, Blalock's minority-resistance theory (1967) argues that as minority numbers increase, majority resistance will increase and minority members will do worse, rather than better. An extension of this theory to women in male-dominated occupations, consistent with Pfeffer and Davis-Blake (1987) and Jacobs (1992), suggests that as women's proportions increase in male-dominated occupations, women should do worse, rather than better. Using the same measures of how well women are doing versus men, I obtain my last hypothesis:

> *Blalock Hypothesis:* As the proportion of women increases over time in computer work, the gender gap in earnings will widen and the degree of gender segregation across specialties, industries, and work activities will increase.

DATA AND METHODS

To test these hypotheses, I drew data on trends in the sex composition of computer specialties from the U.S. Bureau of Labor Statistics (1976–1995), which also provided data on the earnings of computer workers and the civilian labor force. Data on degrees received in computer and information sciences are from Vetter (1992) and the U.S. Department of Education (1992–1993). Data on average annual earnings in computer work were drawn from the Public Use Microdata 1 Percent Sample for the 1980 and 1990 U.S. Censuses (CIESIN 1995).

I also examine micro-level data from the National Science Foundation's Survey of Natural and Social Scientists and Engineers (SSE). The SSE data set contains career histories of 46,049 scientists and engineers who were sampled as part of the 1980 Census and surveyed again in 1982, 1984, 1986, and 1989 (U.S. Bureau of the Census 1991). NSF stratified the sample to ensure sufficient numbers of women, computer specialists, and engineers. They defined scientists and engineers as individuals having a scientific, engineering, or related occupation, having four or more years of college (two, if engineering), and being in the experienced civilian labor force or "labor reserve" (National Science Foundation 1984).[1]

I view computer work as a single occupation[2] whose members support other people's usage of computer systems, because it is one both from Hughes's standpoint (1971) that function should define occupation and from the standpoint of computer practitioners themselves (Denning 1991). One indicator of this internal coherence of computer work is that it is especially difficult to distinguish between specialties (Orlikowski 1988). Debons, King, Mansfield, and Shirey (1981) illustrate this difficulty by identifying over 300 job titles for computer professionals in a national survey of employers in the late 1970s, while reporting great difficulty in categorizing those job titles. Many computer workers' job and occupational titles are assigned to the residual category "not elsewhere classified" or its equivalent. A joint report of the Computer Science and Telecommunications Board and the Office of Scientific and Engineering Personnel of the National Research Council discusses this problem at length (Steering Committee on Human Resources in Computer Science and Technology 1993:12–19).

Combining computer workers into a single field assures capturing respondents as computer workers, even if it is unclear into which specialties they would have categorized themselves. While management analysts sometimes exclude engineers (Orlikowski 1988; Turner and Baroudi 1986), the many close ties between computer science and engineering (Steering Committee on Human Resources in Computer Science and Technology 1993) and the common practice in the 1990s of using the title "software engineer" for workers previously called "programmer/analysts" (King 1994) lead me to include engineers who provide computer support to others.[3]

I therefore include seven computer specialties or sub-occupations: computer programmer, computer systems analyst, other systems analyst, systems engineer, computer scientist, computer engineer, and other computer specialist.[4] This definition yields 6,162 respondents on the SSE who declared a computer specialty in at least one of the four waves: between 3,500 and 3,900 were employed in computer work in each of the four survey years. In each year, roughly 25 percent of the respondents were women and 18 percent were non-white—10 percent Asian, 5 percent black, and 3 percent other. Because the effects of Asian background on technical work are generally unlike those of blacks and other races (Tang 1991), racial analyses within my gender analysis require distinguishing between Asians and non-Asians. Small numbers of respondents limit these analyses to the margin, but I have included them below, where possible.

Figure 3.1. Women's Representation Among Computer Workers and
Computer/IS Bachelors Degree Recipients, 1971–1994

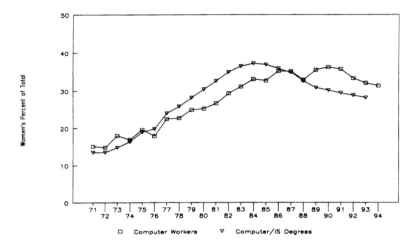

□ Computer Workers   ▽ Computer/IS Degrees

Notes: Computer Worker percentages are based on data for Computer Pro-
grammers, Computer Systems Analysts and Other Specialists, and Operations
Systems Researchers and Analysts (Bureau of Labor Statistics 1976–1995, supplemented by unpublished data for 1971–1974). Details of the calculation are in
Wright and Jacobs (1994). Computer/IS Degree percentages are based on data for
Bachelors Degrees in Computer and Information Sciences (Department of
Education data in Vetter 1992, supplemented by Department of Education
1992–1993 and unpublished data for 1992–1993). The data are for academic years,
marking each by the calendar year in which the academic year ends.

ENTRY AND EXIT RESULTS

Turning to the first set of results, let us explore women's participation in
greater depth. Beyond the few statistics given in the introduction, how has
that participation changed during the 1970s, 1980s, and early 1990s?

Since at least 1970, the first census year to count holders of computer
occupations, women have gained ground in computer work, though they
remain least represented in the engineering-related specialties. Two
related trends illustrate the dramatic increase in women's participation: in
the percentage that women comprise of those employed in computer specialties and in the percentage among those women receiving bachelor's
degrees in computer and information sciences. Figure 3.1 shows the trends
in these two percentages between 1971 and 1994, using data from the U.S.
Departments of Labor and Education.[5]

Women's occupational representation in the areas of computer programming, operations system research and systems analysis, and computer systems analysis and other specialties rose from 15 percent in 1971 to 36 percent in 1990, then fell back to 31 percent in 1994. Women's proportion of computer and information science degrees followed a similar, but earlier, pattern. In 1971, women received 14 percent of these degrees. This figure rose to 37 percent in 1984, but by 1993 had also fallen to 28 percent.

The rise in women's participation in computer work is consistent with women's increasing participation in the general labor force during this period (U.S. Bureau of Labor Statistics 1976-1994) and is less interesting than the subsequent decline. The important question is: Why might women's proportion be decreasing, after two decades of progress? Analysis begins by considering that women's participation can fall in three ways—by fewer women than men entering, by more women leaving than women entering, and by more women than men leaving.

First, regarding women's versus men's entrance rates, we have seen that women's attainment of computer and information science degrees is falling off. This is not the whole entrance picture, however, as men and women also enter in mid-career, as is shown by 47 percent of all entrants to the BLS category of computer systems analysts and scientists in 1986 coming from other occupations within their employing organizations, and 39 percent having left for another occupation and returned (Carey 1989, 1991).[6]

Turning to women's exit versus women's entrance rates and women's exit versus men's exit rates, Table 3.1 compares the exit and entry rates of men and women from computer work into and from the larger SSE panel during 1982–84, 1984–86, and 1986–89. In all three intervals, women leave at higher rates than they enter, and the difference is increasing over successive intervals. In all three intervals, on an absolute basis, men enter more than women enter, and men leave more than women leave. Between 1982–84 and 1986–89, there is no significant difference in either the percentage of men or percentage of women entering, but the percentage of both men and women exiting is significantly increasing. Combining these trends, on a *net* basis, women leave more than men leave. The difference does not change significantly over time, but as a *gender* difference it is significant in two of the three periods. These results complement results from the same data set (Wright and Jacobs 1994), which show that after controlling for differences in background, education, experience, specialty, and industry, women leave computer work more than men.

These results support the Social Control and refute the Male Flight Hypotheses. Independent of the proportion of women, women are less

Table 3.1. Social Control of Women's Progress in Computer Work on the
SSE, 1982–1989

	1982–1984	1984–1986	1986–1989
EXITS FROM COMPUTER WORK [1]			
Percent Men Exiting	27.6	27.2 NS	32.4++
Percent Men Entering	27.9	25.3+	28.5 NS
Net Percent Men Exiting	−0.3	1.9++	3.9++
Percent Women Exiting	21.4	23.0 NS	25.9+
Percent Women Entering	18.8	18.3 NS	20.2 NS
Net Percent Women Exiting	2.6	4.7+	5.7++
Gender Difference in Net	2.9	2.8 NS	1.8 NS
Exit Rates (Women—Men)	**	**	NS
Exit N^2			
Men	2,358	2,449	2,432
Women	772	799	750
Entrance N^2			
Men	2,449	2,432	2,362
Women	799	750	703

Notes: Significance of period difference to 1982–1984
++ $p < .01$ + $p < .05$ NS Not Significant

Significance of gender difference in net exits
** $p < .01$ NS Not Significant

[1] Exits to and entrances from the larger SSE panel of scientific and technical workers in the 1980 Census.
[2] Full- and part-time workers after records with unavailable data removed.

likely than men to enter computer work. Independent of the proportion of women, more women leave than enter the field. On a net basis, women are more likely than men to leave computer work.

Exits from computer work, however, may take many forms: career switches or lateral moves out of computer work, moves into management, job losses (exits to unemployment), and exits from the labor force. These may reinforce each other or they may cancel each other out. Wright and Jacobs (1994) show additional data refuting the Male Flight Hypothesis on these several forms of exit. Drawing from that paper and Wright (1994), Figure 3.2 shows the effects of engineering on the two types of

Figure 3.2. Engineering's Impact on Career Prospects in Computer Work

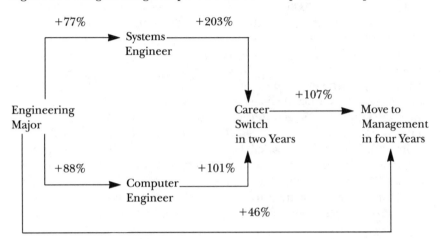

Note: Based on Tables 3–2, 3–14, and 4–4 in Wright (1994); Table 5 in Wright and Jacobs (1994).

exit most important for career progression, career switches and moves to management.

As seen on the figure, having an engineering major increases the likelihood of having an engineering specialist title, in that on the SSE 77 percent of all systems engineers and 88 percent of all computer engineers, respectively, have engineering degrees. Having the title of systems engineer raises, by 203 percent, the odds of making a career switch, or lateral move into noncomputer work, two years after being in computer work, while having the title of computer engineer raises those odds by 101 percent. In turn, making such a career switch in two years raises, by 107 percent, the odds of moving into management in four years, assisted by a 46 percent direct effect of being an engineering major. Not shown on the figure, but pertinent, is the fact that after controls, a direct gender effect appears for making a career switch, but not for moving to management: Being male increases, by 31 percent, the likelihood of making such a move. Similarly, after controls, a direct racial effect shows up for moving to management, but not for making a career switch: Identifying oneself as black lowers the odds of moving by 62 percent, as Asian, by 47 percent.

Is the minority effect related to the engineering effect? How are women of color affected by the fact that computer work rewards engineers? Table 3.2 shows the engineering composition of men and women, by race, in 1984 on the SSE. Non-white computer workers comprise only 18 percent of the men and 15 percent of the women, with Asians outnumbering blacks and other non-whites. These percentages reflect minority under-representation in the field, but slight over-counting in this sample. NSF statistics suggest that only 3 percent of computer specialists are black and 6 percent are Asian (National Science Foundation 1988). In terms of their representation among engineering specialists and majors, non-white computer workers are not disadvantaged vis-a-vis white computer workers. Numbers aside, the only significant racial difference in the table is that Asian men in computer work are more likely ($p < .01$) to be engineering majors than are white men in computer work. The conclusion is that although disproportionately fewer minorities make it into computer work, those who do are at least as likely as whites to be engineers.

More directly pertinent to the gender discussion is the fact that in all racial groups except "other" (which had too few respondents to show sig-

Table 3.2. Engineering Composition By Race of Men and Women in Computer Work on the SSE, 1984

	N^1	*Percent of Gender*	*Percent Who Are Computer or Systems Engineers*	*Percent Who Were Engineering Majors*
MEN				
White	1,955	83	24**	27**
Asian[2]	232	10	23**	38**
Black	106	5	29**	25*
Other[3]	65	3	32 NS	26 NS
Total	2,358	100	24**	28**
WOMEN				
White	657	85	8**	5**
Asian[2]	60	8	9**	7**
Black	33	4	9**	9*
Other[3]	22	3	14NS	14NS
Total	772	100	8**	6**

Note: Significance of gender difference in percent engineer/ing
    ** $p < .01$ * $p < .05$ NS Not Significant

[1] Full- and part-time workers after records with unavailable data removed.
[2] Asian or Pacific Islander.
[3] Hispanic, regardless of race; American Indian or Alaskan Native; Other.

nificance), significantly higher percentages of men than women were engineering specialists and engineering majors. Combining the racial groups, 24 percent of the men versus 8 percent of the women in computer work were either systems or computer engineers, while 28 percent of the men versus only 6 percent of the women were engineering majors. Converting percentages to probabilities, independent of race, a man in computer work is three times as likely as a woman to have an engineering specialty, and 4.7 times as likely as a woman to have been an engineering major.

EARNINGS AND SEGREGATION RESULTS

Having explored women's participation by examining gender differences in exits and entrances, as well as exits to management between engineers and nonengineers, let us now turn to the second set of results, which address women's separation from men while they're both in the field. As noted earlier, previous research has explored two areas of gender separation—the earnings gap between men and women and the degree of segregation between computer specialties. Lack of longitudinal data, however, has made the majority of these studies cross-sectional and difficult to compare.

On the earnings side, there have been a number of studies of the gender gap (Donato and Roos 1987; Glenn and Tolbert 1987; Heywood and Nezlek 1993; Kraft and Dubnoff 1983; Strober and Arnold 1987). None of the combinations of computer workers are directly comparable to the grouping derived from the practitioner definition used here, as none of the calculations include engineers. In addition, only two examine changes over time. Strober and Arnold (1987) find little change between 1970 and 1980, whether they use median hourly or mean annual data, Census reports or the Census PUMS sample. Using Current Population Survey data, Heywood and Nezlek (1993), however, find substantial variation over five-year intervals from 1975 to 1990. Both, interestingly, conclude that there has been little change during those periods.

What happens when segregation, rather than earnings, is examined? There have also been a number of studies in this area (Donato 1990; Donato and Roos 1987; Glenn and Tolbert 1987; Kraft and Dubnoff 1983; Strober and Arnold 1987). Only Strober and Arnold (1987) examine change over time, however, finding little change between 1970 and 1980 in the distribution of men and women across eight computer occupations (including electrical and electronic engineers, and computer and data entry operators) and between end-user and computer manufacturing industries.

Table 3.3. Collective Improvement in Women's Progress in Computer
Work on the SSE, 1982–1989

	1982	1984	1986	1989
EARNINGS				
Median Salary				
Men	35,000	40,000	43,000	50,000
Women	29,187	34,200	38,000	45,000
Median Salary Gap	83.4%	85.5%NS	88.4%**	90.0%**
SEGREGATION[1]				
D Across Industries	13.3	15.6NS	10.7NS	9.4*
D Across Specialties	18.0	18.4NS	18.6NS	[2]
D Across Work Activities	18.1	16.8NS	16.8NS	16.3
Earnings N[3]				
Men	2,671	2,689	2,631	2,532
Women	822	792	748	688
Segregation N[4]				
Men	2,358	2,449	2,432	2,362
Women	772	799	750	703

Note: Significance difference to 1982
  ** $p < .01$　　　* $p < .05$　　　NS　Not Significant

[1] D is the index of dissimilarity, the percentage of women who would have to
  change categories to be distributed like men and vice-versa.
[2] Specialty data not comparable in 1989 due to change in SSE computer categories.
[3] Full-time workers before records with unavailable data removed.
[4] Full- and part-time workers after records with unavailable data removed.

Table 3.3 presents men's and women's median full-time salaries on the
SSE in each of the four years, along with the resultant earnings gap. It shows
a gap of 83.4 percent (women earn 83.4 percent of what men earn) in 1982,
which narrows to 85.5 percent in 1984, 88.4 percent in 1986, and 90.0 percent in 1989. While these gaps are for the SSE panel and exclude labor
force entrants after 1980, a parallel analysis of computer workers in the 1
percent samples of the 1980 and 1990 Censuses yields a mean gap of 79.5
percent in 1979, which narrows to 82.6 percent in 1989 (CIESIN 1995).[7]
The SSE gap is narrower than the Census gap in 1989 because it is based on
medians rather than means and includes engineers who were not available
for the Census calculation. The SSE mean gap in 1989 was 87.3 percent,
within which the gaps for computer and systems engineers were 92.3 percent and 94.2 percent, respectively.

Table 3.3 also shows the index of dissimilarity (the percentage of women who would have to change categories to be distributed like men and vice-versa) in each of the four survey years across three SSE categories: industries, specialties, and work activities.[8] In two of the three cases, specialties and work activities, the index did not change significantly, remaining at 18–19 and 16–18, respectively. Across industries, however, the index declined significantly from 13 in 1982 to 9 in 1989.

On a collective basis, women's earnings were closing the gap with men's. In addition, the segregation of men and women slightly improved across industries, although it remained about the same across specialties and work activities. The declines in both the earnings gap and in segregation indicate collective improvement in women's position. The Kanter hypothesis is supported, while the Blalock hypothesis is not.

WOMEN'S CONTROLLED PROGRESS

Standing back from the two sets of results just reviewed, how can we interpret women's participation in computer work falling off through gender differences in entry and exit rates, when women have made collective progress in closing the earnings gap and reducing the segregation between industries? The results suggest that two different phenomena are occurring—collective progress and social control of individual advancement.

These phenomena support the theories of both Kanter (1977), that there will be collective strength in numbers, and Jacobs (1989), that social control will act to remove individual women from the numbers in question. As a result of these and related findings, I propose a hybrid theory of *controlled progress* for women in feminizing occupations—a theory which combines those of Kanter and Jacobs (Wright 1994). Consistent with Kanter, it predicts that as the proportion of women increases, segregation within the occupation should decline and the earnings gap should narrow. Consistent with Jacobs, however, it asserts that there should be countervailing social control forces operating on an ongoing basis to reinforce the occupation's segregation from other occupations. While there should be slow collective progress, there should also be high mobility into and out of it. Applying the theory to computer work, many women are attracted to it, but many also leave as a result of being made to feel unwelcome.

To understand how this combination can occur, consider first that both men and women enter computer work for any number of reasons. The reason most frequently cited for women is that it is one of the highest-paying occupations for women in the United States (Rytina 1982). As has just been shown, women have also been closing the earnings gap with men. For both men and women, major reasons for entering the field are that computer work is one of the largest technical occupations in the United States, employing one out of every four scientists and engineers (National Science Foundation 1988), and includes the second fastest growing set of occupational specialties in the 1990s—systems analysts and computer scientists (Silvestri and Lukasiewicz 1992).

At the same time that some women enter computer work, however, many women choose *not* to do so, and it appears their numbers are increasing. The reasons most frequently cited for women going elsewhere are socialization away from mathematics and science; software being mostly written by and for men; computer training programs being dominated by boys, men, and male values; and a common perception that computer work is a field for men and antisocial individuals (Committee on Women in Science and Engineering 1991; Decker 1986; Hartman et al. 1988; Newton 1991; Steering Committee on Human Resources in Computer Science and Technology 1993).

Factors put forward for the falloff in women's interest include male backlash (Breene 1993; Faludi 1991) and women's attraction to alternative male-dominated fields such as business (Leveson 1989). There is probably no easy way to measure male backlash, but Jacobs (1995) has shown that the decline of women's entry into computer science is part of a general stabilization in women's entry into male-dominated majors. Reasons suggested for the falloff in both men's *and* women's interest in computer work since the middle 1980s include an increasing misconception of the nature of the occupation (Cale, Mawhinney, and Callaghan 1991); an increase in the number of students taking programming in high school; and the personal computer having demystified, as well as given greater access to, computers (Committee to Assess the Scope and Direction of Computer Science and Technology 1992).

Returning to the results in this paper, that women leave more than they enter the field, leave more than men on a net basis, and leave more than men after controlling for identical characteristics and location may well be related to the perception that computer workers tend to be male and antisocial. Indeed, the perception has been shown to have some justification. Kiesler, Sproull, and Eccles (1985) find an educational "culture of computing," which many girls and young women find male, alien, and intimidating. Turkle (1988) describes its workplace counterpart, finding a general "computer culture" and a "hacker" subculture which dominates the larger culture, although actual hackers are few in number. Hackers are the heroes of the larger culture, who take pride in being antisocial and radically individualistic, as well as leading lives independent of relationships with women.

More generally, because computer work is an offshoot of electrical engineering, the occupation has taken on the culture of that field (Trice 1993). The engineering culture has been shown to be distinctly male in ideology and interactional style, valuing hardware and tinkering over software and problem solving, thus devaluing the gender characteristics of women (Bailyn 1987; Cockburn 1988; Hacker 1990; McIlwee and Robinson 1992). Once women enter computer work, this culture may well act as a vehicle for social control, telling women they are deviant, do not belong, and should avail themselves of the "revolving door" for women in male-dominated occupations (Jacobs 1989).

An alternative possibility may be raised—that women choose not to be engineering majors, the results attributed to differences in gender socialization and human capital (background and investments in education). Women's choice or free will, however, simply cannot be responsible for all of these effects. Once women enter computer work, they face a culture in which engineers are rewarded more than nonengineers. Women in computer work do not fit the engineering cultural mold—they are not male, and most of them are not engineers. Women leave at higher rates than they enter, and women's exit rates (net of entry) are higher than men's. When background, education, experience, specialty, and industry are controlled, women's exit rates are also higher than men's. More must be at work here than choice or free will. Although both men's and women's exit rates are increasing over time, that women's rates are higher than men's suggests that social control operates during, as well as before, women's participation in the workforce (Jacobs 1989). While additional research is necessary to confirm its manner of operation, the engineering culture in computer work appears to be a mechanism effecting that control, leading to women's higher mobility and greater penalties in advancement.

The engineering culture also suggests that the falloff in women's participation in computer work since the late 1980s may be related to the greater deployment of personal computers in a way opposite to the demystification and greater access suggested above by the culturally constrained Committee to Assess the Scope and Direction of Computer Science and Technology (1992). Since the mid to late 1980s, computer downsizing and reengineering have required many, if by now not most, individuals in the computer field to work with personal computers (Anthes 1993; Horwitt 1990). By necessity, supporting others on PCs requires more knowledge of and tinkering with hardware. In a sense, computer work is returning to the

1950s, when hardware knowledge and tinkering were essential to computer work. The engineering culture glorifies such knowledge, and many more men than women have a tinkering socialization (Hacker 1990; McIlwee and Robinson 1992).

Finally, during the 1990s, this culture may be intensifying, rather than lessening, its influence on computer work. Since the middle 1980s, hardware and engineering skills, held by many more men than women, have become even more important for progression in the field, as shown by employers appearing to increase their demand for individuals with formal education in computer science and engineering (Steering Committee on Human Resources in Computer Science and Technology 1993). With formal engineering skills in greater demand, even greater rewards are going to those who have those skills, and the engineering culture of computer work is being reinforced. The field has been engineering in nature since its inception, and may now be becoming even more so.

To close with an analogy: On the race track of computer work, women are increasingly driving cars like those driven by men, and their prize money is edging closer to that paid to men. However, all the cars have been designed by engineers in ways that permit engineers to go faster and enjoy a smoother ride. The track on which they compete has been designed by engineers in such ways that engineers are less likely to crash. While very few women are actually getting run off the track, and some women may simply leave because they're tired of racing, it is hard not to conclude that many women pull out because of a slow and relatively uncomfortable drive.

ACKNOWLEDGMENTS

This research was begun under a dissertation in sociology at the University of Pennsylvania under Jerry A. Jacobs, whose advice and assistance was critical to its completion. Other dissertation committee members were Paul Allison, Ivar Berg, and Chuck Bosk. Elaine Hall, Gary Jaworski, Chris Mills, Laura O'Toole, and Joyce Tang provided helpful comments specific to this chapter.

NOTES

1. The SSE sample was stratified into ten occupational groups, which included computer specialists and engineers. The survey also oversampled women and minorities. NSF's "labor reserve" includes people not currently

in the labor force who have worked in the last five years in a job in a scientific, engineering, or related occupation (National Science Foundation 1984).

2. This analysis uses the term "computer worker" to deliberately bypass the issue of whether or not computer work is a profession by sociological definition. For varying arguments in this regard, see Abbott (1988), Denning (1991), and Orlikowski and Baroudi (1989).

3. Supporting the view of computer work as a single occupation are similarities in self-reported work activities on the SSE between computer engineers and other computer professionals. There were also high rates of mobility between seven computer specialties, including computer and systems engineering, suggesting significant overlap between these fields.

4. The functional definition of computer worker was operationalized by including those SSE occupational titles at least a third of whose holders in each of the survey years gave "computer applications" or "technical development" as their primary work activity, then excluding individuals with Ph.D.s whose primary work activity was teaching or research in an academic setting. As described in Wright and Jacobs (1994), the number of included specialties was six in 1982, seven in 1984 and 1986, and nine in 1989. The seven listed are those in 1984 and 1986.

5. The education data in Figure 3.1 are from Vetter (1992), supplemented by the U.S. Department of Education (1992–1993 and unpublished data for 1992–1993). The data are for academic years starting with 1970–71, marking each by the calendar year in which the academic year ends. The employment data in the figure are a combination of those for all computer categories used in different years by the U.S. Bureau of Labor Statistics (1976–1995 and unpublished data for 1971–1974). Details of the calculation are in Wright and Jacobs (1994).

6. Unfortunately, entrants here "from other occupations" include entrants from other computer specialties, as well as other non-computer occupations. In 1986 computer work continued to feminize in spite of declining numbers of female degree recipients, suggesting that these are not the majority.

7. This narrowing is significant at $p < .10$. These figures combine computer programmers, operations and systems researchers and analysts, and computer systems analysts and scientists (CIESIN 1995). The mean gaps for computer programmers narrowed from 80.6 percent to 85.8 percent ($p < .10$), for operations and systems researchers and analysts remained the same at 78.6 percent and 79.7 percent (not significant), and for computer systems analysts and scientists remained the same at 82.0 and 81.8 percent (not significant).

8. Because industry categories changed in three of the four waves, the industry index was across seven industry groups—manufacturing, professional services, utilities, education, finance/insurance, government, and other. Because specialty categories changed as described in Note 4, the specialty index was across the seven in 1984 and 1986, with one category in 1982 "backed in" from other data as described in Wright (1994). The work activity index was across fifteen primary work activities, which did not change across waves—computer applications, technical development, two categories of management, consulting, design, operations, two categories of research, technical writing, testing, training, distribution, statistical work, and other.

REFERENCES

Abbott, Andrew. 1988. *The System of Professions: An Essay on the Division of Expert Labor.* Chicago: University of Chicago Press.
Anthes, Gary H. 1993. "Feds to Downsize with IT." *Computerworld* (September 13):1,16.
Bailyn, Lotte. 1987. "Experiencing Technical Work: A Comparison of Male and Female Engineers." *Human Relations* 40:299–312.
Blalock, Hubert M., Jr. 1967. *Toward a Theory of Minority-Group Relations.* New York: John Wiley.
Breene, L. Anne. 1993. "Women and Computer Science." *Initiatives* 55:39–44.
Cale, Edward G., Jr., Charles H. Mawhinney, and David R. Callaghan. 1991. "Student Perceptions of Information Systems Careers: Misconceptions and Declining Enrollments." *Journal of Research on Computing in Education* 23:434–443.
Carey, Max L. 1989. "Characteristics of Occupational Entrants." *Occupational Outlook Quarterly* (Summer):9–17.
———. 1991. "Occupational Advancement from Within." *Occupational Outlook Quarterly* (Winter 1991/1992):19–25.
CIESIN. 1995. *Interactive Census Explore Program* (on-line database). Ann Arbor, MI: Consortium for International Earth Science Information Network.
Cockburn, Cynthia. 1988. *Machinery of Dominance: Women, Men, and Technical Know-how.* Boston: Northeastern University Press.
Committee on Women in Science and Engineering. 1991. *Women in Science and Engineering: Increasing Their Numbers in the 1990s.* Washington, DC: National Academy Press.

Committee to Assess the Scope and Direction of Computer Science and Technology. 1992. *Computing the Future: A Broader Agenda for Computer Science and Engineering.* Washington, DC: National Academy Press.

Cournoyer, Paul E. 1983. *Mobility of Information Systems Personnel: An Analysis of a Large Computer Firm's Experience.* Ph.D. dissertation, Sloan School of Management, Massachusetts Institute of Technology, Cambridge, MA.

Debons, Anthony, Donald W. King, Una Mansfield, and Donald L. Shirey. 1981. *The Information Professional—Survey of an Emerging Field.* New York: Marcel Dekker.

Decker, Wayne H. 1986. "Occupation and Impressions: Stereotypes of Males and Females in Three Professions." *Social Behavior and Personality* 14:69–75.

Denning, Peter. 1991. "The Scope and Directions of Computer Science: Computing, Applications, and Computational Science." *Communications of the ACM* 34(10, October):129–131.

Donato, Katherine M. 1990. "Programming for Change? The Growing Demand for Women Systems Analysts." Pp. 167–182 in *Job Queues, Gender Queues: Explaining Women's Inroads into Male Occupations*, edited by Barbara F. Reskin and Patricia A. Roos. Philadelphia: Temple University Press.

Donato, Katherine M. and Patricia A. Roos. 1987. "Gender and Earnings Inequality Among Computer Specialists." Pp. 291–317 in *Women, Work and Technology: Transformations*, edited by Barbara D. Wright et al. Ann Arbor: University of Michigan Press.

Faludi, Susan. 1991. *Backlash: The Undeclared War Against American Women.* New York: Doubleday.

Freedland, Marjorie. 1987. *Computer/DP Professional Career Survey.* New York: Deutsch, Shea & Evans.

Glenn, Evelyn N. and Charles M. Tolbert II. 1987. "Technology and Emerging Patterns of Stratification for Women of Color: Race and Gender Segregation in Computer Occupations." Pp. 318–331 in *Women, Work and Technology: Transformations*, edited by Barbara D. Wright et al. Ann Arbor: University of Michigan Press.

Hacker, Sally. 1990. *Doing It the Hard Way: Investigations of Gender and Technology*, edited by Dorothy E. Smith and Susan M. Turner. Boston: Unwin Hyman.

Hartman, Sandra J., Rodger W. Griffeth, Lynn Miller, and Angelo J. Kinicki. 1988. "The Impact of Occupation, Performance, and Sex on Sex Role Stereotyping." *Journal of Social Psychology* 128:451–463.

Heywood, John S. and George Nezlek. 1993. "The Gender Wage Gap Among Software Workers: Trends Over the Last Two Decades." *Social Science Quarterly* 74:603–613.

Horwitt, Elizabeth. 1990. "Downsizing Quandary for IS Pros." *Computerworld* (March 5):1ff.

Hughes, Everett C. 1971. "The Study of Occupations." Pp. 283–297 in *The Sociological Eye: Selected Papers on Work, Self, and the Study of Society.* Book Two. Chicago: Aldine Atherton.

Hughes, Thomas P. 1987. "The Evolution of Large Technological Systems." Pp. 51–82 in *The Social Construction of Technological Systems,* edited by Wiebe E. Bijker, Thomas P. Hughes, and Trevor Pinch. Cambridge, MA: MIT Press.

Igbaria, Magid and Sidney R. Siegel. 1992. "The Reasons for Turnover of Information Systems Personnel." *Information & Management* 23:321–330.

Jacobs, Jerry A. 1989. *Revolving Doors: Sex Segregation and Women's Careers.* Palo Alto, CA: Stanford University Press.

———. 1992. "Women's Entry into Management: Trends in Earnings, Authority, and Values Among Salaried Managers." *Administrative Science Quarterly* 37:282–301.

———. 1995. "Gender and Academic Specialties: Trends During the 1980s." *Sociology of Education* 68:81–98.

Kanter, Rosabeth M. 1977. *Men and Women of the Corporation.* New York: Basic Books.

Kiesler, Sara, Lee Sproull, and Jacquelynne S. Eccles. 1985. "Pool Halls, Chips, and War Games: Women in the Culture of Computing." *Psychology of Women Quarterly* 9:451–462.

King, Julia. 1994. "Engineers to IS: Drop That Title!" *Computerworld* (May 30):1ff.

Kraft, Philip. 1979. "The Routinizing of Computer Programming." *Sociology of Work and Occupations* 6:139–155.

Kraft, Philip and Steven Dubnoff. 1983. "Software Workers Survey." *Computerworld* (November 14, In-depth Section):1–13.

———. 1986. "Job Content, Fragmentation, and Control in Computer Software Work." *Industrial Relations* 25:184–196.

Leveson, Nancy. 1989. *Women in Computer Science: A Report for the NSF-CISE Cross-Directorate Activities Advisory Committee.* Washington, DC: National Science Foundation.

McIlwee, Judith S. and J. Gregg Robinson. 1992. *Women in Engineering: Gender, Power, and Workplace Culture.* Albany: State University of New York Press.

National Science Foundation. 1984. *The 1982 Postcensal Survey of Scientists and Engineers.* NSF 84–330. Washington, DC: U.S. Government Printing Office.

———. 1988. *Profiles-Computer Sciences: Human Resources and Funding.* NSF 88–324. Washington, DC: U.S. Government Printing Office.

Newton, Peggy. 1991. "Computing: An Ideal Occupation for Women?" Pp. 143–153 in *Women at Work: Psychological and Organizational Perspectives,* edited by Jenny Firth-Cozens and Michael A. West. Philadelphia: Open University Press.

Orlikowski, Wanda J. 1988. "The Data Processing Occupation: Professionalization or Proletarianization?" *Research in the Sociology of Work* 4:95–124.

Orlikowski, Wanda J. and Jack J. Baroudi. 1989. "The Information Systems Profession: Myth or Reality?" *Office: Technology & People* 4:13–30.

Pfeffer, Jeffrey and Alison Davis-Blake. 1987. "The Effect of the Proportion of Women on Salaries: The Case of College Administrators." *Administrative Science Quarterly* 32:1–24.

Reskin, Barbara F. and Patricia A. Roos. Eds. 1990. *Job Queues, Gender Queues: Explaining Women's Inroads into Male Occupations.* Philadelphia: Temple University Press.

Rytina, Nancy F. 1982. "Earnings of Men and Women: A Look at Specific Occupations." *Monthly Labor Review* (April):25–31.

Silvestri, George T. and John M. Lukasiewicz. 1992. "Occupational Employment Projections." Pp. 62–92 in *Outlook 1990–2005,* BLS Bulletin 2402. Washington, DC: U.S. Government Printing Office.

Steering Committee on Human Resources in Computer Science and Technology. 1993. *Computing Professionals: Changing Needs for the 1990s.* Washington, DC: National Academy Press.

Strober, Myra H. and Carolyn L. Arnold. 1987. "Integrated Circuits/ Segregated Labor: Women in Computer-Related Occupations and High-tech Industries." Pp. 136–184 in *Computer Chips and Paper Clips: Technology and Women's Employment, Case Studies and Policy Perspectives,* Vol. II, edited by Heidi I. Hartmann. Washington, DC: National Academy Press.

Tang, Joyce. 1991. *The Career Mobility of Asian American Engineers: Earnings, Career Status, Promotion, and Attrition.* Ph.D. dissertation, Department of Sociology, University of Pennsylvania, Philadelphia, PA.

Tarallo, Bernadette M. 1987. *The Production of Information: An Examination of the Employment Relations of Software Engineers and Computer Programmers.* Ph.D. dissertation, Department of Sociology, University of California, Davis, CA.

Trice, Harrison M. 1993. *Occupational Subcultures in the Workplace.* Ithaca, NY: ILR Press.

Turkle, Sherry. 1988. "Computational Reticence: Why Women Fear the Intimate Machine." Pp. 41–61 in *Technology and Women's Voices: Keeping In Touch,* edited by Cheris Kramarae. New York: Routlege & Kegan Paul.

Turner, Jon A. and Jack A. Baroudi. 1986. "The Management of Information Systems Occupations: A Research Agenda." *Computer Personnel* 10(December):2–11.

U.S. Bureau of Labor Statistics, Department of Labor. 1976–1995. *Employment and Earnings.* January issues. Washington, DC: U.S. Government Printing Office.

U.S. Bureau of the Census. 1991. *Survey of Natural and Social Scientists and Engineers (SSE), 1989.* ICPSR 9504. Ann Arbor, MI: Inter-University Consortium for Political and Social Research.

U.S. Department of Education. 1992–1993. *Digest of Educational Statistics.* Washington, DC: U.S. Government Printing Office.

Vetter, Betty M. 1992. *Professional Women and Minorities: A Manpower Data Resource Service.* 10th ed. Washington, DC: Commission of Professionals in Science and Technology.

Wagner, Jennifer L. and Harry C. Benham. 1993. "Career Paths in Information Systems: A Longitudinal Analysis." Paper presented at the annual conference of the ACM Special Interest Group on Computer Personnel Research, April.

Wright, Rosemary. 1994. *Women in Computer Work: Controlled Progress in a Male Occupation.* Ph.D. dissertation, Department of Sociology, University of Pennsylvania, Philadelphia, PA.

Wright, Rosemary and Jerry A. Jacobs. 1994. "Male Flight from Computer Work: A New Look at Occupational Resegregation and Ghettoization." *American Sociological Review* 59:511–536.

4

Women Dentists

The Social Construction of a Profession

DENNIS O. KALDENBERG, ANISA M. ZVONKOVIC,
AND BORIS W. BECKER

Dentistry, like other professions, is changing. One of the most significant changes that has occurred in the past twenty years is an increase in the number of women in the profession. Using data from a variety of sources, this chapter compares the personal and professional lives of women and men practicing dentistry. When differences are observed, we attempt to account for the extent to which they result from choice and/or structural constraint. With this in mind, we interpret the data using a social constructionist perspective. This perspective acknowledges structural constraints but also recognizes that individuals exercise choice and creativity both when constructing a profession and in their personal lives.

OVERVIEW OF DENTISTRY

Compared to other professions, dentistry is relatively young (Goode 1969). One hundred and fifty years ago, dentistry in the United States[1] was a secondary occupation, performed by itinerant tradespeople who combined personal dental services with such things as barbering, selling medicaments, and performing minor surgery. Today, dentistry is an integral and powerful part of this country's sector of health professions, and dentists enjoy an income, prestige, and legitimacy comparable to medical doctors.[2]

Although not as large as medicine, dentistry is a significant industry. The national expenditure on dental care in 1990 was $34 billion (U.S. Health Care Financing Administration 1991). There are 155,000 active dentists in the United States (U.S. Bureau of the Census 1993), with an average number of three workers per dental office (Bureau of Economic and Behavioral Research 1987). The resulting dental workforce (including dentists) totals about one-half million (U.S. Bureau of the Census 1993).

The Nature of the Dental Practice Today

Like medicine, dentistry is composed of general practitioners (GPs) and specialists. Most dentists (88 percent) are GPs. Specialists include ortho-dontists, oral surgeons, endodontists, prosthodontists, periodontists, and pediodontists. The principal form of delivering dental services in the United States is through private-owned practices operated by solo practi-tioners.[3] Roughly 60 percent of U.S. dentists practice in this arrangement—about 10 percent are employed and 30 percent are partners in a private practice.

Although dental clinics, Health Maintenance Organizations (HMOs), and multi-dentist group practice/partnerships have increased in number over the past twenty years, they have not changed service delivery to any vis-ible extent, for example, in medicine. Complex organizational practice arrangements now dominate service delivery of medical and legal services (such as medical clinics or legal partnerships), but such complex organiza-tional arrangements are rare in dental service delivery. The nature of den-tal work favors the solo practitioner in independent practice; dentistry has been slow to absorb the forces of rationalization/bureaucratization that have transformed service delivery in other professions. Unlike law or medi-cine, independent solo practice is the preferred and most prestigious prac-tice arrangement. Although there is no formal dental career ladder, as seen in law offices, such as progressing from clerk to partner, there recently have been changes in the career paths of new dentists. Whereas dental graduates thirty years ago probably became independent practitioners upon gradua-tion, more recent graduates start in salaried positions. The new dentist may find work as an associate in the office of an established dentist, in public ser-vice (military, public health), or as an employee in a large dental clinic. New dentists may work in these positions for several years, during which time they improve their skills, pay off school debts, and make financial plans for future practice acquisition. Although a few dentists remain in these positions, historically the majority have left to pursue independent practice.

Old Style vs. New Style Dentistry

During the past twenty years there has been a shift in the way services are delivered. At one time, the dentist would have attended to all the patient's treatment needs. Although he or she may have employed a receptionist, the dentist would have performed the activities related to patient preparation and cleanup, and prophylaxis (teeth cleaning). Today, dentists in independent practice are small business operators who manage inventories, equipment acquisition and maintenance, physical facilities, and staff. The staff in a solo independent practice typically includes one or more dental assistants and/or dental hygienists, a receptionist/bookkeeper, and, possibly, a health insurance claims specialist and business manager. This private practice dentist is the CEO of a small business. In this new style of dentistry, a dentist delegates some tasks to dental assistants (patient cleanup, preparation, X-rays, impression taking) and others to dental hygienists (patient education, prophylaxis, injections). This division of labor frees the dentist to perform the more difficult treatment work (fillings, tooth shaping, root canals, surgery). It also means more patients can be processed in the dental office during the day. The use of dental auxiliaries has been hailed as a boon both to public health, as more people can be treated, but also to dentist's incomes, as they are able to collect revenue for these additional services (Chapko et al. 1985; U.S. General Accounting Office 1980).

Roots of the Sexual Division of Labor in American Dentistry

As the folk practice of dentistry yielded to forces of rationalization, the division of labor within the healing professions was hammered out between medical doctors and dentists. The dental practitioners were relegated to treatment of a certain type, within a certain region of the body. As the training of the dental practitioner became more formal, a division occurred between those providers who received more training and served the whole population and those who received less education and served specialized needs or populations. A body of lesser-trained auxiliaries, who were more likely to be female, emerged. In a number of countries, these women provided treatment to children in schools. These people were called dental hygienists in the United States, dental dressers in England, school dentists in Scandinavia, and school dental nurses in New Zealand. Even though these auxiliaries treated a special population or provided only limited services, they served, nonetheless, as potential competitors to the more extensively trained dentists (almost all of whom were male).[4] By the 1920s, the evolution of this form of dental manpower auxiliary in the United States and England was suppressed or discouraged[5] and was not actively resurrected until the 1970s, when the benefits of their contributions were touted (U.S. General Accounting Office 1980). In contrast, the Scandinavian school dentists were integrated into organized dentistry, which may account for the greater proportion of females in dentistry in Scandinavia (Davis 1980). In the United States and most of Europe, the auxiliary dental providers have been subordinated and brought under the direct control of the dentist. Today in the United States, the technically trained dental hygienist typically practices only under the direct supervision of a licensed dentist.[6]

In the early 1970s, females comprised only 1 percent of practicing dentists in the United States, compared to 8 percent in England, 23 percent in Sweden, and roughly 80 percent in Finland, Poland, and the former U.S.S.R. (U.S. Department of Health, Education, and Welfare 1976). While the health professions enjoy high occupational prestige in the United States, the prestige for such providers is much lower in Russia (Tillman 1975).

Since the early 1970s, the proportion of female dentists in the United States has been increasing slowly and is projected to reach 16 percent of all dentists by the year 2000 (U.S. Department of Health and Human Services 1989). This growth is the result of increased numbers of women graduating from dental school in the last twenty years.

From 1950 through 1972, females accounted for less than 1 percent of dental school graduates. In the '70s, the proportion began to increase, reaching one-fifth of all graduates by 1985 and one-third of the class in the 1990s. When compared to the proportions of professional (doctoral) graduates in medicine or law, however, the numbers for females entering dentistry are consistently lower (U.S. National Center for Education Statistics 1993).

The first female dentist was Emeline Rubert Jones of Connecticut (see Bremner 1958 and Sharp 1952 for complete details). After being told by her husband (whom she married in 1854) that dentistry was no occupation for frail and clumsy fingers, Emeline spent time secretly filling extracted teeth and studying anatomy and related fields. She showed her work to her husband, under the pretense that it had been completed by an aspiring dentist. After her husband reported that the work satisfied his professional

Figure 4.1. Dental Degrees Awarded By Sex, 1950–1991

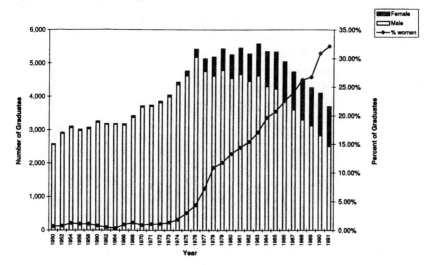

Source: Digest of Educational Statistics (Data prior to 1970 in two-year Intervals).

standards, she informed him that she had done the work. Emeline's husband was won over by the evidence, and Emeline worked with her husband for many years, carrying on the practice even after his death. She participated in the active practice of dentistry for nearly sixty years. Formal recognition of her skills came later in her life. She was elected to the state dental society in 1893 and given honorary membership in the National Dental Association in 1914.

Lucy Hobbs was the first female dental school graduate and first woman to be elected to a state dental society. Dr. Hobbs did not enter dentistry through her husband's office and, consequently, experienced more opposition from men in the organized profession. After she was denied training apprenticeships by many men with whom she applied, a rebel dentist finally gave her an opportunity. Eventually she acquired sufficient skills to open and build her own substantial practice in Iowa. Lucy, like most of her male colleagues, had no diploma to legitimize her skills. She applied to Ohio Dental College after developing her practice and was turned down. Years later, after she was elected to the Iowa State Dental Society (in 1865), she applied again to dental school and was accepted. The doors of some dental schools slowly began to open to women, but until recently most of the schools continued to be populated almost exclusively by men.

CONTEMPORARY COMPARATIVE DATA

This section will compare male and female dentists on a number of dimensions. The data come from a variety of sources. Some of the most representative data come from national probability surveys done by the American Dental Association (Bureau of Economic and Behavioral Research 1987, 1989, 1990). These data are supplemented with data reported in other dental journals and with findings collected by the authors in three separate surveys over a six-year period.[7]

Before comparisons begin, several caveats are in order. First, it is important to remember that the foremost difference between the two groups, which limits direct comparison of all other variables, is the relative difference in age between male and female dentists. Since females have entered the profession in large numbers only recently, the average age of female dentists is significantly lower than that of male dentists. Eighty-eight percent of the females were younger than age forty-five, compared to 50 percent of the males (Bureau of Economic and Behavioral Research 1990). The average female dentist is in a different stage of her personal and professional life cycle than is the average male dentist. To make comparisons more meaningful, we attempt to provide data for a younger age cohort (less than age forty-five) whenever such data are available. Second, although age-specific comparison will reduce some of the bias, the fact that a sizable number of females entered dentistry after working as auxiliaries (Keels et al. 1991; Price 1990) means the average age upon graduation from dental school is likely to be somewhat higher for females than for males.[8]

The Professional Lives of Female Dentists in Traditional Practice Settings

Although the proportion of women in both the dental schools and the profession has been increasing in recent years, there is evidence that women's professional experiences are different from men's. For many women, becoming a dentist is part of climbing up the health career ladder. Both Keels et al. (1991) and Price (1990) found that roughly one-third of female dentists had been employed as either a dental hygienist or dental assistant prior to entering dental school. Virtually no men are employed as dental assistants or dental hygienists.

Once out of dental school, males and females take slightly different career paths. Although the data clearly show a general trend for all new dentists to work as employees before moving into private practices, more young women than men are starting out this way. Nineteen percent of all

Table 4.1. Comparing Male and Female Dentists' Practice and
Professional Characteristics

	Females	Males
For profit setting[2]	95.10%	94.60%
Began career as employee[1]	43%	19%[a]
Began career as employee (age < 45)[1]	47%	31%
Hours in the practice (age < 45)[1]	41.3	43.9
Hours treating patients (age < 45)[1]	31.7	34.8
Hours working with staff[2]	27.70	33.2*
Average appointment length[1]	:45	:40
Appointments (including hygiene) per week[2]	49.6	74.0*
Owns practice (age < 45)[1]	68%	89%
Solo practice (age < 45)[1]	39%	59%
Employs hygienist (age < 45)[1]	53%	67%
Net income (GP age < 45)[1]	$46,120	$75,440
Net income (GP age 30–34)[1]	$45,710	$66,560
Net income (GP age < 45, full time, owners)[1]	$53,260	$73,970
Member of professional association[2]	55.70%	76.30%
Job satisfaction (scale score)[2]	53.3	55.2
Job involvement (scale score)[2]	14.7	15.3
Affective commitment (scale score)[2]	34.9	36.7
Behavioral commitment (scale score)[2]	10.6	11.8
Support independent practice for dental hygiene[3]	31.8%	9.3%*

* $p < .001$

[a] No significant figures were presented for ADA data, although the size of the sample would suggest that even small differences will be significant.

[1] From Bureau of Economic and Behavioral Research, ADA.

[2] From Kaldenberg, Becker, and Zvonkovic (1995).

[3] From Smith and Kaldenberg (1990).

men and 31 percent of men younger than age forty-five began their career as employees. In contrast, 47 percent of the women under age forty-five began their careers as employees.[9] These differences are reflected in the ownership patterns of dental practices. Even though, as stated earlier, the private ownership of dental practices dominates the profession, it is far more common for male (93 percent) than female (70 percent) dentists to own a dental practice, even when controlling for age (for dentists less than age forty-five, 89 percent vs. 68 percent, respectively). In addition, female dentists are more likely than male dentists to relocate their offices, often because of marriage and family demands (Linn 1970).

The hours spent in the practice and in treating patients appear to be quite similar for female and male dentists younger than age forty-five (41.3

Table 4.2. Comparing Male and Female Dentists' Demographic and
           Family Characteristics

	Females	*Males*
Younger than age 45[1]	88.50%	50%[a]
Married[1]	73%	88%
Never married[1]	17%	6%
Average # of children[1]	0.94	2.24
Average # of children (dentists age < 45)[1]	0.85	1.65
Old children[2]	48.60%	78.7%*
Young children[2]	28.50%	35.00%
Spouses with college education[1]	88%	73%
Weeks of leave taken for childrearing[1]	5.8	0.1
Hours spent in child care[1]	22	7.5
Hours spent in housework[1]	8.6	3.5
Hours spent in home maintenance[1]	3	4.8
Other household income[2]	56.20%	17.1%*
Stress[2]	20.5	17.1*

* *p* <.05
[a] No significant figures were presented for ADA data, although the size of the
   sample would suggest that even small differences will be significant.
[1] From Bureau of Economic and Behavioral Research, ADA.
[2] From Kaldenberg, Becker, and Zvonkovic (1995).

vs. 43.8, and 31.7 vs. 34.8, respectively). Women, however, appear to be
spending slightly more time with each patient and have fewer appointments in a one-week period. The latter difference may reflect a different
delivery setting or different style of dentistry—appointments per week will
be higher for dentists in private practice who employ one or more hygienists, since dentists usually provide a short dental exam in conjunction with
the patient's treatment by the hygienist. Waldman (1987), using data from
the Bureau of the Census, reported that the proportion of female-owned
(owned solely or more than 50 percent by females) dental offices with
employees was much smaller than for males (47 percent to 83 percent,
respectively, for 1977). Data collected in 1989 show that among new dentists, 67 percent of men and 53 percent of women employ a hygienist.
    The net incomes of male and female dentists are quite different, even
when controlling for practice circumstances (Strom 1989). Among general
practice dentists in the youngest professional cohort (those between the
ages of thirty and thirty-five), females had net incomes of about $46,000,
compared to about $66,500 for males. Some of the differences in average
income may be related to ownership, hours worked, and style of dentistry.

The disparity remains among full-time dentists (under age forty-five) who own their own practices; males earned $73,970, females earned $53,615 (Strom 1989). In regard to satisfaction with work, Kaldenberg, Becker, and Zvonkovic (1995) found no difference in overall job satisfaction between new male and female dentists. Price (1990) also reported that satisfaction with the practice arrangement increased with a dentist's gross annual income.

Female Dentists in Organizational Contexts

While the glass ceiling may be absent for professionals in small private practices, it is important to remember that the women who work in organizational settings may face barriers to professional advancement. Unfortunately, few studies have been done on dentists who work in organizational settings other than private practice and, consequently, little information exists on the experiences of women in these contexts.

The underrepresentation of women in dental school faculties (Nash 1991) and administration (Solomon 1990), however, may indicate that glass ceilings do exist for female dentists in complex organizational contexts. The barriers that may exist in the organized profession are also unclear. Women are active in professional organizations and have been elected as presidents of both national and state dental associations, suggesting that barriers in these settings have diminished. Women, however, also have their own professional association, the American Association of Women Dentists (AAWD), which publishes a newsletter called the *Chronicle*. AAWD strives to keep the larger professional association apprised of the views and interests of women dentists. Findings from our studies (see Table 4.1) suggest that female dentists are less likely to be members of professional associations.

Personal and Family Lives

Consistent with evidence from other studies of professionals (Uhlenberg and Cooney 1990), male dentists (88 percent) are more likely than female dentists (73 percent) to be married. Seventeen percent of females have never been married, compared to 6 percent of males. Males have an average of 2.24 children, females 0.94; when the comparison is limited to dentists under age forty-five, the averages are 1.65 for males and 0.85 for females. The spouses of female dentists were more likely to have a college education. The female dentists were also more likely than male dentists to live in households that had additional sources of income and to come from families where both parents have a college degree. Forty-seven percent of the females dentists in a national probability study done by Price (1990) reported being married to a health professional, of whom 70 percent were dentists. That is, nearly one-third of the married female dentists in Price's study were married to dentists. Price also reported that many of these private female practitioners were in partnership with their spouses.

Many studies have suggested that women report more interruptions in their professional life than do men. Aside from vacations and illnesses, the primary reasons for these interruptions were marital and family demands (Linn 1970; Rosner 1984). Females spent more time away from work for family reasons. Males averaged 0.1 weeks of leave for child rearing, compared to 5.8 weeks for females. Female dentists who have children reported spending 22 hours per week in child care, males 7.5 hours. Females spent more time each week in housework (8.6 hours) than males (3.5 hours), while men spent more hours per week in home maintenance (4.8 hours) than did females (3.0 hours) (Bureau of Economic and Behavioral Research 1989, 1990). Price (1990) found that the likelihood of a female dentist working more than twenty-nine hours per week decreased as the number of children increased.

ACCOUNTING FOR THE DIFFERENCES

The data suggest women are gaining a foothold in the dental profession, but also that family and professional experiences of female dentists are different from those of their male colleagues. The reasons for the differences, unfortunately, have not been adequately explored. Age differences make comparisons a problem, but even when comparisons are controlled (for age, ownership, and practice setting), there still are differences in practice patterns for male and female dentists, particularly in net income. Differences in shouldering family responsibilities may account for much of the difference in time spent in practice and in net income. Even in today's post-feminist era, family responsibilities constrain women to a greater extent than men, and are likely to impose unique limitations on the female dental practitioner. Many female dentists face conflicts of a personal nature that involve social and interpersonal relationships, marriage, and child-bearing. Tillman and Horowitz (1983) argue that women who are interested in developing a private practice are in a particular bind: "[The] period of intense career building coincides with a woman's peak biological childbearing years, and it is therefore unrealistic to expect that a woman's career could be patterned exactly after the traditional model" (p. 35). These responsibilities may explain why more females than males elect not to pursue the more lucrative forms of practice and remain in salaried or part-time positions for a longer period of time.

Anecdotal accounts have suggested that some women were attracted to dentistry, and the other professions, because the work provided good salaries and schedule flexibility (ideal for family/work juggling). Traditionalists in the professions feared such motivation might represent a shift in priorities from those of male practitioners, suggesting that females would be less committed to their profession. Kaldenberg, Zvonkovic, and Becker (1995) found that new female and male dentists were not significantly different in professional commitment or job involvement. A study that examined the career motivations of female dental students (Austin and Tenzer 1980) concluded that female dental students chose their careers for independence, self-employment, and altruistic reasons. The study, unfortunately, did not compare these responses to male students, which one might conjecture to be quite similar.

Accounting for differences in income among full-time, general practitioners who own their practices is a topic which needs further examination. The difference in income, in fact, may be related to market demand. The gender of the practitioner may influence some consumers' initial selection of a provider. Gender stereotypes held by the general public likely carry over to selection of providers and assessments of their competence. Nimmo (1992) suggests that some patients, as well as some colleagues, perceive the female dentist to be less capable. Consequently, females have a harder time gaining patient and public trust in their knowledge, capabilities, and competence. On the positive side, some preconceptions may help; women dentists may be seen as more caring, with a gentler touch, causing less pain, or being better with children (even though they are not necessarily interested in pedodontics) (Tillman and Horowitz 1983).

Studies of attitudes of patients of male and female dentists (Douglas, Reisine, and Cipes 1985) found no difference in overall satisfaction with dental service provided by males and females. Interestingly, patients of female dentists actually gave their dentist higher marks for accessibility and reasonable cost of treatment than did the patients of male dentists. Judging from the demographics of the patients who participated in this study, male and female dentists treat similar types of patients with one big exception— the patients of female dentists were significantly more likely to report lower incomes. This raises the question about differences in fee structures that may be found between male and female dentists. Based on evidence in the study just mentioned, we hypothesized that women's salaries were lower, at least in part, because their fees were lower. Whether this pricing difference reflected a strategy to attract patients, or a greater sense of altruism in providing access to lower-income populations, or resulted from the female practitioner's lower costs of doing business or lower target income requirements, is an issue which needs further examination.

Women may find it more difficult to start new practices. Cavallaro (1984), for example, suggested that female dentists have more problems than do men in getting bank loans. Females may have greater difficulty connecting to the male professional cliques in which valuable technical and management information is exchanged (Tillman and Horowitz 1983). It is also possible that many females who started as auxiliaries now find themselves unprepared for the position of boss (usually managing a female staff). Statham (1987, 1988) hypothesized that men and women managers in larger organizational settings were held to different expectations and thus performed and were evaluated differently. Women, she argued, were expected to be more person-oriented and thus were judged harshly if they did not meet those expectations. This person-oriented management style is more time-consuming and carries no explicit reward structure. In a study of hygienists and assistants, Zvonkovic and Marks (1990) found some differences in how employees perceived their male or female bosses. Hygienists employed by female dentists viewed them as significantly more task- and person-oriented. Assistants working for female dentists viewed their bosses as more person-oriented than did assistants who worked for males. Staff, regardless of the gender of the boss, reported higher job satisfaction when the dentist was perceived to have a person-oriented management style.

WOMEN DENTISTS AND THE FUTURE
OF THE DENTAL PROFESSION

Another question which begs for additional study is how, if at all, the profession of dentistry will be transformed by the increasing number of female practitioners. Waldman (1981), for example, posited that women, who work in greater numbers as employees and in organizational settings, may be more used to being told what to do and, consequently, may respond more favorably to third-party (government/insurance) intervention into dentistry. In regard to health workforce planning, Waldman (1985) presents data to suggest that the future health workforce projections may be overestimated, owing to gender differences in lifetime productivity. Such projections forecast the health care workforce based on the estimated number of practitioners and their estimated productivity (hours worked, patients treated, full-time years in profession). These estimates have been made based on historical patterns for male practitioners. If females provide less treatment to the public over their career span, it is possible that a future public may be underserved; if females provide more treatment, fewer professionals would be needed.

Another question addresses gender-related dental school enrollment trends for the next twenty years. Since the 1970s we have seen significant increases in the proportions of women entering dental schools. Can we expect these proportions to level off as parity is achieved? Niessen (1991) asks the intriguing question: Are we prepared for a profession that is dominated by females? Such a pattern already is occurring in other fields; females, for example, now receive a greater proportion of the doctoral degrees granted in pharmacy (U.S. National Center for Education Statistics 1993). There is some evidence that occupational prestige of a profession is inversely related to the number of women who practice therein, and may decrease as the proportion of women in the profession increases (Abbott 1988). This hypothesis will be tested in upcoming years as the proportion of women has increased slowly and steadily in many high-prestige U.S. professions such as law, medicine, dentistry, and engineering.

ACTIONS TO REMOVE OBSTACLES

Female dentists are presented with a different set of obstacles than are men (Niessen 1991). The extent to which these obstacles are structural or the result of personal decisions is a matter we have not resolved. When inequities result from differential organization or institutional barriers, corrective actions may be appropriate. To remedy such barriers, Niessen (1991) suggests the following actions: (1) Continue to recruit women and minorities for dental school and leadership positions in the organized profession; (2) Collect representative data on women (using oversamples) to monitor progress; (3) Develop a system of organizational civil rights to encourage women's participation in professional activities/organizations; (4) Encourage schools to take affirmative action seriously when making hiring and promotion decisions; and (5) Develop links between dental associations and other professional associations (i.e., the AMA) which have considerable knowledge on gender-related issues. Neidle (1986) echoes these suggestions as she asserts that young females need more role models in the profession. Furthermore, dentistry would be well-served to consider the proposals that have been outlined for remedying racial and ethnic inequities in the medical professions (Institute of Medicine 1994). These recommendations could be useful both in gender and racial issues[10] confronting the dental profession.

THEORETICAL PERSPECTIVES APPLIED TO WOMEN IN DENTISTRY

While the information we have presented provides insight into the changes that are occurring in a specific profession, it behooves us to use it in conjunction with a larger theoretical framework, in an attempt to gain a broader understanding of how these specific patterns may illustrate the general concepts of gender and profession. In other words, what broader understanding can be derived from the mass of data that we have just presented? Theoretical perspectives, such as tokenism (Kanter 1977) or size discrimination (Blalock 1967), have been used to explain gender-based discrimination in other contexts.

Tokenism might be useful for examining differences in larger organizational contexts (government, education, organized profession) but historically, these contexts have employed a small proportion of dentists—the independent private practice setting is where most dentists work. Size discrimination theories, which expect wage disparities to become more pronounced as the size of the minority increases, are difficult to test owing to the recency of any significant change in proportions and the lack of reliable comparative data from earlier periods in the profession.

Considering the variety of theories that could ground our discussion, we believe the social constructionist theories offer insights for framing the patterns we have observed. The social constructionist perspective sees gender not as a fixed trait but rather as process, fluid, and continuously reconstructed (Gilbert 1993; West and Zimmerman 1987). When gender[11] is fixed, it becomes biological difference; the biological differences between women and men ultimately will dictate what a man's or woman's family and professional life will be like. Gender as process, in contrast, conceptualizes gender as continuously created, constructed, and negotiated. Through social interaction in diverse settings, women and men come to an understanding of what it means to be a man or a woman. Until relatively recently, people understood that to be a woman meant that one could not be a competent dentist; biological differences dictated the differences in work life. The manner in which dentistry and the personal lives of female and male dentists are being reconstructed needs to be considered. The women who selected dentistry as a profession were considered mavericks entering a profession dominated by males. As the proportion of women in dentistry increases, the women who enter the profession may differ from their maverick predecessors. Over time, the way in which the profession is constructed will change in the eyes of men and women. These changes will influence how the profession is seen, both by people who may choose to train as dentists, as well as by practitioners and patients.

Acker (1990) posits that gender may apply not just to individuals, but to organizations. Just as certain organizations come to be gendered as masculine or feminine so can a profession develop a gender. Dentistry's gender, like that of other professions, has been masculine. When viewed as process, the gender of the profession and the individuals who practice in it will interact and be reconstructed as the sexual composition of the professional workforce changes.

Constructing Gender and Dentistry

The data previously presented indicate that women and men do not have similar career paths in the dental profession. Roughly one-third of female dentists first served as dental hygienists and assistants, then retrained as dentists to overcome blocked mobility in the rigid professional division of labor.[12] It would be interesting to investigate further the motives, choices, and barriers that exist for these women and how they may differ from women and men who took a more direct route into the profession. Young women need the same support and mentoring systems that have benefited men, whether financial or symbolic. If a career ladder existed between the paraprofessional women-dominated occupations and the male-dominated professions, more females might enter the profession. Emeline Jones climbed the dental profession ladder provided by her husband, and Lucy Hobbs climbed a ladder provided by a maverick male practitioner, before such ladders were removed by the formalization of training and credentialing within the profession. Davis (1980) suggests that the Scandinavian countries extended the ladder to the paraprofessionals as the profession formalized, thus permitting a greater proportion of men and women in that culture to construct a view of dentistry as more consistent with the female gender.

The social constructionist perspective can provide a new way to understand the transformations that are occurring among professionals and the profession itself. The data we have presented point to numerous differences in the professional lives of male and female dentists. What is uncertain is the extent to which these differences reflect deliberate decisions that the women and men have made about constructing their professional lives.

In this vein, Niessen (1991) argues that direct comparison of the activities of women to men too often, and perhaps incorrectly, implies that the male career pattern is the gold standard. She sees women redefining practice options. As a result of women's activity, dental practice will mean something different tomorrow than it does today. And, likewise, gender will be understood differently tomorrow than it is today. Differences in work hours, time with patients, and types of patients treated reflect the socialization in which women are seen as caregivers to their families and spouses and men are seen as providers. These gender expectations influence the choices that male and female dentists make about their professional lives. Gender expectations also influence doctor-patient interaction—females may spend more time with patients because people spend more time talking to females in general. Each person constructs the profession in view of his or her personal life. For example, given differences in marital status, it appears that more males than females see professional activity and marriage as congruent. When female dentists are married, the income from the practice is less likely to be the only source. Like other dual-career households, the woman dentist is likely to be the secondary wage earner (Gerson 1990; Hertz 1986). Consequently, her construction of her professional life will be different from that of someone who is the sole or primary income provider. If her family structure has less demand for or places less value on her income, she will construct a profession in which part-time, lower income is acceptable. This is consistent with Linn's (1970) observation that most female dentists practice for self-satisfaction rather than for financial gain. As Niessen (1991) points out, the independent practice of dentistry is a laboratory for how women would set rules for careers and families in other contexts, if given the opportunity.

The dental profession will be reconstructed during the next decade as it responds not only to shifts in its sexual composition, but to health care reform and shifting demographics. The role men and women play in this reconstruction will hinge largely on how they construct their gender and on the role that dentistry has in that construction. It is possible the profession will construct multiple tracks which come to be populated disproportionately by men or women. It is equally possible that the multiple tracks are populated by people, who for whatever reason (children, golf, health, lifestyle) choose a limited practice arrangement to a full-time career. The extent of these patterns will become clearer as the present cohort of young, childbearing-age women grow into middle age and empty nests, where family constraints on careers become less imposing.

ACKNOWLEDGMENTS

The authors thank Professor J. Henry Clarke of the Oregon Health Sciences University Dental School for providing a number of documents on the history of women in dentistry.

NOTES

1. This examination focuses primarily on dentists and dentistry in the United States. As with other professions whose natures vary depending on their legitimizing context, the structure and function of the dental profession in the United States will be different from the form it takes in other countries. The relationship between payment mechanisms (self, insurance, government) and treatment will influence both the professional reward structure and the settings in which the dental service is delivered.

2. For a detailed account of the development of the dental profession, see Peter Davis, *The Social Context of Dentistry*.

3. Solo dentists include dentists who share space with another dentist but do not combine management or patients. The designation for the arrangement is "solo/solo share space."

4. Bremner (1958) provides the following account of early views of dental auxiliaries: "But the dental profession as a whole is not yet completely reconciled to these partially trained and legally circumscribed subspecialists. The cleavage seems to be between the school men connected with the institutions which train these young women, the successful practitioners who are able to employ a hygienist profitably in their practice on the one hand, and the average dentist who has sufficient time to do his own prophylaxis. The latter looks upon this new intruder as a competitor, for he feels that if the busy men were unable to delegate the prophylaxis work, some of those patients would of necessity drift into his own office" (pp. 378–379).

5. Gies (1926) reports that the English dental dresser was abolished under pressure from the profession of dentists.

6. There is an effort by hygienists in some states to lobby legislatures to permit the independent practice of dental hygiene. In Colorado, hygienists were granted such independence in 1986.

7. The research methodologies for these studies were reported in Becker and Kaldenberg [1987 survey], Kaldenberg, Becker, and Zvonkovic (1995) [1989 survey], and Kaldenberg and Gobeli (1995) [1992 survey].

8. Unpublished data from surveys conducted by the authors found females to be one year older than males upon graduation from dental school.

9. An attitudinal survey of New Jersey dentists (Quinn 1977), administered as the number of female graduates from dental school was just beginning to increase, reported that these dentists would be willing to hire a female associate and would pay her the same salary they would pay a male associate.

10. We have not examined the issue of race in dental practice. The data on this topic are even more limited than that which is available on gender differences. In a baseline study of the characteristics of women dentists, Keels et al. (1991) reported that 77.1 percent of female dentists were white, 10 percent Hispanic, 7.1 percent Asian, 5.1 percent black, 0.2 percent American Indian, and 0.6 percent other.

11. We make a distinction between sex and gender. Sex is biologically based, gender is cultural expectations applied to sexual differences.

12. This may account for the female dentist's more positive attitudes toward the independent practice of dental hygiene (Smith and Kaldenberg 1990).

REFERENCES

Abbott, Andrew. 1988. *The System of Professions: An Essay on the Division of Expert Labor.* Chicago: University of Chicago Press.

Acker, Joan. 1990. "Hierarchies, Jobs, Bodies: A Theory of Gendered Organizations." *Gender and Society* 4:139–158.

Austin, Grace B. and Amy Tenzer. 1980. "Female Dental Students: Current Status, Motivation, and Future Plans." *Journal of the American Dental Association* 100:353–357.

Becker, Boris W. and Dennis O. Kaldenberg. 1990. "Advertising Expenditures By Professionals: An Empirical Investigation of Dental Practitioners." *Journal of Advertising* 19:23–29.

Blalock, Hubert M. Jr. 1967. *Toward a Theory of Minority Group Relations.* New York: John Wiley and Sons.

Bremner, M.D.K. 1958. *The Story of Dentistry.* Brooklyn, NY: Dental Items of Interest Publishing.

Bureau of Economic and Behavioral Research. 1987, 1989, 1990. *The 1986 Survey of Dental Practice: Employment of Dental Practice Personnel.* Chicago: American Dental Association.

Bureau of Economic and Behavioral Research. 1989. *A Comparative Study of Male and Female Dental Practice Patterns.* Chicago: American Dental Association.

———. 1990. "Practice and Personal Characteristics, 1988 Survey." *Journal of the American Dental Association* 120:407–408.

Cavallaro, Carl J. 1984. "Women in Dentistry: A Study of the Factors That Influence the Utilization of the Professional Degree in Dentistry." Ph.D. dissertation, Department of Women's Studies, George Washington University, Washington, DC.

Chapko, Michael K., Peter Milgrom, Marilyn Bergner, Douglas Conrad, and Nicholas Skalabrin. 1985. "Delegation of Expanded Functions to Dental Assistants and Hygienists." *American Journal of Public Health* 75:61–65.

Davis, Peter. 1980. *The Social Context of Dentistry.* London: Croom Helm.

Douglas, Holly, Susan T. Reisine, and Monica H. Cipes. 1985. "Characteristics and Satisfaction of Patients of Male versus Female Dentists." *Journal of the American Dental Association* 110:926–929.

Gerson, K. 1990. *Hard Choices.* Berkeley: University of California Press.

Gies, W.J. 1926. *Dental Education in the United States and Canada: A Report to the Carnegie Foundation for the Advancement of Teaching.* New York: Carnegie.

Gilbert, L.A. 1993. *Two Careers/One Family.* Newbury Park, CA: Sage.

Goode, William J. 1969. "The Theoretical Limits of Professionalization." Pp. 266–313 in *The Semi-Professions and Their Organizations,* edited by Amitai Etzioni. New York: The Free Press.

Hertz, Rosanna. 1986. *More Equal Than Others: Women and Men in Dual Career Marriages.* Berkeley: University of California Press.

Institute of Medicine. 1994. *Balancing the Scales of Opportunity: Ensuring Racial and Ethnic Diversity in the Health Professions.* Washington, DC: National Academy Press.

Kaldenberg, Dennis O., Boris W. Becker, and Anisa Zvonkovic. 1995. "Work and Commitment Among Young Professionals: A study of Male and Female Dentists." *Human Relations* 48:1355–1377.

Kaldenberg, Dennis O. and David Gobeli. 1995. "Total Quality Management Practices and Business Outcomes: Evidence from Dental Practices." *Journal of Small Business Management* 33:21–33.

Kanter, Rosabeth M. 1977. *Men and Women of the Corporation.* New York: Basic Books.

Keels, Martha A., Linda M. Kaste, Jane A. Weintraub, Dushanka V. Kleinman, Carl Verrusio, and Enid A. Neidle. 1991. "A National

Survey of Women Dentists." *Journal of the American Dental Association* 122:31–41.

Linn, E.L. 1970. "Professional Activities of Women Dentists." *Journal of the American Dental Association* 81:1383–1387.

Nash, David A. 1991. "The Feminine Mystique in Dental Education: A Feminist's Challenge." *Journal of the American College of Dentists* 53:33–36.

Neidle, E. 1986. "To Make Things Right." *Journal of Dental Education* 50:297–299.

Niessen, Linda C. 1991. "Women Dentists: From Here to the 21st Century." *Journal of the American College of Dentists* 58:37–40.

Nimmo, Susan S. 1992. "Where Are All the Women in Dentistry?" *American Dental Association News* 23:4.

Price, Shelia S. 1990. "A Profile of Women Dentists." *Journal of the American Dental Association* 120:403–407.

Quinn, Irwin. 1977. "New Jersey Dentists' Opinions on Women As Associates." *Journal of the American Dental Association* 94:717–718.

Rosner, Judith F. 1984. "Career Patterns of Female and Male Dentists." *Journal of Dental Practice Administration* 1:89–94.

Sharp, Jacob. 1952. "Connecticut Pioneer Woman Dentist—Dr. Emeline Roberts Jones." *Dental Items of Interest* 74:614–622.

Smith, Judith and Dennis O. Kaldenberg. 1990. "The Independent Practice of Dental Hygiene: A Study of Attitudes of Oregon Dentists." *General Dentistry* 38:268–271.

Solomon, Eric. 1990. "Promotion and Appointment to Administrative Positions of Dental School Faculty by Gender." *Journal of Dental Education* 54:530–534.

Spencer, A. J. and J. M. Lewis 1988. "The Practice of Dentistry By Male and Female Dentists." *Community Dentistry and Oral Epidemiology* 16:202–207.

Statham, Anne. 1987. "The Gender Model Revisited: Differences in Management Styles Between Men and Women." *Sex Roles* 16:409–429.

———. 1988. "Women Working for Women: The Manager and Her Secretary." Pp. 225–243 in *The Worth of Women's Work: A Qualitative Synthesis*, edited by Anne Statham, Eleanor M. Miller, and Hans O. Mauksch. Albany: State University of New York Press.

Strom, Tamara. 1989. "Why Are Women Dentists Earning Less?" *American Dental Association* News 20:1, 10, 12.

Tillman, Randi Sue. 1975. "Women in Dentistry: A Review of the Literature." *Journal of the American Dental Association* 91:1214–1220.

Tillman, Randi Sue and S.L. Horowitz. 1983. "Practice Patterns of Recent Female Graduates." *Journal of the American Dental Association* 107:32–35.

Uhlenberg, Peter and Teresa M. Cooney. 1990. "Male and Female Physicians: Family and Career Comparisons." *Social Science and Medicine* 30:373–378.

U.S. Bureau of the Census. 1993. *Statistical Abstract of the United States 1992.* Washington, DC: U.S. Government Printing Office.

U.S. Department of Health, Education, and Welfare, Public Health Service, Health Resources Administration. 1976. *Women in the Health Careers: Chart Book for the International Conference on Women in Health.* Washington, DC: U.S. Government Printing Office.

———. 1978. *Minorities and Women in the Health Fields.* Washington, DC: U.S. Government Printing Office.

U.S. Department of Health and Human Services. 1989. *Seventh Report to the President and Congress on the Status of Health Personnel in the United States.* Washington, DC: U.S. Government Printing Office.

U.S. General Accounting Office. 1980. *Increased Use of Expanded Function Dental Auxiliaries Would Benefit Consumers, Dentists, and Taxpayers.* HRD–80–51. Washington, DC: U.S. Government Printing Office.

U.S. Health Care Financing Administration. 1991. *Health Care Financing Review.* Fall. Washington, DC: U.S. Government Printing Office.

U.S. National Center for Education Statistics. 1993. *Digest of Educational Statistics.* Washington, DC: U.S. Government Printing Office.

Waldman, H. Barry. 1981. "Some Consequences of the Increasing Number of Women Dentists." *Journal of the American Dental Association* 103:563–567.

———. 1985. "Female Dentists: A Factor in Determining Their Available Future Work Force." *Journal of the American College of Dentists* 52:22–27.

———. 1987. "Female Dentists: Practice Plans and Practice Activity." *Annals of Dentistry* 46:37–39.

West, Candace and Don H. Zimmerman. 1987. "Doing Gender." *Gender and Society* 1:125–151.

Zvonkovic, Anisa and Stephen R. Marks. 1990. "Coworker Intimacy in a Small Workplace: A Feminist Inquiry." Paper presented at the Preconference on Theory Construction and Research Methodology, National Council on Family Relations. Seattle, Washington, November 10.

5

Race and Ethnic Minorities and White Women in Management

Changes and Challenges

NANCY DiTOMASO AND STEVEN A. SMITH

Business organizations were the primary targets in the protest movements for civil rights. In the early days of the protests, blacks demanded access to "jobs and freedom." In the subsequent movements by other excluded groups, both white women and other ethnic minorities made similar demands for access to "good jobs." Without doubt, substantial change has occurred over the last several decades in the United States. Both white women and racial and ethnic minorities have moved in unprecedented numbers into jobs from which they were previously excluded, including jobs in corporate management.

There are controversies, however, about how and why such changes have occurred and about both the quality and magnitude of the changes. Some have argued that whatever changes have emerged were the direct result of political protest and its consequences. Recent gains, therefore, are thought to be precarious as political winds shift (Collins 1989). Others have emphasized the effects of changes in the life cycle of the baby boomers in the post-World War II generation, especially the dramatic increase in the labor force participation rates of young (especially white) women (see discussion by Friedland and DiTomaso 1994). Finally, some have argued that the changes have been a consequence of the economic ups and downs that have contributed to tight or slack labor market demands (Farley 1984).

Clearly, all of these factors have contributed to the changes which have been evident in the labor force involvement of white women and racial and ethnic minorities over the last several decades.

In this chapter, we describe those changes with reference to jobs in corporate management, and then we consider some of the explanations for the differences in labor force success for white women and minorities compared to white males in management jobs.

CHANGES IN THE COMPOSITION OF MANAGEMENT JOBS

While it would appear to be rather straightforward to determine who holds what sorts of jobs and how that has changed over time, it turns out to be surprisingly difficult. Data are usually collected for a purpose. When the purpose changes, the data collection procedures may lag behind or not change at all. This has been the case for the kind of government data on which most scholars rely for learning about changes in the structure of occupations and the economy. The most problematic aspect of providing data on trends over time is that the categories change. Such changes have occurred in the categories of occupations, in the classifications of racial and ethnic groups, and in the populations used as the base (e.g., by age category). Further, data available from different sources frequently use variations in definitions. With these caveats, we can provide some general descriptions of the current composition of the managerial labor force and some indication of how it has been changing.

Prior to 1960, there was extensive segregation by race and gender in managerial jobs, with most white women and minorities excluded from such jobs. The level of segregation began to change after 1962, when blacks, who had been concentrated in the lowest status and lowest paid jobs, began to gain access to better jobs (Farley 1984:46–50). The greatest changes were not, however, in managerial jobs, but in those characterized as blue-, grey-, and pink-collar. For example, black men were hired in greater numbers in blue-collar craft and operative and in grey-collar service jobs, while black women were hired in pink-collar clerical jobs. There were increases in the proportion of blacks (especially men) in managerial jobs as well, but because they were such a small percentage of those holding such jobs prior to 1970, they continued to make up a small proportion of the managerial labor force. In fact, blacks comprised only 6 percent of all white-collar workers (managers, professionals, technicians, sales and clerical workers) by 1968 (U.S. Department of Labor 1969:40).

The greater access of minorities to white-collar jobs clearly came about because of the political pressure brought to bear by the Civil Rights movement, and the subsequent legislation. Title VII of the Civil Rights Act became effective in July 1965, and by March 1966, government contractors were required to provide "compliance reports." Stories of blacks who sought management jobs before this legislation show strong evidence of a color bar (Collins 1989; Davis and Watson 1985). Despite the legal mandates, the 1966 Manpower Report of the President gave less than a page to the topic of equal opportunity (U.S. Department of Labor 1966:6–7), and there is no mention of the occupational distribution of blacks compared to whites. By 1969, data were provided on "Improvements in Negro Employment," including on the topic of "Occupational Upgrading" (U.S. Department of Labor 1969:38–41).

During this same period there was rapid growth in the kinds of occupations from which blacks had been excluded, including professional and technical (33 percent), clerical (30 percent), service (20 percent), operative (20 percent), and craft jobs (15 percent). There were slower increases as well in other types of jobs, including managerial (9 percent), nonfarm laborer (5 percent) and sales (4 percent). There were declines during this period in both farm laborer and private household positions, that is, jobs in which blacks had been over-represented (U.S. Department of Labor 1969:36–38). Thus, while occupational opportunities were improved for black workers during this period, it was partly a result of the strong demand for such workers in the growing economy during the Vietnam War. The same kind of trend is evident in subsequent years, as black men and women began to enter various professional jobs. The improved access to such jobs tended to be most evident in those jobs which white men, especially, and white women, to some extent, found less attractive (Sokoloff 1992). Even so, the improvements for blacks in more prestigious and higher-paying jobs during the 1960s occurred at a faster rate than the growth of these jobs in the economy, suggesting that there was indeed a shift in access and available opportunity. The decrease in the level of job segregation occurred more by race among women (e.g., in clerical jobs) than it did among men (Farley 1984:49), but overall, gender segregation continued to be more prevalent than racial segregation after the mid–1960s (Reskin and Padavic 1994:56).

Tables 5.1 and 5.2 provide data on the proportion of minorities and women in white-collar jobs for both 1975 and 1993. Using data from the Equal Employment Opportunity Commission (EEOC), we can see that the increase in the proportion of all minorities (both genders) in jobs classified as "managerial" and "official" increased 100 percent between 1975 and

Table 5.1. White Collar Jobs, 1975–1993, Percent Minority

	Officials & Manager	Professionals	Techni- cians	Sales Workers	Office/ Clerical Workers
1975	5.4	7.5	12.1	9.4	14.4
1993	10.8	14.3	19.9	20	23.7
Percentage Change	100	91	64	113	65

Source: EEOC.

Table 5.2. White Collar Jobs, 1975–1993, Percent Women

	Officials & Manager	Professionals	Techni- cians	Sales Workers	Office/ Clerical Workers
1975	14.2	30	33.3	47.8	80.2
1993	29.9	50.2	46.9	56.5	82.95
Percentage Change	111	67	41	18	3.4

Source: EEOC.

1993. The increase for women (all races) in such jobs was 111 percent, presumably because of the slightly higher rate of increase for white women compared to nonwhite women. In other types of jobs, the representation of minorities increased at a faster rate than the representation of women, for example, sales workers (113 percent for minorities compared to 18 percent for women), professionals (91 percent compared to 67 percent), technicians (64 percent compared to 41 percent), and office and clerical workers (65 percent compared to 34 percent). What appears here to be an advantage for minorities is partly an artifact of small numbers, in that women were already a larger proportion of employees in such jobs in 1975 than were minorities.

Table 5.3 provides data for more detailed racial and ethnic categories in all white-collar jobs covered by the EEOC reporting for 1993. Because EEOC data are derived from government contractors who are required to provide evidence of compliance with affirmative action guidelines, they also present a more favorable view than would be evident from data on the total workforce. We also include, in Table 5.4, therefore, 1993 data from the U.S. Department of Labor, Employment and Earnings Report, on the percentage of women (all races) and blacks and Hispanics (both genders)

Table 5.3. Minority Distribution in EEOC-Covered White-Collar Jobs, 1993
(Percent)

	Officials & Managers	Professionals	Techni- cians	Sales Workers	Office/ Clerical Workers	% Total*
All						
Minorities	10.8	14.3	19.9	20.0	23.7	23.5
Blacks	5.3	5.5	10.5	10.6	14.0	12.7
Hispanics	3.1	2.7	4.7	6.8	6.4	7.2
Asians	2.1	5.8	4.3	2.1	2.9	3.1
Native Americans	0.3	0.3	0.4	0.5	0.4	0.5

Source: EEOC; *Total workforce for EEOC-covered employers.

in all types of executive, administrative, and managerial (EAM) occupations. Compared to their proportion in the total adult workforce, blacks are underrepresented in all types of managerial jobs, except those in the public sector, in education, as personnel specialists (e.g., affirmative action officers), and as inspectors and compliance officers. Hispanics are under-represented in even these types of occupations. They are represented proportionally to their numbers in the labor force only in food service and lodging establishments. Women are also underrepresented in most managerial jobs, with the exception of jobs in education, medicine and health, as accountants and auditors, personnel specialists, and buyers. In more detailed studies of managerial and professional jobs, both women and minorities are concentrated even in these "good" jobs in those with lower status, income, and advancement potential (Reskin and Padavic 1994; Reskin and Roos 1990; Sokoloff 1992).

THEORETICAL EXPLANATIONS FOR INEQUALITY IN MANAGERIAL JOBS

There is extensive theoretical and empirical work on inequality in the labor market, all of which is applicable to managerial jobs (Becker 1957, 1964; Bergmann 1986; Bielby and Baron 1986; Braddock and McPartland 1987; England 1992; Goldin 1990; Jackman 1994; Jencks et al. 1988; Marini 1989; Reich 1981; Reskin and Roos 1990; Sokoloff 1992; Szafran 1982; Tomaskovic-Devey 1993; Von Glinow 1993). Some have restricted the explanations for inequality to market phenomena, and have subsequently

Table 5.4. Percent Women and Minorities in Executive, Administrative, and Managerial Occupations, Age 16 and Over, 1993 (Percent of Total)

Occupation	Women	Black	Hispanic
Officials and administrators, public administration	45.2	11.3	4.5
Financial managers	46.2	4.4	4.2
Personnel and labor relations	60.7	7.9	4.6
Purchasing managers	34.9	8	5.3
Marketing, advertising, and public relations	31.2	3.1	3.5
Administrators, educators and related fields	59.9	13	3.8
Medicine and health	70.5	6.5	4.2
Food service and lodging establishments	43.4	8.1	7.8
Properties and real estate	45.7	6.6	6.3
Funeral directors	18.6	7.1	3.3
Accountants and auditors*	49.2	7	4.2
Underwriters*	69.9	4.9	4.8
Other financial officers*	48.7	5.7	4.8
Management analysts*	33.7	3.9	2
Personnel, training, and labor relations specialists*	64.1	12.5	6
Buyers, wholesale and retail trade, except farm *	48.7	4.8	4.7
Construction inspectors*	5	10.8	4.6
Inspectors and compliance officers, except construction*	25.8	10.9	6.8
Percent of Total Work Force 16 years and Over	45.8	10.2	7.8

Source: U.S. Department of Labor, Employment, and Earnings, January, 1994.
Note: *Management-related occupations.

divided the explanations into "supply side" (e.g., human capital theory) and "demand side" (e.g., discrimination, job queues) explanations (Marini 1989). Human capital theory (Becker 1964) argues that workers receive returns on the value of their investment in their own human capital. Thus, wages vary depending on the levels of education, experience, and effort of workers. In studies of wage differences, human capital models explain about half of the variance, but education itself explains surprisingly little (see summary by Reskin and Padavic 1994).

Demand side explanations assume that the unexplained variance from models of income inequality are due to discrimination (on the assumption that they are "unexplained" by variables that measure contribution). In this regard, the extensive literature on job segregation provides evidence of unequal access to good jobs (Bielby and Baron 1986; Goldin 1990; Tomaskovic-Devey 1993; Von Glinow 1993). Internal and segmented labor market theories, as well as theories of job and labor queues, assume some employers give preference to white males for the best jobs (Hodson 1978; Kaufman 1986; Reskin and Roos 1990). In addition to explicit discrimination by employers, there are also theories which suggest that unequal outcomes are the result of more institutionalized practices, such as the processes used for recruiting (Braddock and McPartland 1987); the relationship between job incumbents and the evaluation of the worth of jobs (England 1992); and theories of pre-labor market socialization practices, which cause women or minorities to seek only certain types of training and jobs (Marini 1989).

In management jobs, human capital explanations focus more on experience, hours worked, and job attitudes than on education. Even so, only recently have women and minorities been receiving the same level of education as white men, and doing so from the same schools. There is still evidence, though, that women and minorities are less likely to major in those fields that are most highly rewarded in business (Spilerman 1988). White women and minorities clearly have less accumulated experience in management jobs than do white men, because of their previous exclusion. This is often taken as an indicator that it is still too early to tell about how things are changing. Various commentaries on this subject, however, have indicated that the rate of change is so slow that the future does not appear especially egalitarian (Kanter 1988; Reskin and Padavic 1994). Further, others have argued that there are enough women and minorities with the years of experience that should have led to their upward mobility in corporate jobs, if they had not been excluded.

Because women's availability both to work long hours and to travel frequently is often constrained by family and child care responsibilities, it is presumed that women workers are less valuable to employers than are men who are not so constrained (Schwartz 1989). Because black women are more likely than white women to be single parents, there may be added burdens for the former in this regard (Smith and Tienda 1988). Also, there is evidence that the patterns of housing segregation work to the disadvantage of blacks in both their search for and ability to work effectively at jobs that are located in white suburbs (Alexis and DiTomaso 1983; Massey and Denton 1993), as are many jobs in corporate management.

Questions have been raised as well about whether white women and minorities have the necessary leadership skills to perform management jobs. For example, some have argued that white women are not aggressive enough to be effective in managerial roles, while minorities are perceived to be too aggressive. While there does seem to be a narrower band of acceptable behavior for white women and minorities than for white men, the evidence does not support an argument that differences in either behavioral style or attitude account for the differences in success levels for women and minorities compared to white men. What differences may exist are minor, and they do not vary systematically with success on the corporate ladder (Davis and Watson 1985; Morrison et al. 1987; Powell 1993). Further, there is still evidence that even when white men are matched with white women and minorities on measurable factors that might suggest differences in "productivity," white men still rise further and faster to the top in corporate hierarchies.

Evidence of job segregation in corporate management is also quite strong. White women and minorities tend to be concentrated in jobs that have shorter career ladders, less decision-making authority, and more vulnerability to shifts in labor market demand (Collins 1989; Kanter 1977; Reskin and Padavic 1994; Sokoloff 1992). For example, Sokoloff found that the professional jobs in which white women and minorities entered between 1960 and 1980 were those jobs which were "deteriorating" in the sense of losing status, income, and opportunity. Like Reskin and Roos (1990), Sokoloff found that in times of major changes in occupational structure, white men still end up in the best jobs. Among women professionals, she found that white women have a more favorable situation in terms of access to good jobs than do black women.

There is additional evidence of other aspects of discrimination in managerial jobs. The best jobs are those which require the use of discretion, and in such jobs, there is a strong preference for hiring people whom one knows and can trust. Thus, social networks are especially important for good jobs (Granovetter 1974; Salancik and Pfeffer 1978). Getting ahead in corporations is also related to the opportunity to do a good job, which is made possible by the kind of position one holds (Kanter 1977). Some jobs carry with them the opportunity to be visible to important people, and therefore, the opportunity as well to be chosen for even better jobs. But jobs do not remain unchanged as new people enter them. As both Reskin and Roos (1990) and Sokoloff (1992) have found, when women or minorities gain access to jobs from which they have been excluded, the jobs themselves are often reevaluated. That is, white men begin to think of them as jobs to avoid, which jobs end up paying and carrying with them less authority than when white men held them (see also England 1992). There are a number of jobs "in transition" which have followed this path. For example, recently the American Psychological Association hired researchers to determine if the influx of women into the field was contributing to the downgrading of the profession and, consequently, to lower pay.

There is still a great deal of controversy regarding why white women and minorities have not yet reached parity with men in managerial jobs. The complexity of the issues involved are, of course, related to the political nature of the subject matter. The questions posed and the answers given are not simply a matter of describing what currently is, because much of the concern has to do as well with what would happen if discrimination were eliminated and people were not constrained from taking advantage of opportunities. An example of this issue can be seen in the controversies about whether women are as involved as men in work outside the home. Past research has found women are less involved than men on standard measures of involvement, but because women are frequently not in the same kinds of jobs, one cannot determine from this research whether differences in attitude have to do with innate gender differences, differences in the roles which women and men are encouraged to play, or differences in the opportunities available to them (see, e.g., Kanter 1977; Powell 1993; and Morrison et al. 1987). When men and women are in the same types of jobs, it has been found that they construct their social identities around work in the same way (Bielby and Bielby 1989). In this case, as presumably is true of other kinds of issues as well, men and women are found to be different, but the differences are primarily because they have different life experiences, with different opportunities and rewards.

The same also could be said regarding minorities. Because whites and nonwhites are distributed differently across the labor force, research that compares averages by group, without taking into consideration these differences, are comparing groups which are not really comparable. The alternative, however, which is to match groups in various ways, then runs the risk of not representing the real economic circumstances for group members. Thus, explanations for inequality have to be contingent and cautious, because different circumstances make predictions about a future of equality that is difficult to gauge.

THE POLITICAL DYNAMICS OF MANAGERIAL JOBS

The current picture of white women and minorities in managerial jobs thus presents a very mixed view. Progress has been made, in that jobs previously unavailable to anyone but white men have now become more diverse. Upward mobility has been slow, but there are some notable exceptions. The income gap has been narrowing for white women and men, yet the gap is still large and seems to widen with career experience. Some have described the picture as a glass both half full and half empty (Sokoloff 1992). The picture is even more complicated, though, because it appears the future will not be like the past. The economic transformation currently underway in the United States and across the global economy toward a knowledge-based economy is changing the structure of organizations, of jobs, and of the labor market. Thus, even more than before, it is difficult to sort out trends from temporary advances or setbacks. In other words, are the changes which we have described just the beginning of a future of full access to good jobs for women and minorities, or are they only the fragile response to government mandates that may be withdrawn or modified? We want, therefore, to look further at what happens on the job by addressing three areas of research that are relevant to sorting out what is happening to white women and minorities in managerial jobs. Specifically, we want to briefly review the research on performance appraisal bias, the "glass ceiling," and the controversies about affirmative action policies.

Performance Appraisal Bias

Neither white women nor minorities have reached parity with white men in management jobs in any sector. Discrimination is one potential explanation, but there is also some who would presume that the reasons for continued inequality is, in the eyes of their employers, women and minorities are not contributing as much as white men. The impact of government pressure to increase the representativeness of the workforce has raised similar concerns (Kluegel 1985). Research on performance appraisal is one means to address the issue of potential differences in contribution, and extensive literature exists on this topic. Most of this literature has focused on the issue of potential bias in appraisals, with the assumption that an environment that had excluded white women and minorities is also one that is likely to evaluate them more severely.

The research on performance appraisal differences, however, underlines the political nature of studies of gender and race and ethnicity. In general, studies done prior to the advent of equal employment legislation show more evidence of bias than studies done subsequently (Chen and DiTomaso 1995). As the legal consequences have grown when evidence of bias is found, it has become more difficult to find evidence that such bias exists. In addition, the Civil Rights movement has contributed to a general understanding in the culture that overt gender and race/ethnic bias is not acceptable. Thus, a new kind of bias seems to be more evident in U.S. culture than the old-fashioned kind, namely, what Gaertner and Dovidio (1986) label, "aversive racism." Their studies have found that whites are increasingly reluctant to disfavor minorities, but express their bias by favoring whites. Results consistent with this claim were found in a study of performance evaluations among scientists and engineers. Net of measures of contribution, whites were favored over others, especially in evaluations of promotability into management (Smith et al. 1995).

There is not clear evidence, however, that white women and minorities are rated lower on performance evaluations. In studies which control for the type of job and the actual performance, women have often been rated as high or higher than men. That women are rarely in the same jobs as men is thus a confounding factor in interpreting this research. Also, some research has found that when clear signals are given of high performance (e.g., by sponsorship, highly visible assignments, or other notable events), women may be rated higher (Heilman et al. 1988). The research on minorities, which has been done mostly on blacks compared to whites, is similar to that on gender, but there are some variations as well. There is more evidence in the performance appraisal literature that blacks are rated lower than whites, especially by supervisors. Studies that have found blacks to be rated higher have generally included peer evaluations by other blacks. Also, high-performing blacks are not necessarily rated higher, but lower-performing blacks tend to be rated more favorably than lower-performing whites (Sackett and DuBois 1991).

A review of the literature on bias in performance ratings shows less evidence of bias than one would expect, given the unevenness in representation in higher-level management positions. In addition, even those effects that are found to account for a trivial amount of variance in most quantitative models. The lack of results can be accounted for, it seems, in part because of social desirability responses on the part of study subjects. In addition, some effects appear to be the result of "aversive racism." Also, the results may be so meager because performance appraisals are really a symbolic rather than a substantive tool for women and minorities in management positions. One study, for example, found that variations in performance evaluations "paid off" more for men than for women: ". . . at managerial levels, the relationship between appraisal ratings and salary was much stronger for men than women. The wage gap favored men by only $342 at lower levels, while it was $2,340 greater for men at higher levels. These findings suggest the salary allocation process, not the performance appraisal process, may be the source of bias in large organizations" (Drazin 1987:157). In addition, the results of such studies may underestimate relevant effects because the comparisons have to be made of those in similar situations, when most white women and minorities are not in the same jobs and performing the same tasks as white men.

The Glass Ceiling, Concrete Walls, and Sticky Floors

As already indicated, there is strong research evidence to show that white women and minorities tend to be concentrated in a limited number of jobs, even within management. For example, minorities tend to be in "segregated" jobs, that is, jobs which Collins describes as "directed at, disproportionately used by, or concerned with" minorities (1983:374). In a subsequent article on black managers, Collins used the term *racialized labor* to describe the jobs of black managers for "white institutional functions that have a manifest or symbolic connection to black constituents or black issues" (1989:326). White women and other minority groups appear to be segregated as well, although not as much as is evident for black managers. Women, for example, tend to be found in "helping" roles (e.g., training, counseling) or those which primarily require social skills (e.g., human resources, public relations, or marketing). Hispanics and Asians, like blacks, are often found in positions that serve or address their own ethnic populations, or alternatively, work in their international divisions.

The issue of a glass ceiling has received prominent attention in the last few years because the federal government has initiated a commission to address the reasons for the absence of white women and minorities in higher level jobs (U.S. Department of Labor 1991). The metaphor of a glass ceiling alludes to women and minorities in management positions being able to see top jobs, but not being able to reach them because of an invisible barrier (Morrison et al. 1987). For example, even in the public sector, where both white women and minorities are disproportionately found, they are still concentrated in lower-level jobs. As reported following one of the hearings of the government Glass Ceiling Commission: "Minorities account for 28 percent of federal jobs but fill only 8 percent of top posts . . . Women make up 44 percent of the workforce, but 87 percent of the top posts are held by men" (Manegold 1994). Others have used the imagery of concrete walls to refer to the segregation into staff jobs, like human resources. And some have used the imagery of a sticky floor to indicate that women and minorities have a difficult time getting beyond entry-level positions (Berheide 1992).

In addition to looking at the proportion of white women or minorities in various levels of management, in comparison with their availability in the labor force, others have looked at specific types of high level positions in major corporations, for example, Chief Executive Officer, member of the board of directors, or member of the top management team. Looking specifically at these types of positions, various studies have found not only that there are few white women or minorities in such positions, but also that not much has changed in terms of their representation at this level of corporate management over the last decades (University of California at Los Angeles/Korn-Ferry International 1993; Von Glinow 1988). One recent report, for example, indicated that half of the top 500 corporations had no women on their boards of directors and most of the others have only one or two.

While there is a popular perception that white women and minorities are doing well in corporate management at the expense of white men, the evidence does not support this. In government jobs, white men still dominate the top-level positions. In corporate positions, white women and minorities are almost absent from the very highest levels and, when represented at the middle level, are most typically in segregated or "racialized" positions that are not avenues to the higher level. While improved access is evident in many types of occupations, women and minorities have gained the greatest foothold into those positions that white men find less attractive. Indeed, when women and minorities begin to appear in new jobs, their very presence often signifies that the jobs are less desirable for white men. There is also a perception among women and minorities that black women are doing especially well. Again, the evidence on almost any indicator does not support such a view. In terms of income, job level, job type, and measures of well-being, black women are almost always in the least favorable situation, with white women and black men taking turns in line, depending on which type of job is at issue.

Among minorities, Asians have much higher representation than do others in professional and technical positions, but are still underrepresented compared to their level of educational attainment, and there are still barriers to their advancement in many types of corporate jobs. The situation for Hispanics is again quite diverse. Those with college educations and lighter skin, especially those who are Cuban in origin, are often indistinguishable from whites, but the majority of Hispanics do not have these characteristics. Hence, we find they are under-represented in almost all areas of management. Discrimination is also apparent regarding national origin, with increasing complaints to the EEOC from foreign-born workers.

A recent article on such complaints indicated that foreign-born workers also face a glass ceiling (Swoboda 1991).

Affirmative Action Policies and Controversies

There is probably no policy that emerged from the Civil Rights movement which has generated more controversy and, among whites, opposition, than affirmative action. At the time of this writing, there is a growing initiative to ban racial preferences in employment and education, namely, to outlaw affirmative action policies (*Business Week* 1995; Holmes 1995). While not part of legislation, the mandate for firms to take affirmative action in compliance with equal opportunity laws is part of an executive order which has the force of law. Survey data indicate that almost all whites are opposed to such policies, including white women who are often the beneficiaries (Kluegel 1985). Conservative groups have recently been working through targeted litigation to undermine these policies.

The legal mandate regarding affirmative action is that government contractors of a certain size are required to provide a plan of action for obtaining compliance with Civil Rights legislation. Unlike the legislation itself, the affirmative action guidelines hold firms responsible for the outcomes, as well as for their good intentions, in personnel decisions ranging from recruiting and hiring to promotion and training (see DiTomaso and Thompson 1988). Further, the guidelines rule out the use of screening devices that have an adverse effect on the selection of minorities or women, and they require that any such procedures must be shown to be directly related to the job tasks for which selection is being made. In the past, both the firms and the federal oversight agencies paid attention primarily to the overall numbers. Only with the advent of the Glass Ceiling Commission has more directed attention been given to the internal processes of upward mobility.

The unpopularity of affirmative action policies, in fact, has made it de rigueur among diversity managers and consultants to downplay affirmative action and to try to distinguish it from diversity as a concept in management practice (Thomas 1990). Focusing on affirmative action is characterized as a lower level of sophistication than is focusing on diversity management "as a business strategy." The rush to broaden the definition of diversity has led one commentator to claim, "Diversity is often all talk, no affirmative action" (Wynter 1994). At least some corporations, however, have taken affirmative action to heart. For example, Xerox Corporation has been noted for both its serious attempt to make a "balanced workforce" part of its management practice at all levels and for its success, especially with black men, in improving the upward mobility of women and minorities in its corporate ranks (Friedman 1991). A key aspect of its success is that it not only held managers accountable for making unbiased decisions, but it also included within its program, the responsibility for managers to provide the necessary training so that a representative pool of employees would be available from which to choose.

There is extensive literature on the effects of affirmative action policies on employment outcomes (Farley 1984; Jencks 1985; Leonard 1984; Molotch 1988; Smith and Welch 1984). This research shows fairly clearly that in the absence of affirmative action policies employers are less likely to hire women and minorities and, where such policies are in place, women and minorities fare better in terms of employment and income. The research also shows, however, that one of the presumed costs of affirmative action is that employers have become more conservative in their hiring practices, for example, with blacks, and have chosen to hire those blacks with higher levels of education. Jencks (1985), for example, argues that because affirmative action policies make it more difficult for employers to get rid of employees who do not work out, and because other screening devices were made more difficult to use, black males with only a high school education or less have had a harder time finding jobs. The study by Smith and Welch, however, found that most of the improvement in both wages and employment occurred early in the 1970s, "before the establishment of an effective monitoring and potential sanctions of the affirmative action programs" (1984:269).

The opposition to affirmative action by whites has been based on a presumption that women and minorities are gaining advantages at the expense of white males. Such views have been widespread, despite the evidence, as already noted, that women and minorities have tended to gain access only to those occupations which were expanding, becoming less attractive to white men, and were less likely to have advantages associated with other good jobs. The most public applications of affirmative action have been in college entrance decisions and in some public sector employment decisions (such as promotion to sergeant in police and fire departments). In these situations, selections have been made for a fixed number of slots for which there is strong competition and high demand among white men, as well as among women and minorities. Even in this situation, however, Dawes (1993), for example, has argued that the few whites who may be adversely affected by giving special consideration to women and minorities are likely to be those in the middle of the distribution of test scores and, thus, those for whom such scores are less reliable. One can also question the utility of relying so heavily on standardized tests, especially given that their origin was to limit the entrance of Jewish immigrants to elite educational institutions. Furthermore, the use of regional preferences in college admissions had the same origin (Sadker and Sadker 1994; Steinberg 1989).

Affirmative action policies are of special concern in management jobs because, like college admissions, these are the jobs in which white men are still very interested. Thus, increasing the pressure on corporations to improve their record of access for white women and minorities directly challenges what has, in effect, been affirmative action for white males (MacKinnon 1987:36). Like most cases where affirmative action has been especially controversial, the overwhelming imbalance in the representation of white men compared to other groups makes the arguments about their disadvantage, in light of affirmative action policies, disingenuous at best. Unfortunately, many of those who have been especially vocal about their views evidently believe white men are somehow paying an undue price for having to share privilege. There does not seem to be as much concern about the price both white women and minorities have paid by being excluded from such privilege, even though hardly any change has occurred across the top management positions in both the private and public sectors.

FUTURE DIRECTIONS FOR MANAGERIAL JOBS

Many management theorists are currently predicting major changes in the structure of both organizations and jobs in the coming decades. The changes underway in organizations have been described in various ways. Organizations are said to be increasingly permeable—the "boundaryless organization" and the "hybrid organization" (Borys and Jemison 1989; Hirschhorn and Gilmore 1992); interconnected—via partnerships, alliances, and networks (Hamel, Doz, and Prahalad 1989; Johnston and Lawrence 1988; Kanter 1989); populated by highly educated and technically trained workers—the "knowledge-based" organization (Drucker 1988); interdependent—the "integrative organization" (Kanter 1983); engaged in customized production—the flexible organization (Piore and Sabel 1984); but also subject to both diversity and tribalism as these changes have brought about greater inequality in class and status—the "politics of secession" (Kotkin 1993; Reich 1991).

In other words, there is a prediction of both the dismantling and decoupling of organizational hierarchy—"de-differentiation" (Clegg 1990) and the emergence of global enterprise webs, both activities of which spill out of formal organizational boundaries (Granovetter 1985; Miles and Snow 1986; Orton and Weick 1990; Reich 1991).

The changes in organizations parallel changes in jobs. In general, the movement is toward work that is more contingent, networked, and self-organized. One might say jobs are increasingly becoming loosely coupled to organizations. Some have even suggested that in the future employees will be prudent to think of themselves as "Me, Inc.," namely, an entreprenuerial company with a workforce of one (Limerick and Cunnington 1993). How minorities and white women may fare in this sort of employment system is not clear. Government policies to protect equal opportunity and the implementation of affirmative action guidelines have all been organizationally based, in that it is primarily large employers who are held responsible for the composition of their workforces.

A labor market system based on individual competition among those who start with unequal advantages or disadvantages could either exacerbate inequality or lead to a situation where people are both more responsible for their own outcomes and also freed from the dependence on closed political networks. At this point, it appears both kinds of effects may be evident. As Reich argues, "Never before in history has opulence on such a scale been gained by people who have earned it, and done so legally" (1991:219). But at the same time, he argues that the kinds of advantages that are carried through access to education in elite schools in the private sector, at primary, secondary, and then college levels, can preclude those who are excluded from such privilege to compete in the new workforce. At this junction, it seems apparent that new thinking should emerge about what kinds of public policies may be needed to preserve the concept of equal employment opportunity.

CONCLUSIONS

The evidence indicates both white women and minorities have gained access to managerial jobs in unprecedented numbers. What is not so clear is whether the gains that have been made are secure and whether the "good jobs" to which women and minorities now have access are as good as they were when white men had them to themselves. Further, the progress white women and minorities have made seems to have a rather low limit. Both women and minorities are still concentrated in lower-level jobs with less opportunity than those held by white men, and there is a point in the hierarchies of most large organizations beyond which it is difficult to find even a single woman or a minority in a position of significant authority and high reward.

The explanations for continued inequality are many. Some have indicated that not enough time has passed for women and minorities to gain parity with white men. Others have pointed to evidence of continued discrimination in both the specific kinds of personnel decisions that are made and in the institutional practices by which women and minorities are recruited, evaluated, and rewarded. Informal practices still favor white men, while formal practices have often had only symbolic effect (e.g., performance appraisal systems). Despite widespread opposition to affirmative action policies, the evidence suggests employers would do much less in providing access to excluded groups unless they had to. Even with the current language about "valuing diversity," few organizations have experienced significant changes unless pressure was brought to bear by lawsuits or government oversight.

Given the current changes in the structure of occupations and organizations, the meaning of managerial jobs is likely to change dramatically as well. Rather than all such positions carrying the connotation of "good job," increasingly such jobs may imply insecurity of employment and instability of income. A few privileged workers with "reputational capital" are likely to be rewarded even more highly, as has been evident in the last few years with the salaries of top-level executives, but such privilege seems to be accompanied by growing inequality across levels. The challenge of public policy in the future is to help shape rather than only respond to the changes underway. An adequate response will not be easy, because the climate for any such response is increasingly tendentious. One hopeful sign for the future, however, is that more white women and minorities have gotten good educations, from good schools, and in some cases, have obtained jobs of significant authority and reward. While not all such success stories provide a pathway for others to follow, by and large, without such diversity at the top, not even this ray of hope would be shining.

REFERENCES

Alexis, Marcus and Nancy DiTomaso. 1983. "Transportation, Race, and Employment: In Pursuit of the Elusive Triad." *Journal of Urban Affairs* 5:81–94.

Becker, Gary S. 1957. *The Economics of Discrimination*. Chicago: University of Chicago Press.

————. 1964. *Human Capital.* New York: National Bureau of Economic Research.

Bergmann, Barbara R. 1986. *The Economic Emergence of Women.* New York: Basic Books.

Berheide, Catherine W. 1992. "Women Still 'Stuck' in Low-Level Jobs." *Women in Public Services: A Bulletin for the Center for Women in Government* 3 (Fall).

Bielby, William T. and James N. Baron. 1986. "Men and Women at Work: Sex Segregation and Statistical Discrimination." *American Journal of Sociology* 91:759–799.

Bielby, William T. and Denise D. Bielby. 1989. "Family Ties: Balancing Commitments to Work and Family in Dual-Earner Households." *American Sociological Review* 54:776–789.

Borys, B. and D. B. Jemison. 1989. "Hybrid Arrangements As Strategic Alliances: Theoretical Issues in Organizational Combinations." *Academy of Management Review* 14:234–249.

Braddock, Jomills H. and James M. McPartland. 1987. "How Minorities Continue to Be Excluded from Equal Employment Opportunities: Research on Labor Market and Institutional Barriers." *Journal of Social Issues* 43:5–39.

Business Week. 1995. "A 'Race-neutral' Helping Hand?" (February 27):120–121.

Chen, C.C. and Nancy DiTomaso. 1996. "Performance Appraisal and Demographic Diversity: Issues Regarding Appraisals, Appraisers, and Appraising." Forthcoming in *Managing Diversity: Human Resource Strategies for Transforming the Workplace,* edited by E.E. Kossek and S. Lobel. Cambridge, MA: Blackwell.

Clegg, S.R. 1990. *Modern Organizations: Organization Studies in the Postmodern World.* London: Sage.

Collins, Sharon M. 1989. "The Marginalization of Black Executives." *Social Problems* 36:317–331.

Davis, George and Glegg Watson. 1985. *Black Life in Corporate America: Swimming in the Mainstream.* New York: Anchor Books.

Dawes, R.M. 1993. "Race Norming: A Debate, Part I." *Academe* May–June:31–34.

DiTomaso, Nancy and Donna E. Thompson. 1988. "The Advancement of Minorities into Corporate Management: An Overview." Pp. 281–312 in *Research in the Sociology of Organizations,* Vol. 6, edited by Samuel Bacharach and Nancy DiTomaso. Greenwich, CT: JAI Press.

Drazin, R. 1987. "Wage Differences Between Men and Women: Performance Appraisal Ratings vs. Salary Allocation As the Locus of Bias." *Human Resource Management* 26:157–168.

Drucker, Peter F. 1988. "The Coming of the New Organization." *Harvard Business Review* 66 (January–February):45–53.

England, Paula. 1992. *Comparable Worth: Theories and Evidence.* New York: Aldine de Gruyter.

Farley, Reynolds. 1984. *Blacks and Whites: Narrowing the Gap?* Cambridge, MA: Harvard University Press.

Friedland, Judith and Nancy DiTomaso. 1994. "What Managers Need to Know About Demographic Projections." Unpublished manuscript.

Friedman, R.A. 1991. "The Balanced Workforce at Xerox Corporation." Harvard Business School Case, No. 9–491–049. Boston, MA: HBS Case Services.

Gaertner, S.L. and J.F. Dovidio. 1986. "The Aversive Form of Racism." Pp. 61–89 in *Prejudice, Discrimination, and Racism,* edited by J.F. Dovidio and S.L. Gaertner. Orlando, FL: Academic Press.

Goldin, Claudia. 1990. *Understanding the Gender Gap.* New York: Oxford University Press.

Granovetter, Mark. 1974. *Getting a Job: A Study of Contacts and Careers.* Cambridge, MA: Harvard University Press.

———. 1985. "Economic Action and Social Structure: The Problem of Embeddedness." *American Journal of Sociology* 91:481–510.

Hamel, Gary, Yves Doz, and C.K. Prahalad. 1989. "Collaborate with Your Competitors—and Win." *Harvard Business Review* 67:133–139.

Heilman, M.E., R.F. Martell, and M. Simon. 1988. "The Vagaries of Sex Bias: Conditions Regulating the Undervaluation, Equivaluation, and Overvaluation of Female Job Applicants." *Organization Behavior and Human Decision Processes* 41:98–110.

Hirschhorn, Larry and Thomas Gilmore. 1992. "The New Boundaries of the 'Boundaryless' Company." *Harvard Business Review* (May–June):104–115.

Hodson, Randy. 1978. "Labor in the Monopoly, Competitive, and State Sectors of Production." *Politics and Society* 8:141–93.

Holmes, S.A. 1995. "Backlash Against Affirmative Action Troubles Advocates." *The New York Times* (February 7):B9.

Jackman, M.R. 1994. *The Velvet Glove: Paternalism and Conflict in Gender, Class, and Race Relations.* Berkeley: University of California Press.

Jencks, Christopher L. 1985. "Affirmative Action for Blacks: Past, Present, and Future." *American Behavioral Scientist* 28:731–760.

Jencks, Christopher, Lauri Perman, and Lee Rainwater. 1988. "What Is a Good Job? A New Measure of Labor-Market Success." *American Journal of Sociology* 93:1322–57.

Johnston, Russell and Paul R. Lawrence. 1988. "Beyond Vertical Integration—the Rise of the Value-adding Partnership." *Harvard Business Review* (July–August):94–101.

Kanter, Rosabeth M. 1977. *Men and Women of the Corporation.* New York: Basic Books.

———. 1983. *The Change Masters.* New York: Simon and Schuster.

———. 1988. "Ensuring Minority Achievement in Corporations: The Importance of Structural Theory and Structural Change." Pp. 331–346 in *Ensuring Minority Success in Corporate Management,* edited by D.E. Thompson and N. DiTomaso. New York: Plenum.

———. 1989. *When Giants Learn to Dance: Mastering the Challenges of Strategy, Management, and Careers in the 1990s.* New York: Simon and Schuster.

Kaufman, R.L. 1986. "The Impact of Industrial and Occupational Structure on Black-White Employment Allocation." *American Sociological Review* 51:310–23.

Kluegel, James R. 1985. "If There Isn't a Problem, You Don't Need a Solution." *American Behavioral Scientist* 28:761–784.

Kotkin, J. 1993. *Tribes: How Race, Religion, and Identity Determine Success in the New Global Economy.* New York: Random House.

Leonard, J.S. 1984. "The Impact of Affirmative Action on Employment." *Journal of Labor Economics* 2:439–463.

Limerick, David and Bert Cunnington. 1993. *Managing the New Organization: A Blueprint for Networks and Strategic Alliances.* San Francisco: Jossey-Bass.

MacKinnon, C.A. 1987. "Difference and Dominance: On Sex Discrimination." Pp. 32–45 in *Feminism Unmodified: Discourses on Life and Law,* edited by C.A. MacKinnon. Cambridge, MA: Harvard University Press.

Manegold, C.S. 1994. "Reich Talks of 'Glass Ceiling' Pervading the Business World." *The New York Times* National Edition. (September 27):B9:1.

Marini, M.M. 1989. "Sex Differences in Earnings in the United States." *Annual Review of Sociology* 15:348–80.

Massey, Douglas S. and Nancy A. Denton. 1993. *American Apartheid: Segregation and the Making of the Underclass.* Cambridge, MA: Harvard University Press.

Miles, R.E. and C.C. Snow. 1986. "Network Organizations: New Concepts for New Firms." *California Management Review* 28:62–73.

Molotch, H. 1988. "The Rest Room and Equal Opportunity." *Sociological Forum* 3:128–133.

Morrison, Ann M., Randall P. White, and Ellen Van Velsor. 1987. *Breaking the Glass Ceiling: Can Women Reach the Top of America's Largest Corporations?* Reading, MA: Addison-Wesley.

Orton, J.D. and K.E. Weick. 1990. "Loosely Coupled Systems: A Reconceptualization." *Academy of Management Review* 15:203–223.

Piore, M.J. and C.F. Sabel. 1984. *The Second Industrial Divide.* New York: Basic Books.

Powell, G.N. 1993. *Women and Men in Management.* 2nd ed. Newbury Park, CA: Sage.

Reich, Robert. 1991. *The Work of Nations: Preparing Ourselves for 21st-Century Capitalism.* New York: Vintage Books.

Reskin, Barbara and Irene Padavic. 1994. *Women and Men at Work.* Thousand Oaks, CA: Pine Forge Press.

Reskin, Barbara and Patricia Roos. Eds. 1990. *Job Queues, Gender Queues: Explaining Women's Inroads into Male Occupations.* Philadelphia: Temple University Press.

Sackett, P.R. and C.L.Z. DuBois. 1991. "Rater-Ratee Race Effects on Performance Evaluation: Challenging Meta-Analytic Conclusions." *Journal of Applied Psychology* 76:873–877.

Sadker, M. and D. Sadker. 1994. *Failing at Fairness: How America's Schools Cheat Girls.* New York: Charles Scribner and Sons.

Salancik, G.R. and J. Pfeffer. 1978. "Uncertainty, Secrecy, and the Choice of Similar Others." *Social Psychology* 41:246–255.

Schwartz, F. 1989. "Management Women and the New Facts of Life." *Harvard Business Review* 67 (January–February):65–76.

Smith, D.R., Nancy DiTomaso, George F. Farris, and R. Cordero. 1995. "Correlated Error and Bias in Performance Appraisals Among Scientists and Engineers." Unpublished manuscript.

Smith, J.P. and F. Welch. 1984. "Affirmative Action and Labor Markets." *Journal of Labor Economics* 2:269–301.

Smith, Shelley A. and Martha Tienda. 1988. "Employment Prospects for Minority Women." Pp. 37–56 in *Ensuring Minority Success in Corporate Management*, edited by Donna E. Thompson and Nancy DiTomaso. New York: Plenum.

Sokoloff, Natalie J. 1992. *Black Women and White Women in the Professions: Occupational Segregation by Race and Gender, 1960–1980.* New York: Routledge.

Spilerman, Seymour. 1988. "Sources of Minority Underrepresentation in Corporate Employment." Pp. 25–36 in *Ensuring Minority Success in*

Corporate Management, edited by Donna E. Thompson and Nancy DiTomaso. New York: Plenum.

Steinberg, S. 1989. *The Ethnic Myth: Race, Ethnicity, and Class in America.* Boston: Beacon Press.

Swoboda, F. 1991. "Foreign-born, Too, Face 'Glass Ceiling' in Job Promotion." *The Washington Post* (March 10):4, 2:2.

Szafran, Robert F. 1982. "What Kinds of Firms Hire and Promote Women and Blacks? A Review of the Literature." *The Sociological Quarterly* 23:171–190.

Thomas, R.R., Jr. 1990. "From Affirmative Action to Affirming Diversity." *Harvard Business Review* (March–April):107–117.

Tomaskovic-Devey, Donald. 1993. *Gender and Racial Inequality at Work: The Sources and Consequences of Job Segregation.* Ithaca, NY: ILR Press.

U.S. Department of Labor. 1966. *Manpower Report of the President.* Washington, DC: U.S. Government Printing Office.

———. 1969. *Manpower Report of the President.* Washington, DC: U.S. Government Printing Office.

———. 1987. *Workforce 2000.* Women's Bureau, (May). Washington, DC: U.S. Government Printing Office.

———. 1991. *A Report on the Glass Ceiling Initiative.* Washington, DC: U.S. Government Printing Office.

University of California at Los Angeles/Korn-Ferry International. 1993. *Decade of the Executive Woman.* Los Angeles: University of California at Los Angeles.

Von Glinow, Mary Ann. 1988. "Women in Corporate America: A Caste of Thousands." *New Management* 6:36–42.

Women on Boards. 1992. *Wall Street Journal* (June 16):A1.

Wynter, L.E. 1994. "Diversity Is Often All Talk, No Affirmative Action." *Wall Street Journal* (December 21):B1.

6

Social Work

The Status of Women in a "Female Profession"

LESLIE LEIGHNINGER

In June 1925, a representative of the American Association of Social Workers (AASW) spoke at an annual professional conference about current trends in social work employment. AASW official Neva Deardorf described the results of the Association's recent survey of working conditions in this expanding field. Paramount in her address was the issue of salary inequities. The median annual salary for women, she reported, was $1,680, the corresponding figure for men a much higher $3,000. Even when they were compared with men of equal educational background and years of experience, women consistently received less pay. "This problem of sex discrimination," Deardorff warned her colleagues, "is [a] question we must face. . . . It is a bald, blatant fact that in a group which presumably stands before the community pleading for the square deal for everyone, we have some very suspicious interior circumstances. . . . One of the simplest remedies which I wish to recommend to some of my men colleagues is the modification of that attitude of mind which assumes, when a job paying more than $3,000 is to be filled, that an ordinary man will be worth that much, but it will take a whale of a woman to earn it" (640–642).

Deardorf spoke with uncharacteristic bluntness for a woman of her times. Many may have recognized the discrepancies between men and women in this "female-identified" profession, but few voiced their criticisms in a public forum. Most practitioners seemed to accept, or at least to acknowledge, the dominant social mores, which stressed the importance of

111

man's position as family breadwinner and which viewed men as more competent than women in administration, fund-raising, and the organization
of social welfare agencies (Brown 1942:178–179).

Even today, when women continue to outnumber men in social work,
men hold a disproportionate share of top administrative positions in social
agencies and professional education, and consistently command higher
salaries. Ironically, women played a major part in the development of social
work from the turn of the century through the early 1900s. In doing so, a
number of women leaders consciously endeavored to create a new profession for women. Yet, by the 1920s, men had become increasingly dominant
in leadership roles. While that dominance has diminished to some degree
in recent years, sexual discrimination in salaries, promotions, and other
areas remains a problem. At the same time, in part because the field continues to be identified with women, social work fails to command the respect
accorded to the more "prestigious," male-identified professions of medicine, science, and law.

Why has social work developed in this way? What accounts for the current status of women in the field, as well as the status and degree of legitimacy of social work in comparison with that of other professions? This
chapter attempts to answer such questions through a historical analysis of
the profession, followed by a review of the demographics of the social work
labor force and educational system from the 1970s to the present. In both
areas, attention is paid to the intersection of race and gender. The chapter
presents theoretical perspectives on the place and role of women in the
profession, as well as on the status of social work in American society. It con-
cludes with speculation on the future of women in social work, citing the
importance of policies on affirmative action and pay equity, as well as
describing the potential of activism by women social workers to recapture
power and influence within this "women's profession."

SOCIAL WORK'S HISTORICAL DEVELOPMENT

Social work traces its history to the confluence of three trends in social welfare which began in the nineteenth century. Women played important
roles in each of these developments, although their involvement took on a
different shape in each. The first movement, the rise of state-supported
charitable institutions in the mid-1800s, represented a scientific response
to the needs of dependent groups. Mental hospitals, state schools for the
blind, and similar institutions constituted an alternative to poorhouses and
meagerly funded local systems of public relief. A woman, Dorothea Dix, was

the movement's major theorist and catalyst. Yet, Dix worked closely with male physicians and legislators to achieve her goals, and the institutions which she helped found were headed by men.

The growth of state-funded institutions prepared the way for the professionalization of the social services through the development of an occupational identity among administrators and staff. This move toward professionalization was greatly enhanced by the rise of a "scientific charity" movement in the private sphere in the 1870s. The movement's leaders believed private, carefully orchestrated relief efforts could eradicate poverty. A Charity Organization Society (COS) would coordinate the work of all private charities to prevent duplication of aid. Each family's application would be systematically investigated by a volunteer "friendly visitor," who would provide practical advice and moral guidance to help families lift themselves out of poverty (Popple and Leighninger 1993:58–61).

Women played several roles in the development of the COS approach. Josephine Shaw Lowell, Mary Richmond, and others joined male leaders in publicizing the movement's mission; Lowell and Richmond wrote seminal books on the philosophy of scientific charity and on appropriate training (Lowell 1884; Richmond 1917). Both headed COSs. Yet, while women had a significant voice in developing the movement, Lowell and Richmond's administrative positions were an anomaly. The predominant pattern was one of male heads of charity organizations, in charge of a cadre of female friendly visitors. As Julia Rauch (1975:243, 253–254) noted in a history of the Philadelphia Society for Organizing Charitable Relief, "women were the foot soldiers" of this war on pauperism. In the Philadelphia organization, the visiting corps was composed entirely of women, the administrative hierarchy and governing board made up entirely of men.

As the COS movement expanded, its leaders recognized the enormity of their task. Individual approaches to poverty failed to stem its growth. In addition to greater attention to broader social reform, the notion of a trained and permanent staff gained popularity. Women leaders like Richmond helped establish training programs in charitable work, such as the New York Summer School of Applied Philanthropy (soon to become the first school of social work in the United States). Yet, men served almost exclusively as the directors of the newly formed schools (Lubove 1969:140–142). Also, women constituted the bulk of the paid staff, which replaced the voluntary friendly visitors (Leighninger 1987:10–11).

This division of labor stemmed largely from prevailing concepts of the proper roles of men and women in society. In what feminist historians have labeled "the cult of domesticity," middle- and upper-class women (who constituted the bulk of female charity workers) were viewed as the caring nurturers of their families and, by extension, of their communities. Men, in contrast, engaged in the rough-and-tumble world of commerce and industry; important characteristics for this engagement were toughness, aggressiveness, and self-assurance (Cott 1977; Harris 1978:32–72). Charitable work with poor families seemed a perfect fit with women's "natural talents" for nurturance and self-sacrifice. Founders of the Philadelphia charity society sought women visitors, for example, because they were "more sympathetic, more self-denying, and gentler" than men; and their domestic responsibilities equipped them for the task of helping the poor to strengthen family ties (Harris 1978:118–119; Rausch 1975:245; but see Ginzberg 1990:200–202 for a different perspective). Charity agency executives, on the other hand, were appointed by community boards or political bodies, who no doubt saw men's energy and power as necessary for this work.

A belief in women's nurturing qualities also helped justify women's participation in settlement work, a third trend in social welfare that began in the late 1800s. The settlement movement, which sought to improve conditions in poor urban communities, stressed the importance of broader social, economic, and political change. Unlike charity work, the movement included a fair proportion of men among its "front line" workers. While men also served in administrative roles, women constituted about two-thirds of all settlement directors and were highly visible advocates for social reform on the local and national level. (Chambers 1986:12). In this endeavor they joined with colleagues in women's trade unions and voluntary organizations. Muncy pictures this interlocking set of women's organizations and agencies as a powerful "female dominion in the mostly male empire of policy making" (1991:xii). The dominion drew upon the concept of women as caring "social housekeepers," but used this imagery in a more conscious way to improve conditions for the poor, and especially for women and children.

Jane Addams was the most prominent and respected of the settlement leaders. A shrewd publicist for the work of Chicago's Hull House, one of the earliest settlements, Addams used concepts of women's nurturing qualities and moral righteousness to legitimize the settlement's efforts at reform. These efforts included tackling bad sanitation and housing conditions, providing health care and day nurseries for children, and supporting women's trade unions. While settlement work attracted both sexes, it offered a particular niche for the growing numbers of college-educated women for whom society offered little challenge outside of the domestic roles of wife and mother (Chambers 1986:14–16; Costin 1983:55; Davis 1973:103–106; Ginzberg 1991; Muncy 1991:3–13).

Addams extended women's social housekeeping role to the hard-hitting world of state and national policy making. The extraordinary cadre of women working with her at Hull House (a group which included physicians, educators, and social scientists) joined hands with other leaders in social welfare to push for legislation and governmental regulation in such areas as child labor and mothers' pensions. Their crowning achievement was the establishment of the federal Children's Bureau in 1912. By institutionalizing women's involvement in national decision making on child welfare, the Children's Bureau legitimized the transfer of women's concerns for children out of the domestic arena and into the public sphere (Costin 1983; Muncy 1991).

Two of Addams' Hull House associates, Edith Abbott and Sophonisba Breckinridge, were instrumental in planning the Children's Bureau's mission and activities. They also played a seminal role in the development of social work as a profession. Where Addams offered a niche for college-educated women in the pursuit of social reform, Abbott and Breckinridge offered a professional career. The two women combined their skills as economist and attorney in a program of social research at Hull House. They also presided over the dissolution of the charity-era Chicago School of Civics and Philanthropy (headed by a man), and transformed it into a university-based professional training program. The goal of the School of Social Service Administration at the University of Chicago was to offer a rigorous and scholarly approach to the study of social welfare and to prepare students for leadership in policy making and social work education. Partly in response to the barriers erected against women in the traditional male professions, Abbott and Breckinridge consciously sought to develop social work as a respected professional career for women. To Addams' rhetoric about women's nurturing qualities, they added intelligence, scholarship, and analytic skills (Fitzpatrick 1990:166–200; Leighninger 1986, 1987:79–80).

It could be argued that the creation of the Children's Bureau, and Abbott and Breckinridge's activities in developing social work as a profession for women, were successful in part because they occurred in an area men had relinquished to women. Muncy (1991:xv, xii) contends that women searching for professional roles in the Progressive Era "discovered that their male counterparts were much more willing to cede professional territory, to acknowledge the female right to expertise in instances where women and children were the only clients." While women might exercise a good deal of control over their separate territories, however, this power "was always limited by the higher authority vested in male legislatures, cabinets, . . . [and] courts." Women soon discovered when they had stepped out of bounds. Jane Addams, for example, was publicly reviled when she openly opposed U.S. entry into World War I; the outraged response of the press reflected a conviction that it was improper for women to speak out on foreign affairs (Davis 1973:212–231).

The boundaries demarking "acceptable activities" on the part of women were even more impenetrable for black American women. Their involvement in social welfare work followed two paths: voluntary charitable activities and mutual aid societies within the black community in the nineteenth century and, eventually, in the twentieth century, professional social service jobs working with black clients. Because the American social welfare system rarely provided for them, blacks developed their own network of charitable organizations early on, in which women played a major role. In 1809, for example, free black women in Newport, Rhode Island, set up an organization to care for each other and for the poor in their community. Similar mutual aid societies sprang up elsewhere in the Northeast; following the Civil War, they were joined by black women's clubs, whose membership was made up largely of educated middle-class women. These clubs, which fostered a number of social welfare activities, were similar to the white women's philanthropic groups from which black women were barred (Gordon 1991; Scott 1990; Higginbotham 1987:74).

In the early 1900s, a small number of educated black women were finally able to breach the walls barring them from the professions. Like their white counterparts, they were usually channeled into the traditional female fields. Unlike white women, however, they were generally confined to work with a black clientele. Those who chose social work thus found themselves restricted to social welfare organizations in black communities and segregated public welfare agencies. Higginbotham (1987:74) uses the term "colonized professionals" to refer to this employment within an "internal colony" of blacks. Sokoloff (1992:6) likens it to the ceding of certain professional areas to women; black social workers were limited to the areas and services where white workers did not want to go.

Most black female (and male) social workers were forced to accept a limited territory in which to work. White female social workers, partly because they did not bear the additional burden of racial discrimination, had more freedom to choose a particular area of endeavor. In the case of the female dominion of reform, they were able to build an important island of control within a larger male world of policy making.

Some white female social workers chose a different path, as seen in the special subfield of psychiatric social work. This specialty developed after World War I and aimed to convert the practice of charity and reform into professional work, based on the principles of psychology and psychiatry (Glazer and Slater 1987). Realizing, however, that they could never achieve equal status with male professionals in the field, psychiatric social workers accepted a role in which they were subordinate to the male psychiatrists and physicians who supervised them. The subordinate role eliminated the need to compete with men, but denied psychiatric social workers the autonomy to shape their field and develop an exclusive expertise.

As social work developed from the 1920s on, its other subfields fell between the subordination model of the psychiatric social workers and the largely separatist approach of the female dominion of settlement work and reform (whose era of activity was coming to an end). Fields like medical social work, school social work, group work, and casework practice in social agencies provided a certain amount of autonomy for women, who were now often supervisors as well as direct service workers. While men remained the majority of agency administrators, the percentage of women directors gradually increased, receiving particular impetus when men left for war in the 1940s (Popple and Leighninger 1993:143).

Up through the mid-1950s, women social workers served as the major theorists of their particular specialties. Women wrote most of the important textbooks in psychiatric social work, casework, and group work. They also shared leadership roles with men in social work education. In 1925, for example, two out of every three schools of social work had a female dean; women still held half of the deanships in 1945. More women than men received social work doctorates in all years but one, between 1935 and the early 1950s (Brandwein 1987:884; Leighninger 1987:37, 87, 132).

The late 1950s and 1960s saw a shift away from women's influence in social work theory and education and a reversal of their progress as agency administrators. Men increasingly took over administrative roles in social service agencies, and soon came to dominate in the social work education hierarchy. They held 48 percent of all agency executive positions in 1950, and 58 percent of those positions a decade later. By 1969, although two-thirds of the members of the National Association of Schools of Social Work (NASW) were women, two-thirds of the administrative positions in social work were held by men (Baker 1965:333; Kravetz 1976:423). In addition, men constituted an extraordinary 91 percent of the social work deans in 1970. The proportion of social work publications authored by women decreased substantially in the 1950s and 1960s, as did the percentage of doctorates earned by women (Brandwein 1987:882, 884).

Varied explanations have been made for these changes. In part they occurred because of the increased numbers of men entering social work. Ironically, by the 1950s, women social workers had concluded that it was necessary to aggressively recruit men into the field in order to enhance the image and status attached to a female profession (Brandwein 1987:884;

Kravetz 1976:422). Recruitment was facilitated by the GI Bill, which provided educational funds to returning veterans. By making social work more
attractive to men through stipends, fellowships, and higher salaries, women
lost ground in the professional territory formerly ceded to them.

Clarke Chambers (1986) suggests additional reasons for the change.
He speculates that women's growing freedom to combine career and marriage may have undercut their chances to rise within the profession. Unlike
earlier unmarried female leaders in social work, married women sometimes took time out for obligations such as child raising, thus found themselves unable to stay on the "promotion track" in universities or agencies.[1]
In addition, the expansion of welfare bureaucracies following the New Deal
opened up positions in public administration that tended to favor men.
Men were attracted to the new types of community planning and community organization work which expanded during the War on Poverty in the
1960s. The development of a conflict-oriented approach to community
organization, for example, was considered to be more in keeping with male
characteristics. Finally, demographics were important. Women who had
held top positions in agencies and schools in the earlier period had begun
to retire; they tended to be replaced by the men who had entered the field
in the 1950s and who were receiving the majority of the doctorates in the
1960s (Brandwein 1987:884, 886).

In the late 1960s, spurred on in part by the women's liberation movement, a number of women social workers (as well as men) became conscious of the continuing power imbalance within the profession. Caucuses
directing attention to women's concerns emerged within NASW, social
work's professional association and its professional education accrediting
body, the Council on Social Work Education (CSWE), in the 1970s. CSWE
added women as a category to an accreditation standard that was initially
set up to bar racial discrimination in the selection of students and the hiring and promotion of faculty. In 1977, the Council mandated content on
women in the social work curriculum.[2] These initiatives have brought some
changes, but the following demographic information indicates the profession still has not achieved gender and racial equality.

DEMOGRAPHIC TRENDS IN SOCIAL WORK, 1970–1994

Size and Gender/Minority Proportions of the Social Work Workforce

The data presented below are from two sources, reports by the U.S. Bureau
of Labor Statistics (BLS) and membership surveys by the National
Association of Social Workers.[3] As indicated in Figure 6.1, the profession of

Figure 6.1. Employed Social Workers, 1970–1990

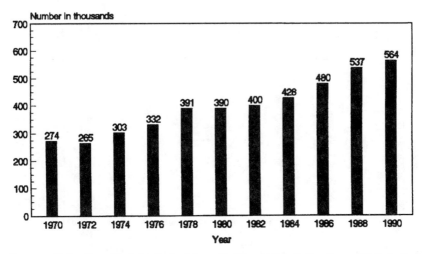

Sources: *Labor Force Statistics Derived from the Current Population Survey: A Data Book,*
Vol. 1, U.S. Department of Labor, Bureau of Labor Statistics, September 1982,
Bulletin 2095, pp. 651–667; *Handbook of Labor Statistics,* U.S. Dept. of Labor, Bureau
of Labor Statistics, August 1989, Bulletin 2340, pp. 79–95; *Employment and Earnings,*
U.S. Dept. of Labor, Bureau of Labor Statistics, January 1991.

social work has more than doubled in size between 1970 and 1990. NASW
membership has grown at an even higher rate, with almost 135,000 members in 1991. The proportion of women in the field has also risen steadily,
with larger figures in the NASW membership. The BLS reports a change
from 59 percent to 68 percent women from 1970 to 1990; periodic NASW
membership studies show a shift from 59 percent in 1972 to over 77 percent
in 1991 (see Figures 6.2 and 6.3). In 1993, the BLS found that 69 percent of
social workers were women, while an NASW study reported that over 81
percent of its sample was female (Gibelman and Schervish 1993b:2–3).[4]
    It is not clear why the proportion of women in social work has been
increasing. Periods of inflation and recession in the 1970s and 1980s may
have spurred men to seek higher-paying fields. The decline of community
organizing, a field dominated by men, may also have been a factor. Whatever
the causes, the discrepancy is continuing; in 1993, women constituted 83 percent of students enrolled in Master of Social Work (MSW) programs.
    Figures 6.2 and 6.3 also depict the percentages of minorities (includ-
ing blacks, Hispanics, Asians, and American Indians) in social work. Blacks
represent about two-thirds of this group. The numbers of minority social

Figure 6.2.   Employed Social Workers, Percentage By Gender and
Minority Status, 1970–1990

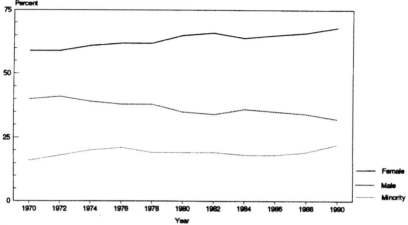

Sources: *Labor Force Statistics Derived from the Current Population Survey: A Data Book,*
Vol. 1, U.S. Department of Labor, Bureau of Labor Statistics, September 1982,
Bulletin 2096, pp. 651–667; *Handbook of Labor Statistics,* U.S. Department of Labor,
Bureau of Labor Statistics, August 1989, Bulletin 2340, pp. 79–95; *Employment and
Earnings,* U.S. Dept of Labor, Bureau of Labor Statistics, January 1991.

Note: 1970 figures include recreational workers, Hispanics, 1984 on.

workers have fluctuated both in the field as a whole and in the professional
association. The proportion of minorities has been consistently lower
within NASW, perhaps in part because of discrimination against minorities
of color in professional education.

Primary Job Function By Gender

Social work job functions can be divided into "direct" and "indirect" practice. Direct practice (referred to, until recently, as "casework"), includes
assessment of personal and social problems, counseling, case planning,
referrals to other services, work with groups, and provision of tangible services such as teaching parenting skills. Indirect practice involves such activities as staff supervision, agency management, program and policy
development, and research. From social work's beginnings, women have

been found predominantly in the direct services area. The trend has continued in the last several decades. In a 1972 study of NASW members, about half of the women respondents identified direct services as their primary job function, compared to a little under one-third of the men. In 1976, those figures were 56 percent for women and 39 percent for men. By 1991, over two-thirds of women members worked in direct services, compared to somewhat over half of the men. In the same period, the percentage of men in administration, policy development, and similar activities varied from 35 to 57 percent, and women 18 to 39 percent (Chernesky 1980:242; Fanshel 1976:449; Hardcastle and Katz 1979:41; Gibelman and Schervish 1993a). These proportional differences in primary function no doubt relate in part to assumptions about women's skills in caregiving and men's capacity for organization and leadership. Reasons for differential involvement in social work administration will be discussed more fully later in this chapter.

Figure 6.3. NASW Members, Percentage By Gender and Minority Status

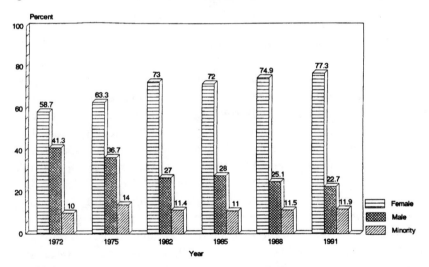

Sources: Henry J. Meyer and Sheldon Siegel, "Profession of Social Work: Contemporary Characteristics," *Encyclopedia of Social Work*, 17th ed., Vol. 2, Washington, DC: NASW, 1977, pp. 1070–1071; June Gary Hopps and Elaine B. Pinderhughes, "Profession of Social Work: Contemporary Characteristics," *Encyclopedia of Social Work*, 18th ed., Vol. 2, Silver Spring, MD: NASW, 1987, pp. 356–357; Margaret Gibelman and Philip H. Schervish, *Who We Are: The Social Work Labor Force As Reflected in the NASW Membership*, Washington, DC: NASW Press, 1993, pp. 20–21.

Primary Auspice and Agency Setting By Gender and Minority Status

NASW delineates several categories for the auspice, or operating authority, of social work practice. These include public local, public state, public federal, private not-for-profit and private for-profit. The 1991 NASW survey was the only one to investigate the relationship between gender, minority status, and primary auspice. It found little differences in agency auspice by gender, but described some important patterns regarding minority status. A significantly higher proportion of minority social workers than white practitioners were employed by local, state, or federal governments. Conversely, higher percentages of white social workers were found in the private for-profit sector. A similar situation existed for agency setting. There were few differences in setting based on gender, but a higher proportion of minorities of color reported agencies as their primary practice setting and a higher percentage of whites cited private solo and private group practice (Gibelman and Schervish 1993a:58–59, 68).

Fields of Practice By Gender and Minority Status

Few researchers have examined the relationship of gender and minority status to social workers' choice of field of practice. Gibelman and Schervish (1993a) examined the topic in some detail, and concluded that "NASW members' selection of practice areas seems to reflect a gender-based role distinction apparent in the population as a whole." Information provided by their respondents reflected the tendency of women in our society to be "the primary caretakers of the family and children, aged, and sick." Women constituted 75 percent of those working with children, and 85 percent of those involved in services to the aged. Proportionately more women than men were represented in the practice areas of family service, school social work, and health care. Men, on the other hand, were overrepresented in corrections, substance abuse, and community organization and planning (Gibelman and Schervish 1993a:82–83).

    Gibelman and Schervish (1993a:82–85) also noted differences in practice areas among minority groups. Asian and Hispanic Americans had a greater tendency to work with children. In keeping with the tradition noted earlier, a higher proportion of blacks than other minorities worked in public assistance, often seen as a less prestigious area of social work.

Social Work Salaries By Gender and Minority Status

Of all the data on gender differences in social work, the statistics on salary differentials are the most publicized, consistent, and dramatic. Women social workers have made less than men from the early years of the profession to the present. Broad studies using NASW membership data give the following picture: In 1961, men made a median annual salary of $7,700, while women made $6,600. In 1968, the median salary for men had risen to $1,500 more than that of women social workers. Men earned a median monthly salary of $1,600 in 1976, women, $1,250. A 1987 study showed one-half of the male respondents but only one-quarter of the female respondents bringing home more than $25,000. In 1991, the median income of female respondents was in the $17,500 to $19,999 range, the median for males in the $20,000 to $24,999 range (Baker 1965:537; Fortune and Hanks 1988:221; Hardcastle and Katz 1979:48; Gibelman and Schervish 1993a:109).

Other studies with smaller samples have found similar patterns. Most of these studies have focused on the reasons behind the salary differentials, and have controlled for various factors which could be expected to affect them. Jennings and Daly (1979) surveyed 1971–1976 graduates from a Texas school of social work. Overall, male graduates made almost $900 more than females in their first job, and over $1,600 more in their current job. Yet, when job type was controlled for, no significant differences were found. Large salary differentials existed between administrative and direct service jobs. Because men obtained entry-level administrative-support positions much more often than women and moved into administrative and supervisory positions at a much faster rate, men as a group had significantly higher salaries. However, while this survey suggested that differential career development accounted for most of the salary differentials by gender, a number of other studies found significant salary differentials even when job type was controlled for. Brownstein and Hardcastle (1984) concluded, for example, that women social work managers made less than male managers even when controlling for job experience, suggesting that discrimination was a factor (see also Fanshel 1976; Sutton 1982; York, Henley, and Gamble 1987).

Studies looking at other job aspects, such as rank, position, part-time vs. full-time work, and type of agency achieved similar results; while these variables explained some salary inequities, gender remained the most important predictor (see, for example, Belon and Gould 1977). Researchers focusing on personal factors, such as family commitments and aspiration for high-level positions, produced the same findings: salary differences remained when these variables were ruled out (Williams, Ho, and Fielder 1974). One is left with the inevitable conclusion that sex discrimination is a factor in the salary differences between men and women in social work.

The picture is less clear in the case of minority social workers. The 1987 NASW salary study showed an average salary for the total membership of $27,800, with a mean of $31,500 for blacks. Most other minority groups also averaged more than the Association's mean. However, these averages were based on a small number of cases and may not have been representative (Williams and Hopps 1990:294). The Gibelman and Schervish survey (1993a:111) found few differences in income by ethnicity, and those that existed were not significant. Data based on larger samples is necessary for a better understanding of the salary status of minorities in social work.

TRENDS IN SOCIAL WORK EDUCATION
BY GENDER AND MINORITY STATUS

As Figure 6.4 indicates, the dominant pattern in student enrollments in masters' level social work programs is the steady increase in women and decrease in men from 1970 to 1992. The picture is similar to that in the employment world, although the proportion of women students is even higher than that of women practitioners. An educational phenomenon that may be related to this change is the fairly steady and sizable rise in the number of students choosing to specialize in direct practice and clinical work (from 36 percent of all graduate students in 1970 to 54 percent in 1992) and the slightly smaller decrease in the number of those specializing in community organization/administration/planning (from 11 percent to 8 percent) (*Statistics on Social Work Education* 1970–1992).

As shown in Figure 6.4, the proportion of minority students in MSW programs has remained remarkably stable between 1976 (when this data was first gathered by CSWE) and 1992. The percentages for minorities are much higher for students enrolled in baccalaureate social work programs, which grant the BSW, or first professional degree. In 1992, 27 percent of BSW students were minorities. Higher minority enrollments suggest that baccalaureate education is a more accessible level of professional social work education for many minorities (*Statistics on Social Work Education* 1976–1992).

While the majority of students and practitioners are women, women are underrepresented as social work faculty members, and particularly as

Figure 6.4. Full-Time Student Enrollment in MSW Programs, Percentage By Gender and Minority Status

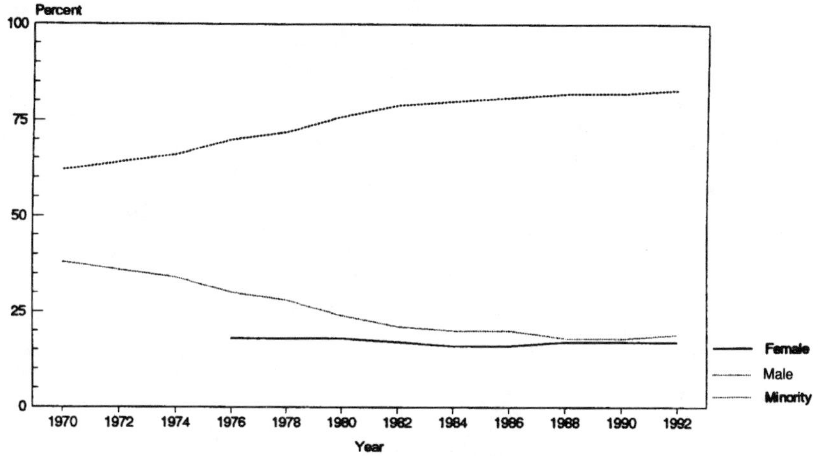

Sources: Statistics on Social Work Education, NY: Council on Social Work Education, 1970–1982; and Washington, DC: CSWE, 1984–1992.

upper-level administrators. Women constituted between 45 percent and 50 percent of graduate social work faculty members from 1972 to 1986; the percentages have risen slightly since then, reaching 58 percent women in 1992. The gender differences seem not to relate to the size of the pool of eligible women, since from 1984 on, women have earned 60 percent or more of social work doctorate degrees and have constituted about two-thirds of all doctoral students (*Statistics on Social Work Education* 1972–1992).

The discrepancies are more pronounced among educational administrators. As Figure 6.5 shows, women have made progress in achieving social work deanships, yet the figures for women deans remain the lowest on the chart. Particularly interesting is the relatively high proportion of women in assistant dean positions, suggesting a traditional pattern of women administrators clustered in the lowest administrative echelons. Women have also fared better as directors of undergraduate social work programs, which tend to be viewed as less prestigious posts than deans of graduate schools. The undergraduate programs also report greater percentages of women and minority faculty.

Analysis of faculty salaries for gender and minority differentials is difficult, since a large number of variables (degree, experience, publications, job responsibility, and rank) are involved. Nonetheless, women appear to

Figure 6.5. Administration in Schools of Social Work, Percentage By
Gender

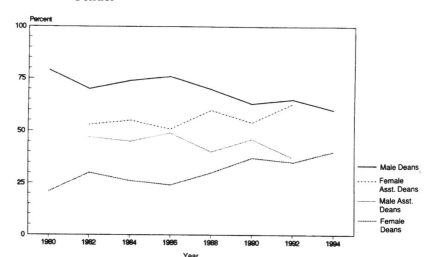

Sources: Statistics on Social Work Education, NY: Council on Social Work Education,
1980–1992; *Directory of Colleges and Universities with Accredited Social Work Degrees,*
Alexandria, VA: Council on Social Work Education, 1993–1994.

be rewarded at a lower salary level than men across academic disciplines,
even when these variables are controlled for. While the evidence is as yet
inconclusive, it is likely that minority women fare least well in the area of
salaries (Sowers-Hoag and Harrison 1991; *Statistics in Social Work Education*
1984–1992).

MEN AND WOMEN IN LEADERSHIP AND ADMINISTRATIVE
ROLES IN SOCIAL WORK

As in social work education, women are far less likely than men to be in
management, particularly in the higher ranks of agency administration. In
1968, 43 percent of women NASW members held administrative posts,
compared to 58 percent of men. Women were more likely to be in lower-
level positions, such as supervisors of direct service workers. Among NASW
members in 1976, less than one-third of all social work administrators were
women. In that same year, only 16 percent of the top administrative positions in non-profit social welfare agencies were occupied by women, a drop
from 60 percent in 1957. By 1984, only 13 percent of female NASW mem-

bers were administrators. In 1991, although there were proportionately more women in social work, the percentage of administrators among women had risen only to 19 percent (Brandwein 1987; Sutton 1982; Chavetz 1972; Dressel 1987:298; Gibelman and Schervish 1993a). Leadership patterns within social work professional organizations, especially the educational association, have been similar.

What accounts for the continued dominance of men in social work administration? While many of the explanations reflect the general position of men in American society, some relate more specifically to social work. Brandwein (1987) suggests dividing explanatory theories into individual, sex role socialization, and structural approaches. Using this framework, one can make the following groupings.

Individual explanations include the notion that women are more suited to counseling and other nurturing positions, while men are more equipped for leadership roles. Whether or not this is true, the majority of women social work students specialize in direct practice rather than administration and policy, and take direct practice jobs after graduation. Career behavior also differs between men and women social workers. Women change jobs less often than men, and men are more likely to leave jobs for positions with higher salaries (Williams, Ho, and Fielder 1974). Men may have higher aspirations for career advancement. A 1979 study of social workers found 36 percent of female respondents aspiring to administration as a career goal, compared to 56 percent of the males (Sutton 1982). However, later studies have questioned this finding (see Kravetz and Jones 1982). Finally, men in a women's profession may "deal with role strain" by gravitating toward the traditional male activity of administration (Kadushin 1976).

Individual analyses easily shade into sex role socialization explanations, however. Women students may gravitate toward direct practice concentrations because this is an area of activity commonly expected of them. Men and women may choose (or be "guided into") employment positions based on sex role stereotyped beliefs that men are "more likely to exercise leadership traits while women [lack the] necessary aggressiveness" for management (Brandwein 1987:887). Male decision makers may carry these beliefs into their choices regarding promotions. Society may expect women to put family obligations ahead of career advancement, although this idea has probably become less prevalent and less likely to be considered a barrier by women social workers (Sutton 1982).

Sex role socialization theories link individual and structural explanations. The latter focus on conditions at the organizational or societal level. A major structural component in the increase of male administrators in the last several decades was the recruitment of men into the profession and into leadership roles, beginning in the 1950s. Such recruitment was based on the expectation that men, with their perceived higher status, would bring a more positive image to the profession they joined. Current structural barriers to women's advancement include the fact that women are less likely to be groomed for administrative positions, to be given such supports as paid time off for continuing education, and to be part of mentoring systems. While informal support networks for women social workers have increased in recent years, they are a far cry from the network formed within the earlier female dominion of reform.

Kanter's seminal study (1977) of men and women in the corporation also has a bearing on the position of women in social work. Kanter identifies lack of power and opportunities and the phenomenon of tokenism as major barriers to women's advancement in organizations. When women are small minorities in high level positions, they often experience isolation and marginality, and sometimes develop rigid behavior patterns in response. In social work and other fields, this makes it harder for women to take on mentoring responsibilities further down in the professional school or agency, and makes the development of affirmative action measures and support networks even more necessary.

THEORETICAL PERSPECTIVES ON THE PLACE AND ROLE OF WOMEN IN THE SOCIAL WORK PROFESSION

More and more women are entering social work; men still hold the majority of high-level positions; and the field itself occupies a fairly marginal position in the professional hierarchy. Why is this so? Two broad arguments can be made. First, sex role stereotyping and behaviors continue to play a significant role in shaping the careers of men and women in social work, as well as the public's perception of the profession. Identification of social work as a "caring profession" and women as "carers" encourages many females to choose social work as a career and to elect direct practice as an area of employment. Stereotypes about men being more decisive, assertive, and rational beings, while diminished somewhat in the new sensibilities of the 1990s, still influence decisions about who is best equipped for leadership roles in professional education programs and social agencies. Society's ambivalence about the importance of the "feminine" activity of caretaking leads to a devaluing of a profession seen as having this activity at its core.

A related, but darker, explanation stems from a political economy perspective on social work and social welfare. Dressel (1987) and others have argued that social work and the broader field of social welfare are examples of the production and reproduction of patriarchal relations in the work place. "Under capitalism," Dressel writes, "the power of men to control women's labor power extends beyond the family to the labor market in the form of occupational sex segregation and the devaluation of female-intensive work" (295). This sex segregation is grounded in part in ideologies about men's and women's differing capabilities, ideologies which justify sex-based differences in jobs and job functions. From social work's beginnings, there has been a noticeable division of labor between male and female workers, with men generally in charge. Women have participated in this domination through their tendency toward altruism and self-sacrifice. Men have been able to control the field of social welfare, including both its practitioners and its predominantly female clients.

Both the sex role stereotyping and the political economy explanations should be viewed with a certain degree of caution. Just as social work historians have begun to question the dominant explanation of client as "victim" (Gordon 1988), so analysts of the position of women in social work should acknowledge the existence and power of activist stances on the part of women social workers (and sympathetic male colleagues). As early as 1973, the leadership of NASW voted to add eradication of sexism and sex discrimination to the Association's major legislative priorities (Sutton 1982). Women's caucuses within CSWE and NASW have helped create mandates for material on sexism and other women's issues in the social work curriculum, establish guidelines for affirmative action in hiring faculty, and set up an affirmative action program for NASW staff. Women social workers have developed new models of feminist therapy and successfully challenged "male models" of quantitative research (Davis 1986; Van Den Bergh and Cooper 1987). Finally, support systems in social work education, agencies, and professional associations have begun to help women define their priorities and build an equal power base for themselves within this "women's profession."

ACKNOWLEDGMENTS

Paula Dressel read an earlier version of this material and offered helpful suggestions.

NOTES

1. Studies of social work employment in the 1960s have noted the effects of family obligations on women's salaries and career advancement (see, for example, Williams, Ho, and Fielder 1974).

2. Similar moves were made regarding minorities of color.

3. These sources yield different figures. The BLS defines social workers in terms of job title rather than professional degree. Since some social work jobs have always been open to those without social work degrees, BLS figures are higher than those of the professional organization and reflect a different mix of workers. In 1991, the BLS estimated that only about half of those whose positions had social work titles held professional social work degrees (Gibelman and Schervish 1993a:19). NASW studies produce a more selective picture. The organization requires a professional social work master's or baccalaureate degree for membership, and constitutes roughly 20 percent of the total social work population. NASW members are predominantly MSW rather than BSW workers.

4. This sample differed from the total membership, however, in that half of those surveyed were entry-level workers.

REFERENCES

Baker, Mary. 1965. "Personnel in Social Work." Pp. 532–540 in *Encyclopedia of Social Work*. 15th issue. New York: National Association of Social Workers.

Belon, Cynthia J. and Ketayun H. Gould. 1977. "Not Even Equals: Sex-Related Salary Inequities." *Social Work* 21:466–471.

Brandwein, Ruth. 1987. "Women in Macro Practice." Pp. 881–892 in *Encyclopedia of Social Work*. 18th ed. Vol. 2. Washington, DC: National Association of Social Workers.

Brown, Esther. 1942. *Social Work As a Profession*. New York: Russell Sage Foundation.

Brownstein, Cynthia D. and David A. Hardcastle. 1984. "The Consistent Variable: Gender and Income Differences of Social Work Administrators." *California Sociologist* 7:69–75.

Chambers, Clarke A. 1986. "Women in the Creation of the Profession of Social Work." *Social Service Review* 60:1–33.

Chavetz, Janet S. 1972. "Women in Social Work." *Social Work* 17:12–18.

Chernesky, Roslyn H. 1980. "Women Administrators in Social Work." Pp. 241–262 in *Women's Issues and Social Work Practice*, edited by Elaine Norman and Arlene Mancuso. Itasca, IL: F.E. Peacock.

Costin, Lela B. 1983. *Two Sisters for Social Justice: A Biography of Grace and Edith Abbott*. Urbana, IL: University of Illinois Press.

Cott, Nancy F. 1977. *The Bonds of Womanhood: Women's Sphere in New England, 1780–1835*. New Haven, CT: Yale University Press.

Davis, Allen F. 1973. *American Heroine: The Life and Legend of Jane Addams*. New York: Oxford University Press.

Davis, Liane V. 1986. "A Feminist Approach to Social Work Research." *Affilia* 1:32–47.

Deardorf, Neva. 1925. "The Objectives of the Professional Organization." Pp. 636–643 in *Proceedings, National Conference of Social Work*. Chicago: University of Chicago Press.

Dressel, Paula. 1987. "Patriarchy and Social Welfare Work." *Social Problems* 34:294–309.

Fanshel, David. 1976. "Status Differentials: Men and Women in Social Work." *Social Work* 21:448–454.

Fitzpatrick, Ellen. 1990. *Endless Crusade: Women Social Scientists and Progressive Reform*. New York: Oxford University Press.

Fortune, Anne E. and Lou L. Hanks. 1988. "Gender Inequities in Early Social Work Careers." *Social Work* 33:221–226.

Gibelman, Margaret and Philip H. Schervish. 1993a. *Who We Are: The Social Work Labor Force As Reflected in the NASW Membership*. Washington, DC: NASW Press.

———. 1993b. *What We Earn: 1993 NASW Salary Survey*. Washington, DC: NASW Press.

Ginzberg, Lori D. 1990. *Women and the Work of Benevolence: Morality, Politics, and Class in the Nineteenth Century United States*. New Haven, CT: Yale University Press.

Glazer, Penina M. and Miriam Slater. 1987. *Unequal Colleagues: The Entrance of Women into the Professions, 1890–1940*. New Brunswick, NJ: Rutgers University Press.

Gordon, Linda. 1988. *Heroes of Their Own Lives: The Politics and History of Family Violence*. New York: Penguin Books.

———. 1991. "Black and White Visions of Welfare: Women's Welfare Activism, 1890–1945." *The Journal of American History* 78:559–590.

Hardcastle, David A. and Arthur J. Katz. 1979. *Employment and Unemployment in Social Work: A Study of NASW Members*. Washington, DC: National Association of Social Workers.

Harris, Barbara J. 1978. *Beyond Her Sphere: Women and the Professions in American History.* Westport, CT: Greenwood Press.

Higginbotham, Elizabeth. 1987. "Employment for Professional Black Women in the Twentieth Century." Pp. 73–91 in *Ingredients for Women's Employment Policy,* edited by Christine Bose and Glenna Spitze. Albany: State University of New York Press.

Jennings, Peter L. and Michael Daley. 1979. "Sex Discrimination in Social Work Careers." *Social Work Research and Abstracts* 15:17–21.

Kadushin, Alfred. 1958. "Prestige of Social Work: Facts and Figures." *Social Work* 3:37–43.

———. 1976. "Men in a Woman's Profession." *Social Work* 21:440–447.

Kanter, Rosabeth M. 1977. *Men and Women in the Corporation.* New York: Basic Books.

Kravetz, Diane. 1976. "Sexism in a Woman's Profession." *Social Work* 21:421–426.

———. and L.E. Jones. 1982. "Career Orientations of Female Social Work Students: An Examination of Sex Differences." *Journal of Education for Social Work* 18:77–84.

Leighninger, Leslie. 1986. "Bertha Reynolds and Edith Abbott: Contrasting Images of Professionalism in Social Work." *Smith College Studies in Social Work* 56:112–121.

———. 1987. *Social Work: Search for Identity.* Westport, CT: Greenwood Press.

Lowell, Josephine S. 1884. *Private Charity and Public Relief.* New York: Putnam's.

Lubove, Roy. 1969. *The Professional Altruist: The Emergence of Social Work As a Career, 1880–1930.* New York: Atheneum.

Muncy, Robyn. 1991. *Creating a Female Dominion in American Reform, 1890–1935.* New York: Oxford University Press.

Popple, Philip R. and Leslie Leighninger. 1993. *Social Work, Social Welfare, and American Society.* Boston: Allyn and Bacon.

Rauch, Julia B. 1975. "Women in Social Work: Friendly Visitors in Philadelphia, 1880." *Social Service Review* 49:241–259.

Richmond, Mary. 1917. *Social Diagnosis.* New York: Russell Sage.

Scott, Anne F. 1990. "Most Invisible of All: Black Women's Voluntary Associations." *The Journal of Southern History* 59:3–22.

Sokoloff, Natalie J. 1992. *Black Women and White Women in the Professions: Occupational Segregation By Race and Gender, 1960–1980.* New York: Routledge.

Sowers-Hoag, Karen M. and Diane F. Harrison. 1991. "Women in Social Work Education: Progress or Promise?" *Journal of Social Work Education* 27:320–328.

Statistics on Social Work Education in the United States. Annual Series, 1970–1992. New York and Washington, DC: Council on Social Work Education.

Sutton, Jacquelyn A. 1982. "Sex Discrimination Among Social Workers." *Social Work* 27:211–217.

Van Den Bergh, Nan and Lynn B. Cooper. 1987. "Feminist Social Work." Pp. 610–617 in *Encyclopedia of Social Work, 18th Edition*, Vol. 1. Washington, DC: National Association of Social Workers.

Williams, Leon F. and June G. Hopps. 1990. "The Social Work Labor Force: Current Perspectives and Future Trends." Pp. 289–306 in *Encyclopedia of Social Work, 18th Edition 1990 Supplement*, edited by Leon Ginsberg, Shanti Khinduka, Judy A. Hall, Fariyal Ross-Sheriff, and Ann Hartman. Silver Spring, MD: NASW Press.

Williams, Martha, Liz Ho, and Lucy Fielder. 1974. "Career Patterns: More Grist for Women's Liberation." *Social Work* 19:463–466.

York, Reginald O., H. Carl Henley, and Dorothy N. Gamble. 1987. "Sexual Discrimination in Social Work: Is It Salary or Advancement?" *Social Work* 32:336–340.

7

Serving Our Country

African American Women and Men in the U.S. Military

EARL SMITH

> *I'm an active duty officer, not engaged in political matters.*
> —General Colin L. Powell (1990)

> *One's economic class position determines in major measure one's life chances, including the chances for external living conditions and personal life experiences.*
> —William J. Wilson, sociology professor (1978)

> *The problem, then, was one of justice within our existing institutional framework . . . That no more generally satisfactory solution to these conflicts emerged within the army only reflects the inability of a single segment like the army to accomplish what the larger society has yet to achieve.*
> —Stouffer et al., *The American Soldier* (1949:599)

INTRODUCTION

African American women and men struggled to participate in America's war efforts. The profession of full-time soldier has served the African American community well—both in the past and well into the twentieth century. With the cry of full equality by one of America's largest native-born population groups, the question for future research is, how long will African Americans accept differential treatment at the hands of the military establishment?

Table 7.1.   African Americans in the U. S. Military, 1989

	Women		Men	
Officers	4,226	6%	17,975	5%
Enlisted	66,207	94%	341,531	95%
Total	70,433	100%	359,506	100%

Source: U. S. Office of Assistant Secretary of Defense, 1988–1989.

Of critical importance to African American people is their sense of pride, peoplehood, and deliverance (Dyson 1993). This sense of pride has been firmly established in several institutional and quasi-institutional settings, beginning long before the contemporary era: on the eastern seaboard, from New England, to the Sea Islands, off the coast of Georgia, African American women, men, and children set about to establish themselves as new, viable communities of people disfranchised from their motherland by force (Aptheker 1951). This effort produced churches, community, governing structures, schools, places of employment and, in some communities, a standing militia.

This chapter, while capturing only a small segment of this long and variable struggle, looks closely at the establishment of a tradition among African American people—their acceptance of military service, which is firmly rooted within the established institutional structure of African American society.

The work ethic remains a central theme in both the American and African American experience (Rodgers 1979). While this is not the place to recapture the history of African Americans in American society, I will note here that African Americans came to these shores as a captured people for the most part, enslaved to the dominant majority (Aptheker 1951; Patterson 1991; Takaki 1989). While the twenty slaves put ashore at Jamestown in 1619, after traveling on a Dutch freighter for many months, were not *legally* slaves, all who come to understand African American history know these ex-Africans are, in fact, slaves (Franklin 1947). In the colonies of Virginia and Maryland, and in the neighboring islands of the Caribbean, African Americans were identified by the color of their skin, labeled non–Christian, and worked until they were exhausted. African American labor, as Harold Baron points out, was precisely what the colonies needed to clear the fields and forests and cultivate large crops of tobacco, rice, indigo, and cotton. Like the plantations that were set up in Virginia and Maryland, soon thereafter African Americans were being imported into both North and South Carolina, as well as Georgia. The

Carolina colonies had, by the early 1700s, established controls through legislative enactments, thus bringing about full-scale social control. This control soon took place all across the South.

To round out the picture, we know from the work of Greene (1942) that not only were African Americans brought to the eastern seaboard aboard large sailing vessels, but that some black slaves were transported to states like New Hampshire, Massachusetts, Connecticut, and Rhode Island. Although the primary goal of the enslavement of African Americans in colonial New England was not to set up and reproduce a plantation economy, early slaves in these states were placed on the auction block (e.g., traded for cash and goods) and used as laborers in the burgeoning New England shipbuilding industries. According to Greene:

> The relatively small number of Negroes in New England during the colonial period raises the question of their economic importance. The answer is to be sought in the occupational development of this section and in the extent to which Negro slaves proved adequate to its labor demands. The opulence that the plantation barons obtained from their extensive domains, the enterprising New Englanders secured largely from maritime pursuits and from the slave trade. (1942:100)

The early history of the African American in America is a history rife with contradictions. A perusal of any of the great documents—the Constitution and its many amendments, the Bill of Rights, or a score of other documents that were drawn up to ensure the freedom of speech, religion, association, and other activities—were central to day-to-day existence. Not one of the aforementioned documents applied to the status of African American people, however.

The necessity of introducing this essay by speaking to the *devaluation* (as Orlando Patterson of Harvard calls it) of freedom is important as we examine African American women and men in the U.S. military. It is in the late 1980s and early 1990s that we begin to see questions arising from the general public, the elected legislature, and on college campuses and elsewhere, which have forgotten what the historical trajectory has been for African Americans. When you see questions about affirmative action and various entitlement programs (e.g., the "Great Society Programs") that serve as safety nets to bring African Americans and others on par with the larger majority, one can only question whether or not people too quickly forget the history of a given situation and, in this context, the history of the incorporation and then neglect of African Americans into American society.

We cannot forget that the forces which operated on the backs of the African American people for centuries were of such magnitude as to create a distinctly separate African American community within the larger American community. This separate world, especially around the 1860s as the Civil War was drawing to an end, was very problematic for Americans in general. This problem is captured by historian John Hope Franklin:

> In the period following the Civil War, white America was compelled to consider the problem of the extent to which blacks would be permitted to move into the mainstream of American life. There was no general agreement on the way in which the problem would be solved, and the heritage of the slave period merely served to inhibit any movement towards integration. It was not a problem that Negroes could themselves solve, for it involved acceptance. Blacks continuously sought opportunities to participate more fully in the affairs of American life, but the overtures were more frequently spurned than not. They [were] forced back into their own world, and as they erected more institutions and ways of life uniquely their own, the prospect of full equality became more remote. (1947:381)

One of the major ways the African American community attempted to bridge the gap between total separation and a move toward limited integration was to participate, at all times in American history, in the various skirmishes and wars in which the larger American community was involved. This includes, but is not limited to, the War of 1776, the Civil War, World War I, World War II, the Korean War, and the Vietnam War. We also know, based on live television coverage from Kuwait, that fighting African American men and women participated in one of the last wars, Desert Storm.

This essay is an overview of the way in which African American women and men participated in the wars to end all wars and to bring about freedom for American society. Early on, we are reminded that while African American women and men were in uniform, fighting on distant shores, the basic rights, birth rights that are inherent in U.S. citizenship, were not totally given to African Americans.

THE EARLY AFRICAN AMERICAN SOLDIER

A critical component in understanding the social relationships of professional military service and the African American soldier is to examine, from a sociohistorical perspective, this evolving relationship. Details of the genesis of this relationship are critical if we are interested in understanding today's contradictory relationships of acceptance and rejection, at a time when all laws and covenants open the way to full U.S. citizenship for all Americans.

When Abraham Lincoln headed for Washington in February 1861, the nation he was going to administer to was rapidly deteriorating (Franklin 1947:181). At the beginning of the Civil War, African Americans were not permitted to fight for either side. When they were finally permitted to enlist in the Union Army they did so with pride and enthusiasm. African American leaders such as Frederick Douglas were involved in large-scale recruitment efforts. Other African American leaders such as Harriet Tubman, herself born into slavery, served the Union Army as a spy scout and nurse (U.S. Department of Defense 1985). Being female and African American exerted a great deal of difficulty upon soldiers such as Harriet Tubman. The historian Aptheker says:

> The contributions of African American women during the Civil War are not well documented. Because of her reputation [Harriet Tubman] helping runaway slaves escape through the underground railroad, federal officers requested Tubman to organize an intelligence service that provided tactical information on confederate forces. Neither Taylor, Tubman, nor other African American women who participated in the Civil War were given official recognition for having served—partly because they were women and partly because they were black. (1945:205)

These deeds of heroism were welcomed. And, while this is not the place to detail the nature of the Civil War or its larger meaning to American society, one should be clear that it was intersectional strife that did have an implicit impact on the future of the American nation-state. One of the best analyses of the nature of the Civil War was initiated, in the form of a newspaper submission by Karl Marx. In a submission to *die presse*, November 7, 1861, Marx and Engels (1937) note the following:

> On the day when it shall be decided that either slavery or the Union must go down, on that day sentence of death is passed on slavery. If the North can not triumph without emancipation, it will triumph with emancipation.

Marx saw the struggle between North and South as nothing but a struggle between two social systems, the system of slavery and the system of free labor. He felt the struggle had broken out because the two systems could no longer live peacefully, side by side, on the North American continent.

After it became clear that African American soldiers would actually see combat in the Civil War, hardly a battle was fought, until the end of that war, where African American troops did not meet enemy forces. According to Franklin (1947), African American troops were involved in at least 250 skirmishes. Many testimonies were given at the end of the Union Army victory regarding the honorable role African American soldiers played. Approximately 38,000 to 40,000 African American soldiers lost their lives in the Civil War. The estimates found in Franklin (1947) are approximately 40 percent greater than the mortality rate of white troops. So great was the contribution of African American troops that Franklin closes his discussion of the Civil War as follows: "There can be no doubt, therefore, that Negroes contributed heavily to the victory of Union forces in the second great war for freedom."

It would be important to suggest that the heroic participation by African Americans, in a variety of roles in the Civil War, ensured their full freedom after the war was over. This was not the case. In the end, African American participation was grossly overlooked and, until this day, one has to search to find a record of this participation.

MILITARY SERVICE IN A NONSEGREGATED ARMED FORCES: THE POST-WORLD WAR II ERA

When Europe was pulled into the Second World War because of Hitler's invasion of Poland in 1939, the United States was faced with a crucial decision—a dilemma. This decision became even more crucial with the fall of France in 1940. Over 200,000 African Americans served in World War I (but were limited in their participation by various decrees which stipulated the number of African Americans, in proportion to their numbers in the population). By the time the United States entered World War II, the drive to end official segregation was moving full blast.

Although the segregation of troops existed during World War II, thousands of African American women and men stepped forward to serve their country. This period also saw the beginning of large-scale mass social protests by major civil rights organizations such as the National Association for the Advancement of Colored People (NAACP). Additionally, A. Philip Randolph threatened to hold a march in Washington, D.C., to end racial apartheid. All of these actions were escalating as the United States prepared for World War II.

Over 90,000 African Americans served in segregated units during World War II. It was not until 1948, when President Harry Truman issued Executive Order 9981, that the deep-seated, visceral, social segregation of the U.S. armed services came to an "official" end. An abbreviated quote from the order says:

This policy shall be put into effect as rapidly as possible, having due regard to the time required to effectuate any necessary changes without impairing efficiency or morale. (Davis 1971:652)

The large-scale effect of President Truman's executive order did not take hold until the Korean War era. An accepted fact of American military might is that the honing of the "military machine" came full force in the period to end all wars. After World War I, America set out to ensure American troops never be embarrassed in battle. This dictate, along with Executive Order 9981, was an expedient way to "offer to all persons in the armed services, without regard to race, color, or national origin" full access to equal opportunities. Conversely, the order was also an attempt to beef up American forces thus, in the end, ridding America of the inability to enter battle at full strength and bring an end to institutional discrimination.

Executive Order 9981 officially ended the segregation of the U.S. armed forces. The decision not only had an important impact on the African American presence within the U.S. armed forces, but it also affected African Americans in civilian life. To establish a precedent that allowed full and open participation in the total institutional structure of American society—via the U.S. military service—meant hope for African Americans outside the institution of military service. One columnist saw it this way:

After our armies have marched on Berlin and Tokyo, if the G.I. Joes, both colored and white don't turn around and march on Washington and drive out the Fascist coalition of Southern Democrats and Republicans who are trying to Nazify America, they will not have learned what they were fighting for. (T. Smith 1988:275)

That hope established itself in many ways, including the escalation of the soldiering role that African American women would and could play in the U.S. military establishment.

THE DOUBLE AND/OR TRIPLE BURDEN: AFRICAN AMERICAN WOMEN AND MILITARY SERVICE

The roles and responsibilities African American women played in military service is an important piece of the puzzle on the institutional impact addressed above. Critical to this section of the chapter is an analysis of the notion of a "double/triple" burden faced by African American women in their pursuit of social, economic, and political equality.

When discussing military service, often we are talking about "fighting men." Women contributed very little to the advancement of the U.S. military effort and did not do so until the end of the nineteenth century, and contributed only slightly more since. It is rare to see pictures, movies, and books, or hear ordinary people holding conversations about the efforts of fighting women. While we finally acknowledge that the advent of the women's movement and media presentations such as *Rosie, the Riviter* brought to the American consciousness the American women's efforts in U.S. military service, it is still rare to see any systematic treatment of women's participation in military service.

The U.S. military forces have traditionally been cast in the image of predominantly white males. Women, and especially racial minority women, have not been accorded any treatment of their participation in the U.S. military war effort, even though women (and African American women) have participated in all of America's wars.

Documentation of the historical contribution of African American women in America's war efforts is sparse. As mentioned above, one does find treatment of such gallant heroes such as Harriet Tubman, who served in the Union Army in a variety of roles, but especially as a spy. It is because of such recognition that we have a scattered record on the participation of African American women.

Although women in America have historically participated in the U.S. armed forces, it was not until World War II that they began serving in numbers worth noting. There are excellent accounts of women who distinguished themselves during the American Revolution, the Civil, Korean and Vietnam Wars. Many of the African American women who served in the more contemporary war effort, beginning in the First World War and up to the Vietnam War served as nurses.

These nurses, showing they were worthy of first-class citizenship, took their assignments all over the United States and abroad with the utmost urgency. During the First World War, African American nurses were assigned to Camp Sherman in Ohio and Camp Grant in Illinois. The Women's Army or Auxiliary Corps (WAAC), assigned to such places as Arizona, Ohio, and Illinois, took these young African American women and molded them into some of the most exceptionally prepared soldiers. The 6888th Central Postal Battalion was the only African American WAAC Battalion to serve overseas during the Second World War (Treadwell 1954).

Like their male counterparts, African American women were segregated during their stint in the pre-1948 U.S. armed forces. In many of the official military settings, African American women were forced to live and socialize in a socially segregated arena. In the civilian community, African American women experienced many of the same injustices as did African American men. Some communities that surrounded the U.S. military installations were very hostile to both men and (especially) African American women who were in uniform. Gender, as such, did not shield African American women from these onslaughts (Holm 1982). The institutional structure of the armed forces have not been very hospitable to African American women, in terms of career mobility. Like the *Bell Curve: Intelligence and Class Structure in American Life* argument[1] of the 1990s, the arguments for mental deficiencies against African American women loomed large in the 1940s. It was during the 1940s that the Armed Forces Qualification Test (AFQT) was used to demonstrate the lower cognitive abilities of African American women.

The belief system was that most of the jobs women would and could do in the armed forces required a high aptitude score on the AFQT. White women tended to score higher than African American women and, as a result, African American women were regulated to the lower, more menial, types of jobs. African American women were assigned to tasks such as kitchen help and cleaning details. Many of these women were never given the opportunity to continue in their service occupation once their term of enlistment was over. It is the belief herein that the occupational opportunities for African American women in the post-1930s armed forces were no better than the occupational opportunities for African American women in the civilian labor force. It is, to be sure, the intersection of both race and gender that seems to have limited the occupational mobility for these women.

Table 7.2. AFQT Scores for African American Women and White Women, 1988

	AFQT Category (%)			
	I	II	III	IV
African American Women	0.7	19.9	79.2	0.2
White Women	5.8	45.3	48.8	0.1

Source: U. S. Office of Assistant Secretary of Defense, 1988–1989.

Note: AFQT is scored from highest (I) to lowest (IV). Individuals scoring in categories I and II are considered above-average. Scoring in category III is considered average. Individuals scoring in category V (not shown here) are considered to be unfit for military service. The aptitude tests are actually sets of tests for arithmetic reasoning, word knowledge, paragraph comprehension, and numerical operations.

Table 7.3. African American Women and White Women in Officer Ranks, 1988

	N	%
African American Women	4,226	6%
White Women	26,949	19%

Source. U. S. Office of Assistant Secretary of Defense, 1988–1989.

The ascribed characteristics of race and gender worked against African American women who sought career opportunities in the U.S. armed services. Some analysts would have us believe that with the introduction of the All-Volunteer Army in 1973 (Gates 1970), many of the opportunities that were blocked for African American women would indeed open up to them at this time (Moskos 1986).

In concluding this discussion of African American women in the military service, it should be added that, like their male counterparts, African American women are found in the U.S. Army. One of the main considerations in terms of who is selected to participate in a given branch of service is the possibility of skills attainment. It is well-known that the U.S. Air Force is one of the most technically skilled branches of the armed services. One finds few African American women who are enlisted in the U.S. Air Force and/or in the U.S. Navy (Butler 1992).

In terms of level of rank, African American women are more likely than white women *not* to be officers in the U.S. armed forces.[2] In all branches of the U.S. armed services, African American women comprised less than 10 percent of officers.

The route to obtaining a commission for African American women has usually been regulated to Reserve Officer Training Corps (ROTC), whereas white female officers usually obtain their commission after having been students in Officer Candidate School (OCS). On first examination, this distinction may seem trivial. Yet, when one understands mobility in the U.S. armed forces, we are more likely to understand that advancement up the ranks as officers is critical to where one begins this process. Students entering the career mobility track from OCS have a better chance than those entering from ROTC programs.

We must also keep in mind that until recently (1960–1994) most, if not all, African American women who attend the ROTC program did so at the Historically Black College and University (HBCU). It has been argued that students coming from this type of institution are not well-prepared to do above-average academic work. These views then spill over to the HBCU-educated ROTC students. In a special edition of *Black Issues in Higher Education* (April 12, 1990), Ed Wiley III repeated this allegation about the lack of training for African American officers. While the allegation may be

Table 7.4.   African American and White Women Officer Job Classifications, 1988

| | African American | | White | |
	N	(%)	N	(%)
General/Executive	0	0	269	0.1
Tactical Operations	207	4.9	2,102	7.8
Intelligence	173	4.1	1,725	6.4
Engineering	583	13.8	2,802	10.4
Scientific/Professional	97	2.3	1,051	3.9
Medical	1,504	35.6	11,534	42.8
Administrative	938	22.2	4,823	17.9
Supply/Procurement	676	16.0	2,344	8.7
Nonoccupational	29	0.7	431	1.6
Unknown	8	0.2	53	0.2

Source: U. S. Office of Assistant Secretary of Defense, 1988–1989.

open to discussion and debate, it is consistent with the larger allegation about the relationship between the level of resources and the level of training for African Americans who attend HBCUs. It would seem that most of the allegations are not true, especially when one looks at the kinds of studies that trace the baccalaureate origins of African American science and engineering Ph.D.s (Pearson and Pearson 1985). While there are factors contributing to the lack of mobility and status attainment for African American soldiers, African American women rose to the occasion and went on to serve their country with valor.

As we get closer to our time period and examine mobility and entry into the officer ranks, it may be important to show just where African American women work once they enter military service.[3] In looking at the types of employment held by African American women in the U.S. armed services, we see that their institutionalized place in the U.S. armed forces looks very similar to white women, except in areas such as engineering, medical, and administration. I would add here that, like their African American male counterparts, African American women have had to struggle to obtain whatever career progress they have made. The rest of this chapter discusses African American men in the U.S. military.

AFRICAN AMERICAN FIGHTING MEN

While African American women rose to the occasion to take their places alongside their male counterparts, African American men also participated in, as was discussed earlier, all of America's wars. Like African American women, their biggest challenge and opportunity came at the beginning of

World War II. It is not until the Second World War that African American men are given the full opportunity to participate in the American war effort (Butler 1992).

Like the sporting community, the military institution has always been accorded the status of being an egalitarian institution. Yet, it is only recently that we begin to learn that the term *egalitarian* does not adequately fit. By the time the U.S. military was preparing for battle in Korea in 1950, African Americans had been integrated into the armed forces with considerable speed. Approximately five years prior to the historic case *Brown vs. Topeka, Kansas Board of Education*, which went before the U.S. Supreme Court, and which said, in part, that equal education opportunities were inherently unequal, the integration of the military had proceeded apace. President Truman's executive order brought African Americans into the *secondary* mainstream of American military life. The period between 1950 and 1953, also known as the Korean Conflict, was the period which finally brought Jim Crow to his knees. It was during the Korean War that the need to bring African Americans and whites together to fight a common enemy also brought an end to segregation and a realization of Truman's executive order to the U.S. military. According to Executive Order 9981:

> It is the declared policy of the President that there shall be equality of treatment and opportunity for all persons in Armed Service, without regard to race, color, or national origin. (Executive Order 9981, *Federal Register*, Number 13, July 28, 1948, p. 4313)

A few years after the Brown decision, the U.S. military was desegregated.

The period between 1955 and 1965 was very intense in terms of African American participation in the armed forces. In 1965, for example, African Americans comprised 10 percent of the enlisted ranks of all of the U.S. armed services and approximately 2 percent of the officer ranks. Early in the 1960s, President John F. Kennedy appointed an equal opportunity commission to monitor and advise him on race relations in the U.S. military. Much of the discussion that ensued from 1955 through the early 1960s was positive. Many of the skirmishes that had taken place in the post-World War II period, both in the United States and abroad, had been alleviated. Many of the troops in uniform firmly believed African American participation in the armed services was good for the country. Most consistently the belief was that by working hard and doing a good job in the field, carrying out training missions, and behaving in an acceptable manner, African American soldiers would in fact advance in rank.

This perceived opportunity for African American men did not go unnoticed in a major publication, *The Atlantic* (1986). Military sociologist

Charles Moskos produced a story that had significant impact not only on the sociological community but on the reading public at large. In the article "Success Story: Blacks in the Military," Moskos painted a story of the utmost positive impact that the military service had on African American men. He began his discussion by noting that Defense Secretary Casper Weinberger had attended a dinner at the National Guard Armory in Washington, D.C., in which none of the national media paid attention to the event. The nature of the event was a banquet for African American officers who were generals and admirals and who were being received by the African American community. Moskos also noted that the African American press was absent at this affair.

The meaning of this comment by Moskos is very clear. While the armed services still had race problems (e.g., there were still skirmishes taking place, especially at bases located in the South and the Pacific), the U.S. military had achieved a high level of success that no other institution in American society had achieved. African Americans were occupying management positions in the U.S. military, whereas in the rest of American society, they were hardly visible in management positions at all. Moskos tells us this:

A visitor to a military installation will witness a degree and a quality of racial integration that are rarely encountered elsewhere. At many points in their terms of military service, whites are sure to be commanded by black superiors. In their performance of their military duties, blacks and whites typically work together with little display of racial animosity. Not only do whites and blacks inhabit the same barracks but also equal treatment is the rule in such non-duty facilities as chapels, barber shops, post exchanges, movie theaters, snack bars, and swimming pools. (1986:64)

While Moskos may have taken the observed situation a bit beyond what the data would have suggested, he does raise a critically important question. While American society portrays itself as a participatory democracy where all institutions accord all Americans equal treatment under the law, it was in the military service that African Americans first obtained a level of freedom unprecedented in U.S. history.

One of the continuing battles that African American men in the military face (similar to their female counterparts a few decades ago) is the notion that they are less intelligent than white men. This argument comes full circle in Herrnstein and Murray's *The Bell Curve* (1994). The authors constantly point toward standardized tests as the way to understand geneti-

Table 7.5.   African American Percent (%) of Officers and Enlisted Personnel,
            1991

Rank	All Services	Army	Marines	Navy	Air Force
Officers	6.8	11.1	4.5	4.0	5.6
Enlisted	22.6	31.6	20.0	17.7	17.3
Total	20.3	28.6	18.5	15.9	15.1

Source: Adapted from Butler, 1992.

cally inherited intelligence. One of the tests featured in the volume is the
AFQT.[4]

The consequences of such widespread beliefs is that African American
men having huge numbers in the U.S. military were regulated to positions
of servile status. While Moskos could write about the success in 1986, what
he did not write about were the long years of neglect and servitude. Much
of this treatment still lives on in the modern military institution. Butler
(1992), in his study of affirmative action in the military, shows a chart
wherein African Americans (both male and female) comprise less than 8
percent of all officer ranks, with the largest number of officers in the army
(11 percent). To be sure, African American men held one job—and one
job only—in the U.S. military, that of combat infantry soldier. The combat
infantry soldier was the "occupation" for the majority of African American
men in the military, since his participation in America's wars came full circle during the era of the Vietnam War.

VIETNAM

It was during the Vietnam War that the African American soldier came full
circle with her or his ability to fight on all fronts (air, sea, land) without
being discriminated against. It was also at this time that African American
soldiers were able to live the full life of a GI, thus accepting the responsibilities and rewards that accrued to service personnel in uniform. Yet, problems remained for those wedded to this profession.

From the Vietnam era on, many legends and myths have circulated
surrounding African American participation. Are these soldiers coura-
geous? Should African American GI's constitute the bulk of the frontline
troops? Does the minority status of African American soldiers place them in
a positive or negative position for dealing with the Viet Cong? And, what is
the reception for the African American soldier once they return home?

These legends set the tone for the folklore of the Vietnam War. Here we examine just what the role of the African American soldier was and how fully the African American soldier was accepted during and after the Vietnam War.

Prior to Vietnàm, many public and private citizens in the United States felt that African American participation in the U.S. military would eventually make right the many wrongs and, over time, this would not be an issue as to whether or not their participation would be, in fact, full participation. What these pronouncements did not entertain is that at about the same time the Vietnam War entered the public's view in the United States, the modern Civil Rights movement also entered the conscience of the nation. Around 1955, under the leadership and direction of individuals such as Rosa Parks, the Reverend Martin Luther King Jr., and other vigilant African Americans and whites, the Civil Rights movement ignited the struggle for freedom. When Ms. Parks decided not to give up her seat on the bus, the Civil Rights Movement began. Other events, like the Greensboro, North Carolina, Woolworth's sit-in and some sit-ins spearheaded by African American soldiers in uniform, had an awakening effect on the long, slumbering giant of discrimination against African Americans.

In Herbert Aptheker's *A Documentary History of the Negro People in the United States* (1951, 1973, 1974), from the beginning of the New Deal to the end of the Second World War (1933–1935), there were scores of petitions and histories of the vigilant acts of African Americans to undo the distortion and segregation heaped upon African American people in general and African American soldiers in particular.

This is evidenced in a speech by Charles H. Huston, who spoke at a conference held under the auspices of the *Nation*, entitled "Conference on America's Opportunity to Create and Maintain Lasting Peace." The conference was held in New York City on October 7 and 8, 1944. A quote from the Huston speech suggests:

> I want to speak in particular on the subject of the armed forces. Here, after nearly three years of war, Negroes are still insulted by the navy's barring all Negro women, except those now passing for white, from the Waves, the Marines, and the Spars. We have officers in the army and the navy; but there is still not a single Negro Lieutenant in the U.S. Marines. The Army puts Negroes in uniform, transports them South and then leaves them to be kicked, . . . , and even murdered with impunity by white civilians. In places, Negro service men do not have as many civil rights as prisoners of war. In at least one army camp down South for a time there was one drinking fountain for white guards and German prisoners, and a segregated

fountain for Negro soldiers. The Negroes know that just as soon as the shooting stops many Americans will give the same Germans, Austrians, Italians, Rumanians and others who were trying to kill them preference over Negroes who were defending them, simply because these Germans and others are white. (Charles H. Huston, "The Negro Soldier", quoted in Aptheker 1974:508–509)

African American soldiers in Vietnam claim some of the same injustices as African American soldiers did in World War II. During Vietnam, the African American presence was well-established. As the war escalated, so too did the casualties among African American soldiers. In fact, all who write about the Vietnam War have made notice that the casualties among African Americans were disproportionate to their numbers in the fighting ranks (Moskos 1986). While the Vietnam War continued to escalate and the high casualty of African American soldiers grew, at home, the Civil Rights movement was gaining in momentum, unprecedented in the history of the United States.

Just as the civil rights marchers were being combined with the anti-war effort, shown to us on national TV in the form of protest marchers, we also saw a lot of racial conflict on the war front in Vietnam. One of the more highly discussed incidents took place at Long Binh in 1968. In Long Binh, racial clashes among African American and white soldiers were the talk of many, both in and out of Vietnam. The same type of clashes was also being recorded aboard naval vessels and at other U.S. military installations throughout the Pacific.

This racial polarization grew out of long-standing ethnic relations in the military. The variety of tensions at one end of the spectrum was the inability for career officers to move up the career ladder and, at the other, the tensions grew out of symbolism, as seen in the various popular culture depictions such as the movie *Platoon*. These tensions grew out of such symbolism as the "Afro" hairstyle, the "Black Power" handshake/salute, and terminology like "soul brother."

In my estimation, while these concerns with symbolism seemed to be correct and may have triggered some of the skirmishes that took place in Vietnam between African American and white soldiers, the bottom line is more complex. In the final analysis, one finds lack of credibility and respect for the African American soldier and the devaluing of the African American soldier, who had grown dependent on the U.S. military to sustain himself in terms of rank, prestige, and power.

DISCUSSION AND CONCLUSION: OF CHANGING
SOCIAL RELATIONS

Does a changing economic and political climate and social unease impact African American soldiers differently than others? With so many new issues taking place (from high rates of unemployment, military base closings, and downsizing of major U.S. corporations, to an increase in racism and hate), it is necessary to conclude this chapter by looking at the future of African American soldiers and asking: "What will it be?"

In his paper, Williams (1989) draws an assessment of the two-volume study entitled *The American Soldier*, published in 1949. The *American Soldier* analyzed a large body of data about racial attitudes. Many of the conclusions that came out of the book showed that African American soldiers held strong views against social segregation and discrimination.

These soldiers felt by enlisting in the military (as was the case prior to 1973 with the advent of the All-Voluntary Army), they would at least have increased opportunity for career mobility than those African Americans in civilian society.

What is important about the revisitation by Williams is that embedded within the *American Soldier* are several ideas and elaborations about group dynamics. Williams draws the conclusion that the military is just another type of professional organization within American society. In his opinion, given its organizational basis and principles of organizational management prior to 1950, Stouffer et al. were correct in assuming that, since racial relations were moving in a positive direction, one would find an organizational structure welcoming African American soldiers. Williams, like others who are interested in the military service, dismisses some of the aberrations that have taken place inside the contemporary military organization.

Like Williams, Moskos makes a similar assessment. According to Moskos:

> But I think there is more to it than that. The interracial leveling of military service gives black soldiers a prospect on society less easily acquired by black nonveterans. Just to have completed a tour of duty means that a black soldier has competed, and competed successfully, with whites. The army experience emphasized the correlation between reward and effort (as opposed to reward and race). (1986:68)

While interesting, Moskos has it wrong. Complexities of race relations in American society, regardless of the institutional structure and setting, have not been adequately worked out.

Hochschild (1995) argues that the American public is confused about the nature of race relations. Citing public opinion poll data from the 1950s onward, she shows that equality is an illusive concept. Whites have not changed much in their view of African Americans. When looking at how African Americans view whites, the polling data show that African Americans hold similar views about whites. What can one make of these similarities? Nothing, according to Hochschild. What we have is a nation-state of people of different races and ethnic groups who do not understand each other. Hochschild notes that African Americans are succeeding more but enjoying it less. This sums up the kind of experience that African Americans have had with the U.S. military.

Who can deny the fact of a General Colin Powell or General Fred A. Gorden, Commandant at the U.S. Military Academy at West Point? Both Generals Powell and Gorden had extensive and distinguished military careers. Holding both of these men up to the general populace shows that African American men can succeed in the U.S. military, regardless of all the negative odds.

Yet, one has to be careful of these types of super role model exceptions. General Powell graduated from the City College of New York in 1958. He had an extensive career in the U.S. Army, and won the Purple Heart in 1963 for his service in Vietnam. Powell was also the assistant to National Security Advisor Frank Carlucci, and was an aide to former Secretary of Defense Casper Weinberger. Additionally, Powell had extensive administrative and field experience. When George Bush was president of the United States, Powell became Chief of all U.S. armed forces (Kennedy 1990).

Likewise, General Fred A. Gorden advanced through the ranks and became the Commandant at the U.S. Military Academy at West Point. Gorden, like Powell, had an extensive administrative and field background, and was an early graduate of the West Point Academy. Both of these men epitomize successful striving and successful career mobility. Yet, most African American fighting women and men have no, and will never have, such backgrounds. The accomplishments of these two men (and I am sure others) are not typical of the experiences of ordinary African American soldiers.

In 1989, Defense Secretary Richard Cheney announced that the government would seek to reduce approximately $180 billion from the next

several defense budgets (Willis 1989). The research shows that the perceived *overrepresentation* of the African American soldier makes it more
likely that they will be separated first when such downsizing takes place.
Much of the expected and continued budget cuts (see Butler 1992;
Janowitz and Moskos 1974) will not only close military installations that are
deemed not necessary, but in a world that now considers the Soviet threat
dead, most of these budget cuts will have a major impact on U.S. military
personnel. Could it be that personnel reductions within the U.S. military
institution will embrace the age-old adage "last hired, first fired?"

Finally, it is important to note that, while affirmative action within the
U.S. military has brought many advancements to African Americans,
women, and others, it is hard to believe that different groups are now on a
level playing field. This, for sure, would make it possible to miss my central
point. It is one thing to see a General Colin Powell commanding all U.S.
armed forces. It is another thing altogether to try to understand the opportunity structure of military life for ordinary African American soldiers.

NOTES

1. *The Bell Curve* is written by Richard Herrnstein and Charles Murray
(1994). This very controversial book has generated voluminous responses,
reviews, and critiques. *The Bell Curve* argument—as it pertains to this chapter—is this: With little supporting data, Herrnstein and Murray argue that
African Americans are less cognitively developed than whites. Membership
in the "cognitive elite" say Herrnstein and Murray, rests on having a high
IQ. According to them, whites have these high IQ's—blacks don't. This
note, then, summarizes the 552-page text (including 110 pages of appen-
dices, 168 pages of notes, and a 57-page bibliography). Of the many reviews
of *The Bell Curve*, the best is by James Heckman in *Reason* (1995).

2. African American women are at a disadvantage because of their
point of origin. They start out in the military, more often than their white
counterparts, as Reserve Officer Training Corps (ROTC) students, whereas
white women students are more often in Officer Candidate School (OCS).

3. The data are for officers only.

4. Herrnstein and Murray (1994) (pages 73, 120, 277, 278), (pages
579–592) note that as a proxy for all intelligence tests, the AFQT (like other
IQ tests) shows us the mediocrity of African American intelligence.

REFERENCES

Aptheker, Herbert. 1945. *Essays in the History of the American Negro.* New York: New World Paperbacks.

———. Ed. 1951. *A Documentary History of the Negro People in the United States, 1661–1910.* Volume I. Secaucus, NJ: The Citadel Press.

———. Ed. 1973. *A Documentary History of the Negro People in the United States, 1910–1932.* Volume II. Secaucus, NJ: The Citadel Press.

———. Ed. 1974. *A Documentary History of the Negro People in the United States, 1933–1945.* Volume III. Secaucus, NJ: The Citadel Press.

Butler, John. 1976. "Inequality in the Military: An Examination of Promotion Time for Black and White Enlisted Men." *American Sociological Review* 41:807–818.

———. 1992. "Affirmative Action in the Military." *Annals of the American Academy of Political and Social Science* 523:196–206.

Darity, William. 1983. "The Managerial Class and Surplus Population." *Society* 21:54–62.

Daula, Thomas, D. Smith, and R. Nord. 1990. "Inequality in the Military: Fact or Fiction." *American Sociological Review* 55:714–718.

Davis, John P. 1971. *The Negro Reference Book.* Englewood Cliffs, NJ: Prentice Hall.

Davis, Mike. 1986. *Prisoners of the American Dream.* London: Verso.

Dyson, Michael. 1993. *Reflecting Black: African-American Cultural Criticism.* Minneapolis, MN: University of Minnesota Press.

Farley, Reynolds. 1984. *Blacks and Whites: Narrowing the Gap?* Cambridge, MA: Harvard University Press.

Federal Register. 1948. Executive Order 9981. Number 13 (July).

Foner, Jack. 1974. *Blacks and the Military in American History.* New York: Praeger.

Franklin, John Hope. 1947. *From Slavery to Freedom.* New York: Random House.

Gates, Thomas. 1970. *Report of the President's Commission on an All-Volunteer Armed Forces.* Washington, DC: U.S. Government Printing Office.

Gibbs, Jewelle. Ed. 1988. *Young, Black, and Male in America: An Endangered Species.* Dover, MA: Auburn House Publishing Company.

Greene, Lorenzo. 1942. *The Negro in Colonial New England.* New York: Columbia University Press.

Heckman, James. 1995. "The Cracked Bell." *Reason* (March).

Herrnstein, Richard and Charles Murray. 1994. *The Bell Curve: Intelligence and Class Structure in American Life.* New York: Free Press.

Hochschild, Jennifer. 1995. *Race, Class, and the American Dream*. Princeton, NJ: Princeton University Press.

Holm, Jeanne. 1982. *Women in the Military: An Unfinished Revolution*. CA: Presido.

Jaynes, Gerald and Robin Williams. 1989. *A Common Destiny: Blacks and American Society*. Washington, DC: National Academy Press.

Kanter, Rosabeth. 1993. *Men and Women of the Corporation*. New York: Basic Books.

Kennedy, Randall. 1990. "Taking Powell Seriously." *Reconstruction* 1:49–51.

Marx, Karl and Frederick Engels. 1937. *The Civil War in the United States*. New York: International Publishers.

Moskos, Charles. 1966. "Racial Integration in the Armed Forces." *American Journal of Sociology* 72:132–148.

———. 1986. "Success Story: Blacks in the Army." *The Atlantic Monthly* 257:64–72.

Patterson, Orlando. 1973. "The Moral Crisis of the Black American." *The Public Interest* 23:43–69.

———. 1991. *Freedom in the Making of Western Culture*. New York: Basic Books.

———. 1993. "Blacklash." *Transition* 62:4–26.

Pearson, Willie and LaRue Pearson. 1985. "Baccalaureate Origins of Black American Scientists." *Journal of Negro Education* 54:24–34.

Rodgers, Daniel. 1979. *The Work Ethic in Industrial America*. Chicago, IL: University of Chicago Press.

Smith, Earl. 1988. Editor and Contributor. "Black America in the 1980s." *Humboldt Journal of Social Relations* 14(1&2).

———. and Dan Green. 1983. "W. E. B. Du Bois and the Concepts of Race and Class." *Phylon: The Atlanta University Review of Race and Culture*, Vol. XLIV, No. 4:262–372.

———. and Stephanie Witt. 1995. "The Experience of African American Women in the Academic Workplace: Doubly Disadvantaged or Meeting the Challenge of Greater Opportunity." *Review of Public Personnel Administration* 15:24–40.

Smith, Thomas. 1988. "Outside the Pale." *Journal of Sport History* 15:259–277.

Stouffer, Samuel et al. 1949. *The American Soldier*. Princeton, NJ: Princeton University Press.

Takaki, Ronald. 1989. *Strangers from A Different Shore*. Boston: Little, Brown, and Company.

———. 1993. *A Different Mirror*. Boston: Little, Brown and Company.

Treadwell, Mattie. 1954. *U.S. Army in World War II.* Washington, DC: Department of the Army.

U.S. Department of Defense. 1985. *Black Americans in Defense of Our Nation.* Washington, DC: Office of Deputy Assistant Secretary of Defense.

U.S. Office of Assistant Secretary of Defense. 1988–1989. *Population Representation in the Active Duty Military Service.* Washington, DC: Department of Defense.

Williams, Robin. 1989. "The American Soldier: An Assessment Several Wars Later." *Public Opinion Quarterly* 53:155–174.

Willis, Grant. 1989. "Army Slashing 12,000 More." *Army Times* 25 (December).

Wilson, William J. 1978. *The Declining Significance of Race: Blacks and Changing American Institutions.* Chicago: University of Chicago Press.

8

Native Americans in Higher Education

ALLAN LISKA

INTRODUCTION

Education is a very effective way of assimilating any group into mainstream society. Governments are very aware of this and, in North America, domineering groups, from missionaries to businessmen, have tried to use education to "subdue" or "civilize" Native Americans[1] since before the creation of the United States (Carnegie Foundation for the Advancement of Teaching 1989:7).

Education is an important part of life to most Native American societies. In cultures with no written language, the only way tradition and learning were transmitted from one generation to the next was through oral education. Therefore, education became an integral part of life. People who can tell a story effectively and pass that story on to others are vital, because they are transmitters of the culture.

The strong histories of education led many Native societies to initially accept the schools set up by Europeans. However, this initial excitement soon vanished. Treatment of American Indians by some white school administrators and by the system has often been harsh (Littlefield 1989). This has led to a paradox faced by many families and groups. There is a desire to learn, but many American Indians distrust schools and the educational system. However, without education, it is nearly impossible to escape from the rampant unemployment that exists on many reservations. So tribal leaders have to work to make the educational system more appealing to Native American students, and more responsive to the needs of the students. This chapter deals with higher education. It is important to first place in context, although greatly simplified, the situation faced by most Native American students. The chapter will not only focus on Native American college students, but Native American professors as well, since professors are extremely important in helping to define the situation faced by the students. Also discussed, briefly, will be the role that Tribal Colleges and the American Indian Higher Education Consortium (AIHEC) play in helping with the definition of not only the student's role, but the faculty's as well.[2] While I am speaking in general terms throughout this chapter, because of space limitations, each Native culture faces different challenges when it comes to educating their children and adults. What is described here is meant to be an overview of the entire situation and not a discussion of the unique problems faced by each group.

COLLEGE LIFE

Before entering into a discussion of the problems faced by American Indians on college campuses, it is necessary to define the type of discrimination that will be discussed. This chapter focuses on *indirect institutionalized discrimination*.[3] That is, discrimination that is not intentional, but instead is built into the existing system (Feagin and Feagin 1986:16). Indirect institutionalized discrimination applies to the current educational system because there are no guidelines designed to keep Native Americans, per se, out of the educational loop. However, many rules and regulations involved in the educational bureaucracy work against the American Indian student. For instance, the high cost of most universities is a force working against many American Indian students. This is not a force that expressly forbids Native Americans from going to college. However, because of the relatively poor socioeconomic status of most American Indian college students, there is difficulty in getting an education at a large university. Even if scholarships or loans are made available, these can only cover a limited amount of the costs of education. Any other activities would have to be paid out-of-pocket.

Beyond the economic factors that keep American Indian students from getting to college, there are many cultural obstacles that must be faced. One of these cultural obstacles is the persistence rates of high school and college students. Native American college students had a 27 percent persistence rate in 1993 (Carter and Wilson 1994). In other words, only 27 percent of students who start college finish with a degree. This compares to 30 percent of African American students, 41 percent of white students, and

63 percent of Asian American students. Native Americans have the lowest rate of college completion of any group in this country.

Just as the lack of Native American professors is hinged on the lack of available Native American college students, a reason for the low rate of college completion by Native American students is the low rate of high school completion. The 1990 census shows that only 65.5 percent of Native Americans complete high school; this translates into a smaller pool of college candidates and lowers their chances for completing college. Objectively, a lower number of high school graduates should not lower the persistence rate of college students. However, when the eligible candidate pool is lowered, the support base of the students is damaged. If a student does not perceive that there are people like him or her facing the same problems, then that student will be less likely to remain in the college environment.

The fact that there is such a low rate of high school and college completion is often attributed to a cultural bias that is found in our educational system (Benjamin, Chambers, and Reiterman 1993; Gardner 1994; Liska 1994). Most professors in mainstream colleges are not aware that there are cultural differences between American Indian college students and white students. Even fewer professors are aware that there are differences between different Native American societies.

There are also some professors who will actively work against multicultural education, feeling that it detracts from time spent discussing traditionally important issues. There is a misconception that since there is only so much classroom time, and a course has already been plotted out to include the highlights of an area, then many important aspects of the course would have to be dropped to make it more multicultural (Dennick-Brecht 1994). Failure to incorporate other cultures into a curriculum not only alienates the students whose culture is being ignored, but it also leaves large gaps in students' perceptions of reality (Dennick-Brecht 1994).

The idea of cultural barriers hindering college completion is also hinged upon the amount of acculturation experienced by each individual student. A survey done by Tate and Schwartz (1993) of American Indian college students indicated that the greater the cultural isolation a student felt the more likely he or she would fail to complete a professional program. It appears that, in many cases, the more acculturated a student is the more likely he or she is to remain in college (Benjamin, Chambers, and Reiterman 1993).

Native American college students and professors also have to face the possibility of being asked to become cultural spokespeople. Especially in classes that focus on cultural differences, once it is found that a student is Native American, he or she may be asked to speak for all American Indians, from all nations (Cross 1991). This is an unfair burden to place on any-

Figure 8.1. Native American Participation in College

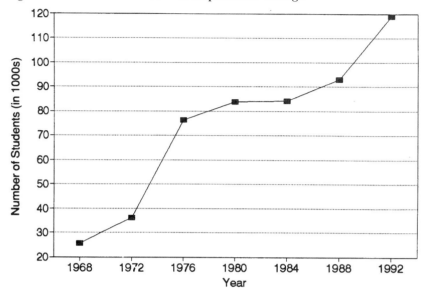

body, especially a student who may already be feeling alienated from university life.

TRIBAL COLLEGES

The terms associated with Native Americans in social science literature tend to be negative. Usually when American Indians are mentioned it is in conjunction with terms like alcoholism, infant mortality, disease, and poverty. Even this chapter is largely negative. It is necessary to note that there are many problems faced by American Indians today, and no one should try to dismiss these problems as trivial. However, it is also important to remember that there are also many positive aspects of American Indian culture. The Tribal Colleges are one example.

Native American college enrollment has increased dramatically since the 1960s. In the early 1980s, when college enrollment was declining for many ethnic groups, American Indian enrollment, especially for women, was actually on the rise. As Figure 8.1[4] illustrates, between 1968 and 1992, enrollment for Native Americans increased over four times, in a pattern similar to African Americans. What the chart does not illustrate is the percentage of increase of American Indians in college enrollment, from 3.28 percent of the population in 1968, to 6.12 percent in 1992. This is almost a 100 percent increase! While there are many reasons for this increase, surely one of the most important is the role the tribal colleges and AIHEC have played.

The tribal colleges are one of the best-kept secrets in academia (Carnegie Foundation for the Advancement of Teaching Report 1989). The first tribal college was the Navajo Community College, established in 1969, with less than 100 students. Today, there are over thirty colleges with a total of more than 5,000 students.

This remarkable growth of the tribal colleges has mirrored the increase in enrollment of Native Americans in college. In fact, the growth in American Indian participation in higher education is due, in large part, to the increase in student population at the tribal colleges, because the colleges serve as a bridge between reservation life and life at a larger university. There is, currently, a movement, which started with the Navajo Community College, to become fully accredited four-year institutions; the idea behind this is to allow American Indian students to learn in a culturally familiar environment. This form of education allows for a much higher retention rate and better overall performance by the students.

Tribal colleges are by no means typical colleges. The mean age of students is twenty-seven. In fact, most of the students are holding down full-time jobs while they are attending these schools. There are more women enrolled in tribal colleges than men, and the majority of the presidents of the thirty-one tribal colleges are women (Cordero 1994). In addition to cultural familiarity, another advantage of tribal colleges is price. Since most of the colleges are small and very community-oriented, they strive to keep their tuition down so most people will have a chance to attend. This, obviously, isn't always easy. With limited government funding and a heavy reliance on charitable contributions, it is often a struggle to make ends meet. So far, the colleges have met the challenges and continued on (Boyer and Boyer 1994; Boyer 1994).

These challenges explained why the AIHEC was developed. It acts as a communication tool between the thirty-one colleges, even publishing its own magazine, *Tribal College*. Not only does the AIHEC help obtain and distribute funds to the different colleges but it also acts as a warehouse of information. If a tribal college wants to start their own radio station, they can go to the AIHEC and find out which colleges have done this before, what their start-up costs were, if there was available funding, and any other information that may be relevant. At the same time that the AIHEC is helping the tribal colleges, it is also working with the federal government. The Council's main office is in Washington, D.C. From there, members can keep abreast of pertinent issues affecting American Indian higher education in general, and tribal colleges, specifically (Cordero 1994). With very limited resources and exploding enrollments, tribal colleges are trying their best to meet the needs of the students with what limited resources they have available. Their success is vital to continued increases in enrollment by Native Americans in higher education.

PROFESSORIATE

The success of American Indian students determines the quality and range of American Indian professors. Currently, because of the low number of Native American college students, there are disproportionately low numbers of associate and full professors in the academic setting. Before discussing the implications of this cycle, I will examine the trends in degrees received by Native American graduate students.

Between 1981 and 1991 the number of masters and doctoral degrees conferred upon Native American students more than doubled (Carter and Wilson 1994). This is exceptional news and very significant. However, bear in mind that because the numbers are so small they are not as indicative of trends as the statistics might suggest. To demonstrate: In 1992, there were a total of 38,814 doctoral degrees awarded to students. Of those 38,000+, only 150 were conferred on Native American students. In other words, only .39 percent of the doctoral degrees presented in 1992 went to Native American students, but American Indians comprise roughly 2 percent of the U.S. population, so this figure should be about five times higher than it is.

Many Native American students are driven by a need to help within their communities. Educating other people in their society is one of the most obvious modes of assistance, so doctorates in the field of education are the most commonly earned by Native Americans. Of the 150 doctorates earned in 1992, fifty were in the field of education, demonstrating the commitment of American Indians to education. In fact, speaking strictly in terms of proportions, this 33 percent is the lowest portion of education Ph.D.'s presented to American Indians in over twenty years. In 1980, when there were only seventy-five doctoral degrees received by American Indians, forty-three were in education-related fields (Carter and Wilson 1994).

Figure 8.2.   Doctoral Degrees By Field: Native Americans, 1992

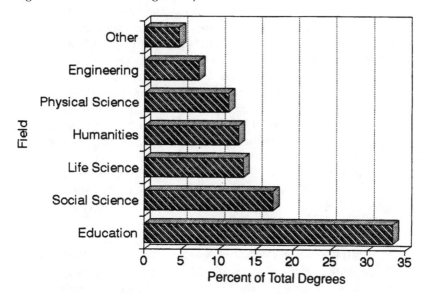

The breakdown of 1992 doctoral degrees conferred on Native American Students is shown in Figure 8.2. Notice that, aside from education, social science degrees constitute the largest field, making up 17.3 percent of doctorates received by Native Americans. The fields of education and social science constitute over 50 percent of all doctoral degrees received by Native Americans. Research on Native American education has suggested that this represents the need of most American Indian college students to work for the benefit of their people (Cross 1991; Kirkness and Barnhardt 1991). Education and social sciences or social work are fields that bring tangible benefits to the tribe, and thus are greatly prized. Medical doctors and physicians are also greatly prized by the different nations. Unfortunately, because the cost of receiving a medical degree is so high, there are very few Native Americans in medical schools. In fact, there are no reliable data sources that list the number of American Indian medical school students.

Equally as important as lack of research is the lack of voice that Native Americans have in their professional associations. For instance, in 1992, only .6 percent of the members of the American Sociological Association were Native American and .45 percent of the American Psychological Association members were Native American (Smith and Winje 1992). Thus, the amount of research in these fields that addresses Native American issues is relatively small. The research is often carried out by scientists who are not American Indian. This may cause the problems associated with any research that is done by an outside source. A non-Native American may have inaccurate, preconceived stereotypes about his/her subjects that will taint the research. Also, when drawing conclusions, while it is possible to empathize, it is not possible to understand exactly how each experience has affected the subjects. While a researcher can record the objective experiences of the Navajo or Cherokee, that researcher will not know what it is like to be a Navajo or Cherokee. Does this mean outside research should not be done? Of course not. There is a lot of very good outside research carried out all the time, but research about Native Americans, done by Native Americans, provides clearer insights into issues affecting the different societies. In a way, this is reflective of the larger society. Native Americans rarely have their voices heard in matters of politics, law, the economy, or the environment. The situation of Native American professors is analogous.

A 1992 report by the Equal Employment Opportunity Commission (EEOC) placed the number of Native American faculty members at about 2,500. Many of these faculty are affiliated with the tribal college system. Because of tight budgets and the lack of strong general education programs, most tribal colleges are unaccredited. Without accreditation, it is difficult to attract funds. Therefore, very little research is done on tribal colleges. Generally, the way to achieve "success" in the academic domain is through research, followed by publication of that research. A faculty member who takes a position at a tribal college may be stagnating her or his career. In addition, because of the small size of tribal colleges, the monetary rewards are minimal. However, as mentioned earlier, most faculty do not choose tribal colleges for financial gain. There are many advantages for faculty who choose to teach at tribal colleges.

Tribal colleges do offer faculty the same advantages they offer students. Many American Indians feel a strong commitment toward their community (Cross 1991). Teaching at a tribal college can help to fulfill this commitment. Also, many tribes are socialist in nature. The success of the group is more important than the success of any one individual. These phenomena highlight a key aspect of many American Indian societies: The idea of the collective over the individual; it is more important to work for the success of the group than for any one individual. It is the greatest strength of tribal colleges and it is almost diametrically opposed to some of the goals in a typical academic setting. In academia, what matters is your class rank and your ability to get published or acquire research grants (Cross 1991). Many American Indian faculty prefer tribal colleges for these reasons and choose them over larger, more traditional, universities.

However, some American Indian faculty elect to remain in a more "traditional" academic setting. This can be equally fraught with dangers. A major obstacle that must be overcome by Native American faculty members is that their research, if it focuses on Native American issues, is often considered irrelevant to the larger population. This inaccurate perception of insignificance held by many people in academia leads to limited sources of funding and fewer chances for publication. Even if a faculty member manages to obtain funding, there is often little time for research. Just as Native American students are forced into the role of cultural spokespersons, Native American professors are often asked to function in the same way. Whether they are asked to serve on bureaucratic committees, counsel Native American students, or moderate American Indian groups on campus, valuable research time can be squandered. Not that these activities are not important, but being forced to spend inordinate amounts of time participating in them can be detrimental to one's career.

The rewards for all of the research and publication done by academics revolve around tenure. The number of tenured faculty members who are American Indian is very small. In fact, the 1992 EEOC report referred to earlier did not list the number. Because many American Indian faculty are affiliated with small tribal colleges, or are forced into the "cultural spokesperson" role and have little time for research or publication, there is little chance to achieve tenure.

CONCLUSION

This chapter has been very circular in nature. The external forces that exist in our society create a situation that makes it difficult for most Native Americans to attend and complete college. The culturally hostile environment at most universities, coupled with the economic strain as well as the unfamiliarity associated with most new places, creates a difficult learning arena. This causes a disproportionately large dropout rate among American Indian students. Those few who do complete college and go on to graduate school are almost forced into two situations: students either fade into obscurity at small tribal colleges, or choose to stay at larger universities where they are often forced into ineffectiveness by a system that has allowed so few Native Americans through. This is the effect that indirect institutionalized discrimination has on groups. There are no laws forbidding Native Americans from going to college or becoming tenured professors. However, because of external forces, Native Americans' academic opportunities are limited and, therefore, their life chances are limited.

The solution? I do not know if there is an easy solution, or one that will fit into the pages of this chapter. From the information gathered for this chapter, the best hope for continued improvement in the higher education of Native Americans lies in the tribal colleges. While it is true that most of the colleges are still fledgling, the Navajo Community College is an example of what the others could become: fully accredited, four-year institutions that work with other universities to produce research which addresses issues that are important to Native Americans and, therefore, to the rest of society.

ACKNOWLEDGMENTS

I would like to thank the American Indian Higher Education Consortium for their assistance in both locating and verifying sources for this project.

NOTES

1. In this text, I have chosen to use the terms Native American and American Indian interchangeably.

2. It is important to note two things. The first is that this is hardly a definitive work. In less than twenty pages, it is impossible to capture all of the positive and negative situations facing all American Indians in every college in the United States. This chapter attempts to give an overview and to encourage more research and support focused on American Indians and academic life. The second is to remember that Native Americans are not a homogeneous group.

3. While this chapter focuses only on one type of racism, this does not mean that there are not other types. The relatively high status of college students and professors keeps them shielded, for the most part, from the threat of physical violence. There still are, however, many incidents of verbal violence reported (Huffman 1991).

4. Figures 8.1 and 8.2 are both derived from information gathered by the American Council on Education in its report, *Minorities in Higher Education.*

REFERENCES

Benjamin, Don-Paul, Stephen Chambers, and Gary Reiterman. 1993. "A Focus on American Indian College Persistence." *Journal of American Indian Education* 32:24–40.

Boyer, Ernest L. and Paul Boyer. 1994. "Tribal Colleges: Shaping the Future of Native America." *Winds of Change* (Special Issue):37–38.

Boyer, Paul. 1994. "Tribal College Celebrates Five Years of Publication." *Tribal College* 5:4.

Carnegie Foundation for the Advancement of Teaching. 1989. *Tribal Colleges: Shaping the Future of Native America*. Princeton: Princeton University Press.

Carter, Deborah J. and Reginald Wilson. 1994. *Minorities in Higher Education*. American Council on Education Twelfth Annual Status Report. Productions Department, Washington, DC.

Cordero, Carlos. 1994. Telephone interview. August 12.

Cross, William T. 1991. "Pathway to the Professoriate: The American Indian Faculty Pipeline." *Journal of American Indian Education* 30:12–24.

Dennick-Brecht, Katherine. 1994. "Multicultural Education: Preparing for the 21st Century." Paper presented at the Lowell's Conference on MultiCulturalism and Transnationalism, October 14–16.

Eller, Jack David. 1994. "Anti Anti-MultiCulturalism." Paper prepared for presentation at the Lowell's Conference on MultiCulturalism and Transnationalism, October 14–16.

Feagin, Joe R. and Clairece Booher Feagin. 1986. *Discrimination American Style: Institutional Racism and Sexism*. 2nd ed. Malabar, FL: Robert E. Kriger Publishing Company.

Hoover, John J. and Cecelia Jacobs. 1992. "A Survey of American Indian College Students: Perceptions Toward Their Study Skills/College Life." *Journal of American Indian Education* 31:21–29.

Huffman, Terry E. 1991. "The Experiences, Perceptions, and Consequences of Campus Racism Among Northern Plains Indians." *Journal of American Indian Education* 30:25–35.

Kirkness, Verna J. and Ray Barnhardt. 1991. "First Nations and Higher Education: The Four R's—Respect, Relevance, Reciprocity, Responsibility." *Journal of American Indian Education* 3:1–15.

Liska, Allan. 1994. "Ghost Dancers Rise." *Humanity and Society* 18:100–121.

Littlefield, Alice. 1989. "The B.I.A. Boarding School: Theories of Resistance and Social Reproduction." *Humanity and Society* 13:428–447.

Smith, H. Lovell and Carolyn Winje. 1992. "August Biennial Report on the Participation of Women and Minorities in ASA." Unpublished manuscript.

Tate, Donald S. and Charles L. Schwartz. 1993. "Increasing the Retention of American Indian Students in Professional Programs in Higher Education." *Journal of American Indian Education* 33:21–31.

9

Medical School Faculty Then and Now

JOYCE TANG

Minorities comprise about 14 percent of the medical school faculty and 35 percent of medical school applicants in the United States (Association of American Medical Colleges [AAMC] 1993a, 1993b). Over the past decades, there has been a steady increase in the proportion of underrepresented minorities[1] and women in medical school training.[2] Yet, we know very little about the growth and participation of minorities, both male and female, on medical school faculties. In fact, based on the current literature, we may know more about minority faculty in other academic disciplines than we do in medicine.[3] Analyses pay more attention to women on medical school faculties than to minorities.[4]

One reason for this lack of knowledge is the small numbers of minorities on medical school faculties. Between 1980 and 1993, the number of full-time salaried medical school faculty in AAMC's Faculty Roster System had increased by 66 percent, from 45,220 to 75,144 (AAMC 1990, 1993a). However, in 1993, when 17,642 medical school faculty members were women, less than 10,000 full-time members were minorities (AAMC 1993a:2).

Another reason is that social scientists and policy makers tend to focus on how to increase the numbers of minorities applying, matriculating, and graduating from medical schools. Only a few recent studies address another important aspect of minority participation in medicine—that of medical school faculty (American College of Physicians [ACP] 1991; Bickel 1991:255; Petersdorf et al. 1990:667).

In recent decades, federal and other institutional efforts to establish and expand medical schools have opened up more opportunities for minorities in training, and perhaps in teaching as well. For example, according to AAMC President Robert G. Petersdorf (1989), there is declining interest in medical careers among twenty-two-year-olds. Yet, minorities continue to improve their representation in medicine. Meanwhile, medical school faculty continues to grow. Nonetheless, we do not know whether minorities with medical training have made substantial progress in this predominately white male-dominated profession, nor do we have any updated knowledge of any subgroup differences in career achievements.

Despite the end of mandatory retirement,[5] the aging of the medical school faculty has generated a steady but growing demand for younger medical school faculty (Jones 1991). Demographic trends also suggest that underrepresented groups will increase their relative proportions in medicine. However, the report by the ACP (1991), which revealed that minorities on medical school faculties have not made as much progress as women, implies that there may be insufficient institutional effort to recruit and promote minority faculty. Results of a recent AAMC survey of medical school graduates reveal racial differences in career plans. Underrepresented minorities show a stronger preference for clinical practice than for a full-time academic career (Petersdorf et al. 1990:666). These career pattern variations may reflect underrepresented minorities' concern about "making a contribution" to their community—especially in the socially deprived areas—as well as reflect their higher level of indebtedness upon graduation from medical schools (ACP 1991:66). Meanwhile, in a survey study of a medical school on the West Coast, Osborn, Ernster, and Martin (1992) found that women medical students were also less interested in pursing academic careers. They contended that, in addition to women's strong commitment to family, lack of mentors might present barriers to female medical students choosing academic careers. Lack of role models or mentors may also explain why underrepresented minorities do not have a strong desire to pursue academic medicine. If this is the case, combining with a growing but small pool of underrepresented minority medical graduates, there may be very little change in the level of representation of minorities on medical school faculties. Furthermore, it would be interesting to see if there is a discernable pattern of similarities or differences in participation in academic medicine among underrepresented minorities—blacks and Hispanics.

More significantly, there is virtually no available information as to how different racial groups fare in their promotion to higher ranks and in their involvement in administration, compared to whites. A combination of factors, such as comparative group size and concentration in certain types of schools, may affect their career prospects in different ways. For example, 10 percent of medical schools employ 40 percent of minority faculty (Petersdorf 1991:667). In 1993, 18 percent of black faculty ($N = 1,748$) was found in predominantly black medical schools, such as Howard, Meherry, and Morehouse. Sixty percent of the Puerto Rican faculty was employed by Ponce, Puerto Rico, and Central Del Caribe (AAMC 1993a:2). This pattern of minority concentration suggests that black and Hispanic minority faculty may be more likely to occupy administrative positions in minority-concentrated medical institutions than in other medical schools. On the other hand, their small numbers at predominately white medical schools may help, or hurt, their overall chances of getting promotions.

Two theories can be used to explain these phenomena: the tokenism and size-discrimination arguments. Some scholars have forcefully argued that low visibility of a group—minorities or women—would lead to stereotyping its members, increased performance pressure, and heightened differences with the dominants (Kanter 1977). A small minority group size also lowers its members' possibility of seeking role models or mentors from similar backgrounds. Further, forming and expanding professional networks would be difficult. Thus, based on this "tokenism" thesis, underrepresented minorities—blacks and Hispanics—would be most disadvantaged when seeking career advancement, compared with other minorities—Asians.

Contrary to the notion that "small is vulnerable," Blalock (1967) and others (Frisbie and Neidert 1977) have found that there is a negative impact on members' career attainment when the size of a minority group is increased. They contend that a larger minority group (e.g., Asians) would pose a greater (perceived or actual) threat to the majority group (e.g., whites) than would a smaller minority group (e.g., blacks). The result is greater resistance from the majority against a larger minority group than a smaller minority group. Based on this "size-discrimination" argument, underrepresented minority medical school faculty would fare better in their promotion to higher professional ranks, including administration, than would other minority faculty.

Finally, what is lacking in current literature about minority medical school faculty is an examination of the career status of black, Hispanic, and Asian females in relation to white females. Tracing the growth of women on medical school faculties from 1978 to 1989, Whiting and Bickel (1990) found very little change in the proportion of minority women on faculties. However, the rate of increase in the actual number of minority women was greater than that for white women faculty. Unfortunately, this observation tells us very little if there are variations in the rates of growth among minority women. Besides, there is no attention to the progression of minority women faculty to higher professional ranks. The experience of underrepresented minority women in academic medicine may be quite different than that of white and Asian women. Black and Hispanic female faculty may perform better, or worse, than other female counterparts in both representation and promotion.

Building on Kanter's notion of "tokenism," some researchers have suggested that being both a racial minority and a woman may have a devastating impact on the careers of educated minority women. For example, Sokoloff (1992) found that black female professionals were at the bottom of the occupational hierarchy, compared to white males, black males, and white females. Black women, according to Cunningham and Zalokar (1992), are still more economically disadvantaged than other groups with similar qualifications. There is also evidence that minority women are doubly disadvantaged in certain academic settings (Kulis and Miller 1988). Nonetheless, this "double whammy" theory has been tested empirically in nonacademic settings and has not always been applicable to black women. There is no indication that black female chemists are in double jeopardy (Koelewijn-Strattner, Lengermann, and Adler 1991; Smith and Witt 1995). Epstein (1973) found that being a double token might help, rather than hurt, the careers of professional black women. According to Lebra (1981) and others (Loos 1986; Yamanaka and McClelland 1994), Asian women have circumvented the cultural barriers against their professional advancement. However, it is important to keep in mind that both of these studies examine the status of minority women in nonacademic settings.

In fact, opposing the double jeopardy view, proponents of the "size-discrimination" thesis argue that being both a racial minority and a woman benefits minority women, especially women of underrepresented minorities. The very small number (in both absolute and relative terms) of minority women would convey a lesser threat to the dominants. Compared to minority males and white females, an extremely small group size might make minority women stand out even more in a predominantly white male profession. The dearth of minorities and women on medical school faculty may set them apart from their peers in terms of characteristics and performance. Hence, when it comes to appointments and promotions, minority women might be viewed more favorably. Unfortunately, no studies in the medical or academic community have evaluated the validity of this "small is valuable" argument. Additionally, treating all minority women faculty as a monolithic group obscures differences in their experiences and comparative group sizes. It is very likely that the comparative advantage of being a minority woman may not equally apply to blacks, Hispanics, and Asians.

This chapter examines the changing role of minorities, both male and female, in academic medicine since 1980. It focuses on their progress in terms of entry and career patterns. Data in AAMC's recent reports[6] will be used for this purpose (1990, 1993a). I first look at the overall rate of increase in the proportions of blacks,[7] Asians, Hispanics,[8] and Native Americans[9] on medical school faculties. Relevant is whether there is any sign of departmental segregation among these racial groups. Then I examine evidence of (lack of) improvement in recruiting and promoting minorities to higher academic ranks. Factors underlying career differentials between races in academe are explored. Also addressed is the issue of whether, and to what extent, minorities have kept up with whites in their involvement in administration. Because my emphasis is on the intersection of race and gender, I will compare the career achievements not only between races, but also between minority males and females and white males and females. In addition to addressing these questions, the AAMC data provide a context for evaluating several concepts derived from the literature on career mobility.

Comparing the representation and career attainment of whites and minorities on medical school faculties has enormous implications for medical schools and the medical community. If certain minority groups are not doing as well as whites and other minority groups (as measured by representation, tenure status, academic rank, and involvement in administration), medical schools may want to readdress their policies or procedures regarding appointments and promotions. Medical school faculty not only contribute their services to the society through teaching, research, and/or clinical practice, but also educate and prepare those who would be practitioners and medical faculty. Continuous underrepresentation of minorities on medical school faculties offers fewer role models and mentors for minorities pursuing medical education and teaching careers.[10]

RECENT TRENDS IN PARTICIPATION

Table 9.1 presents the distribution of full-time medical school faculty by sex and race in 1980, 1990, and 1993. The data reveal white dominance in medical school faculty over the years. Over the past decade, the involvement of minorities in medical teaching careers has not changed appreciably. The

Table 9.1. Distribution of Medical School Faculty By Race and Sex in 1980, 1990, and 1993

Race / Sex	1980 N	1980 %	1990 N	1990 %	1993 N	1993 %	% Change 1980–90	% Change 1990–93	Total % Change 1980–93
White	37,442	89	53,120	87	59,925	86	42	13	60
Male	31,744	85	42,598	80	46,387	77	34	9	46
Female	5,698	15	10,522	20	13,538	23	85	29	138
Black	748	2	1,274	2	1,748	3	70	37	134
Male	529	71	815	64	1,097	63	54	35	107
Female	219	29	459	36	651	37	110	42	197
Asian	3,004	7	4,905	8	6,029	9	63	23	101
Male	2,340	78	3,668	75	4,425	73	57	21	89
Female	664	22	1,237	25	1,604	27	86	30	142
Hispanic	1,021	2	1,659	3	2,087	3	62	26	104
Male	841	82	1,281	77	1,530	73	52	19	82
Female	180	18	378	23	557	27	110	47	209
Native American	34	0	60	0	76	0	76	27	124
Male	28	82	43	72	53	70	54	23	89
Female	6	18	17	28	23	30	183	35	283
Total	42,249	100	61,018	100	69,865	100	44	14	65
Male	35,482	84	48,405	79	53,492	77	36	11	51
Female	6,767	16	12,613	21	16,373	23	86	30	142

Note. Excludes faculty who declined to identify their race.

overall representation of minorities on medical school faculties increased from 11 percent to 14 percent between 1980 and 1993. Minority growth in representation seems to have leveled off since 1990. Although the numbers of blacks and Hispanics in medicine continue to grow, these groups remain severely underrepresented on medical school faculties, a pattern similar to that in medical school enrollment. Blacks and Hispanics, respectively, account for 12 percent and 9 percent of the U.S. population, yet each group comprises about 3 percent of medical school faculty. In contrast, although Asians constitute less than 3 percent of the population, they make up 9 percent of medical school faculty. The proportional disparity in academic medicine for Native Americans is less pronounced. The relative proportions of minorities on medical school faculties are somewhat similar to those in the hard sciences (National Science Foundation 1992).

Data in Table 9.1 reveal a substantial increase in the proportion of women on medical school faculties, from 16 percent in 1980 to 23 percent in 1993. Also of interest is that women in general fared better than did minorities in gaining entry to academic medicine during this thirteen-year period. There is a higher proportion of women among minority faculty than among white faculty. However, regardless of racial background, the rate of increase in the number of women was greater than that of men. This is an encouraging sign for female students who are contemplating medical careers. The gaining share of women's participation reflects increasing female interests, and probably career opportunities, in academic medicine (Eisenberg 1991). Although there are still relatively few women on medical school faculties, the rate of growth in the 1980s suggests that women's participation in academic medicine has changed.

Despite a continuous low representation of blacks, Hispanics, and Native Americans on medical school faculties, there are a few optimistic readings of these trends. First, the numbers of underrepresented minorities (irrespective of gender) on medical school faculties grew faster than did those of whites and Asians. The surge was the greatest among blacks, an increase of 134 percent in a thirteen-year period. Demographic changes suggest that underrepresented minorities may be able to sustain this level of growth for some time.

Second, most of the growth in women's representation has been made by underrepresented minorities. Women of underrepresented minority groups, especially Native Americans, have entered medical school faculty in great strides. The number of black, Hispanic, and Native American women on medical school faculties tripled (and nearly quadrupled for Native Americans) in thirteen years. There is evidence against the double whammy thesis but for the double minority argument. Comparing the magnitude of changes since 1980, there also is an indication that underrepresented minority females have made more progress in appointments than any other groups. Between 1980 and 1993, the rate of increase in the number of black (197 percent) and Hispanic (283 percent) females was greater than that of white males (46 percent), minority males (from 82 percent to 107 percent), white females (138 percent), and Asian females (142 percent). Minority females as a group made significant gains in entry to academic medicine, though they still lag far behind white males.

Third, there is a higher female ratio among blacks than among other groups. In 1993, 37 percent of black faculty was female, compared to 30 percent for Native Americans, 27 percent for Hispanics and Asians, and 23 percent for whites. As mentioned earlier, compared to other medical school graduates, blacks may be less likely to enter teaching careers, partly because of a strong desire to help the socially disadvantaged through clinical practice. Still, black females maintained the largest proportion in medical teaching, while the opposite was true for black males. This interesting phenomenon can be attributed in part to the fact that, since the 1970s, most of the gains in medical school enrollment among blacks were made by women (Ready and Nickens 1991). In fact, the number of black men in medical training has declined. Further, a relatively high representation of black women on medical school faculties may reflect an extension of racial and gender roles (Perrucci 1970). Women or minorities are more likely than men or the majority to have a "typically female or minority" career—that of teaching. Applying the underlying logic to the medical profession, teaching may become a more natural career path for medically trained black women than for black men. One can also argue that medical schools have increased the number of minority women faculty to fulfill two affirmative action goals—women and minority medical school faculty.

Differential departmental concentration may affect the professional development of minority and women medical school faculty. Based on opposing views of relative group size, competition for (internal and external) funding support, laboratory space, and tenure track positions for minority faculty may vary across departments. According to an AAMC survey of senior medical school students, there is no significant difference in specialty selection between entering white and minority medical students. Racial divergence in specialty preference occurs later among medical school graduates and in graduate school education (Petersdorf et al. 1990:666). This situation may result from the influence of academic advisors and peers at medical schools. Additionally, it has been suggested that the favorite specialty for female medical school graduates is internal medicine—a traditionally lower—paying specialty (Relman 1980). In a study of medical school faculty in internal medicine, Levey et al. (1990) found that, after controlling for age differences, female faculty still received less grant support from the National Institutes of Health than did their male counterparts. They also noted that women were less likely than men to have laboratory space for research. Differences in the allocation of financial and physical resources may explain, in part, why women lag behind men in research productivity in academic medicine (ACP 1991:64). Ironically, there is evidence that gender difference in rank attainment is smaller in internal medicine than in radiology (Dial et al. 1989).

To see if there was any tendency for a particular group to concentrate in certain medical departments, I calculated the indexes of dissimilarity (*D*) for women and minorities separately in 1980, 1990, and 1993.[11] The data[12] show that departmental segregation by race has declined since 1980, especially for Hispanics and Native Americans. The same is true for women. However, departmental segregation by gender or race among medical school faculties remains very low, reflecting a high degree of integration of women and minorities in medical teaching. This is an interesting finding. Female medical students tend to concentrate in low-status, low-paying fields, such as internal medicine and pediatrics. Nevertheless, there is no indication of an uneven departmental distribution, by sex, among medical school faculty. A steady increase of women in academic medicine has not resulted in departmental sex segregation. This phenomenon does not sit well with the prevailing assumption that rising female participation in traditionally male-dominated professions necessarily leads to their concentration in low-status fields (Epstein 1993; Reskin and Roos 1990).

Generally, the trend data suggest that minority females have been more successful in gaining entry to this prestigious profession, when compared to their minority male and white female counterparts. Nonetheless, for women or minorities, gaining entry may be just the first step to gaining structural assimilation in medical professions. We should also look at what happens to these groups after they become a part of the medical school faculty. It is premature to conclude that they fare better or worse than other groups without examining two standard measures of success in academia—the relative representation of minorities on each track (tenure vs. nontenure track)[13] and the academic advancement of minorities.

TENURE STATUS AND ACADEMIC RANK

This section addresses the question of whether minority faculty have achieved parity of tenure status, as well as academic rank, with white faculty.

Research on minorities and women in general academic careers shows that they are disproportionately found in lower ranking, nontenure positions (Chamberlain 1991; Haas and Perrucci 1984; Jackson 1991; Smith and Tang 1994). Approximately 95 percent of all the accredited medical schools in the United States offer tenure to faculty (Jones 1993:588). However, our country's definitions of tenure track and tenure in academic disciplines may be somewhat different than those of academic medicine's. Bickel (1991) points out that because of differences in the characteristics and guidelines of medical schools, the term *tenure* or the title *professor* in one institution does not necessarily mean the same in another. For example, a small number of medical schools grant tenure only to basic science faculty (Jones 1993:588). For budgetary concerns and other reasons, some medical schools have extended the probationary period beyond seven years (e.g., the University of Pennsylvania School of Medicine). Thus, there might have been few changes in the ranks of different groups in the last decade. Meanwhile, some medical schools provide tenured faculty with financial guarantees, while others offer clinical faculty only the academic title and support for teaching and research (ACP 1991; Bickel 1991). Because of enormous variations in the definitions of tenure and tenure track among medical schools, the ACP (1991) contends that tenure status and academic rank may not be comprehensive measures of the status of minorities and women on medical school faculties.

On the other hand, one could argue that although tenure in academic medicine may not provide faculty with economic security, it does offer individuals stability and academic freedom for innovative research or the exploration of new ideas. One can also consider awarding tenure as an indicator of a medical school's commitment to its faculty (Bickel 1991). The academic title and higher ranks may entail additional internal support for research, such as laboratory space and, in turn, improve one's prospects of securing external research grants, contracts, and clinical work (Jones 1993:591). That is why I would argue that tenure status and promotions (at least in most faculty's minds) remain two of the most important indicators of achievements among medical school faculty.

Table 9.2 reports the distribution of tenure status and academic rank of medical school faculty. Being appointed to a tenure track position and/or obtaining tenure is the first indicator of the career success of medical school faculty. The data reveal that the proportion of medical school faculty on tenure track, irrespective of race and gender, dropped precipitously between 1980 and 1990, which may be an outcome of financial retrenchment in higher education over the last decade. Careful examination also reveals convergence in the levels of representation on tenure track

Table 9.2. Academic Rank and Tenure Status of Medical School Faculty By Race and Sex in 1980, 1990, and 1993 (in Percent)

	White		Black		Asian		Hispanic		Native American	
	Male	Female	Male	Female	Male	Female	Male	Female	Male	Female
1980 (N)	30,508	5,252	501	206	2,241	624	816	170	25	6
Professor	34	11	23	7	16	3	22	5	32	0
Associate Professor	25	22	28	17	26	14	24	15	16	17
Assistant Professor	34	46	34	44	45	59	40	49	36	50
Instructor	7	21	15	32	13	24	13	31	16	33
Total	100	100	100	100	100	100	100	100	100	100
Tenured	31	21	31	14	21	10	23	19	40	17
On Tenure Track	22	28	24	20	26	33	30	26	16	67
Not on Tenure Track	46	51	45	67	52	56	47	55	44	17
1990 (N)	41,261	10,081	798	430	3,590	1,200	1,259	367	42	15
Professor	34	11	19	6	23	6	24	8	45	13
Associate Professor	26	20	21	14	27	21	25	19	21	7
Assistant Professor	34	51	44	54	40	56	39	52	24	67
Instructor	5	18	16	26	10	17	11	21	10	13
Total	100	100	100	100	100	100	100	100	100	100
Tenured	35	17	24	12	25	12	25	13	31	13
On Tenure Track	15	17	15	14	14	16	16	15	14	7
Not on Tenure Track	50	66	61	74	61	72	59	72	55	80

(Continued on next page)

Table 9.2. (*continued*)

	White		Black		Asian		Hispanic		Native American	
	Male	*Female*	*Male*	*Female*	*Male*	*Female*	*Male*	*Female*	*Male*	*Female*
1993 (*N*)	45,871	13,024	1,081	625	4,286	1,536	1,508	537	53	21
Professor	34	10	15	4	24	8	24	6	36	10
Associate Professor	26	21	24	14	24	21	23	23	21	10
Assistant Professor	33	50	46	55	41	55	41	51	38	48
Instructor	7	19	16	27	11	16	11	20	6	33
Total	100	100	100	100	100	100	100	100	100	100

Notes: Excludes faculty who declined to identify their race, academic rank, or tenure status. Data on tenure status by race and sex for 1993 are not available.

positions between races and sexes. With the exception of Native American females, the portion of faculty on tenure track ranged from 16 percent to 33 percent of overall faculty in 1980, compared to 14 percent to 17 percent in 1990.

During the same period, the proportion of faculty with tenure increased for some groups and decreased for others. A drop in the proportion of faculty on tenure track among white males, Asians, and Hispanics can be attributed in part to promotions.[14] Indeed there was a small-to-moderate percentage increase in the associate professor rank among these groups. However, the same cannot be said about white females and blacks. Between 1980 and 1990, the proportion of white female and black professors declined substantially, while there was little or no change in their proportion in higher ranks (full and associate professors).

The data also reveal considerable inter- and intra-gender differences in tenure status during both periods. Although the gender gap in tenure status has been reduced somewhat since 1980, female faculty continue to trail their male counterparts in obtaining tenure. Minority women have also consistently fallen behind white women and other groups in increasing their proportions with tenure. Among males, whites had the highest proportion of tenured faculty, followed by Native Americans. Despite differences in the level of representation on medical school faculties, a comparable percentage of blacks, Asians, and Hispanics held tenured positions in 1990.

Next, I address the question of whether there were any changes in the ranks of different groups over the last decade. Between 1980 and 1990, minorities, especially females, were consistently less likely than whites to be full professors. In 1993, however, among males, Native Americans had the largest proportion (36 percent), and blacks the lowest proportion (15 percent) at the highest academic rank. For females, whites were more likely than minorities to hold the rank of full professor. In 1993, only 4 percent of black females—but 10 percent of white females—were full professors.

Data in Table 9.2 also indicate that academic rank distributions of whites remained fairly constant over the thirteen-year period, with approximately 34 percent of males and 11 percent of females holding full professorships. However, changes in other groups were far from uniform. Between 1980 and 1993, there was a declining representation of black faculty at higher ranks. The proportion of black males and females who held full professorships dropped from 23 percent and 7 percent, respectively, in 1980 to 15 percent and 4 percent in 1993. Meanwhile, an increasing number of blacks were concentrated at the lowest academic rank—that of assistant professor. In contrast, Asians, both male and female, made steady gains in promotions. This is also true for Hispanic faculty, though to a smaller extent. In 1993, 24 percent of Asian and Hispanic male faculty were full professors, compared to 8 percent of Asian females and 6 percent of Hispanic females. Also interesting is that a greater proportion of women (minorities in particular) than men were instructors during this period. Therefore, a relevant issue is whether certain groups had faster or slower rates of promotion.

Table 9.3 reports the relative increase of race/gender groups at each rank between 1980 and 1993. Although the proportion of certain race/gender groups in higher ranks was decreasing, the actual numbers of each group at each rank continued to grow. However, the most striking finding was that women, regardless of their racial background, showed the largest increase at each academic rank during this period. Comparing the

Table 9.3. Medical School Faculty By Academic Rank, Race, and Sex in 1980, 1990, and 1993

	1980	1990	1993	% Change 1980–90	% Change 1990–93	Total % Change 1980–93
Academic Rank / Race / Sex						
PROFESSOR						
White	10,789	15,186	16,805	41	11	56
Male	10,227	14,107	15,440	38	9	51
Female	562	1,079	1,365	92	27	143
Black	127	174	186	37	7	46
Male	113	149	161	32	8	42
Female	14	25	25	79	0	79
Asian	389	898	1,140	131	27	193
Male	369	821	1,023	122	25	177
Female	20	77	117	285	52	485
Hispanic	191	334	402	75	20	110
Male	182	306	369	68	21	103
Female	9	28	33	211	18	267
Native American	8	21	21	162	0	162
Male	8	19	19	138	0	138
Female	0	2	2	—	0	—
Total	11,504	16,613	18,554	44	12	61
Male	10,899	15,402	17,012	41	10	56
Female	605	1,211	1,542	100	27	155

(Continued)

Table 9.3. (*continued*)

	1980	1990	1993	% Change 1980–90	% Change 1990–93	Total % Change 1980–93
Academic Rank / Race / Sex						
ASSOCIATE PROFESSOR						
White	8,920	12,778	14,572	43	14	63
Male	7,744	10,719	11,884	38	11	53
Female	1,176	2,059	2,688	75	31	129
Black	178	232	345	30	49	94
Male	142	171	257	20	50	81
Female	36	61	88	69	44	144
Asian	665	1,212	1,372	82	13	106
Male	577	957	1,049	66	10	82
Female	88	255	323	190	27	267
Hispanic	219	389	477	78	23	118
Male	194	318	354	64	11	82
Female	25	71	123	184	73	392
Native American	5	10	13	100	30	160
Male	4	9	11	125	22	175
Female	1	1	2	0	100	100
Total	9,987	14,621	16,779	46	15	68
Male	8,661	12,174	13,555	41	11	57
Female	1,326	2,447	3,224	85	32	143
ASSISTANT PROFESSOR						
White	12,698	19,331	21,913	52	13	73
Male	10,269	14,167	15,366	38	8	50
Female	2,429	5,164	6,547	113	27	170
Black	262	584	838	123	43	220
Male	172	352	492	105	40	186
Female	90	232	346	158	49	284
Asian	1,368	2,105	2,584	54	23	89
Male	1,002	1,439	1,738	44	21	73
Female	366	666	846	82	27	131

(Continued)

Table 9.3. (*continued*)

	1980	1990	1993	% Change 1980–90	% Change 1990–93	Total % Change 1980–93
Academic Rank / Race / Sex						
ASSISTANT PROFESSOR *(Continued)*						
Hispanic	413	687	887	66	29	115
Male	330	496	612	50	23	85
Female	83	191	275	130	44	231
Native American	12	20	30	67	50	150
Male	9	10	20	11	100	122
Female	3	10	10	233	0	233
Total	14,753	22,727	26,252	54	16	78
Male	11,782	16,464	18,228	40	11	55
Female	2,971	6,263	8,024	111	28	170

Note: Excludes faculty who declined to identify their race or academic rank.

overall rates of female increase across ranks suggests that women faculty as a whole did slightly better at the lowest academic rank (170 percent) than they did at higher ranks (143 percent to 155 percent). Despite a faster rate of growth of female faculty at each rank, data in Table 9.3 reveal considerable inter- and intra-gender variations in progress.

Among full professors, Asians, especially females, made the largest gain. The total number of Asians holding the highest academic rank tripled in thirteen years. The rate of increase for Asian females at the professor rank is phenomenal. The number of Asian female full professors increased from twenty in 1980 to 117 in 1993—five times greater. Hispanic females also demonstrated an exceptional rate of growth in holding full professorships. Nonetheless, despite a 267 percent increase during this period, the actual number of Hispanic women holding this rank remained very small. Compared with other groups, blacks made the smallest gain at the highest academic rank. More important is that there has been little or no change in the number of black faculty holding full professorships since 1990. Based on the actual and relative proportions of Native Americans, they are indeed severely underrepresented at the highest rank.

At the associate professor level, Native Americans, as a group, fared better than did others in terms of growth. However, among all race/gender groups, Hispanic females became the fastest-growing group at this academic rank. Their numbers increased by nearly 400 percent, from twenty-five in 1980 to 123 in 1993. Their Asian female counterparts also made impressive gains, though at a smaller scale, followed by black females. Also noteworthy is that black, Asian, and Hispanic males had identical rates of increase in this thirteen-year period (81 percent to 82 percent). Unexpected is that white faculty, especially males, showed the smallest increase.

Black medical faculty showed their largest increase at the lowest academic rank. Specifically, black females made huge gains at the assistant professor rank. The number of black women appointed assistant professors nearly tripled between 1980 and 1993. There also was a sizeable increase in the appointment of Hispanics as assistant professors. However, among Hispanics, the rate of increase was substantially higher for females than for males. In comparison, whites and Asians had substantially lower rates of increase at this rank.

In short, comparing the overall rates of increase across ranks reveals a somewhat different pattern of growth for each racial group. Much of the progress made by blacks in academic medicine over the past thirteen years was at the junior academic rank. The rates of increase at each level for Hispanics and Native Americans were comparable. Asians made disproportionate gains at the highest ranks. And compared with minorities as a group, whites were the slow-growing group at each academic rank.

AGE AND YEAR OF FIRST APPOINTMENT

Some of the differences in the rates of increase at each academic rank between races and sexes may be a result of cohort effects. A disproportionate growth in minority and female representation on medical school faculties suggests that many are newcomers in academic medicine. They might have entered academic medicine too recently to advance to higher ranks. The distribution of age and the year of first faculty appointment for 1980 and 1990 (Table 9.4) confirms the widely held speculation that minorities, except for Native Americans, are younger than whites. In 1990, a larger proportion of minority faculty (except Native Americans) than white faculty began their careers in the 1980s. One-half of black, Asian, and Hispanic males received their first faculty appointment after 1979. The proportion of recent appointments of female faculty is even greater. In 1990, with the

Table 9.4. Age and Year of First Academic Appointment of Medical School Faculty By Race and Sex in 1980 and 1990 (in Percent)

	White		Black		Asian		Hispanic		Native American	
	Male	Female	Male	Female	Male	Female	Male	Female	Male	Female
1980 (N)	31,731	5,697	529	219	2,340	664	840	179	28	6
Under 30	1	4	0	4	1	2	1	2	4	33
30–39	34	41	27	42	37	49	36	37	43	33
40–49	32	26	37	29	45	35	33	34	36	17
50–59	23	20	25	18	14	12	25	23	7	17
60+	10	8	10	7	3	2	5	4	11	0
Total	100	100	100	100	100	100	100	100	100	100
Appointed Before 1970	43	32	41	26	27	17	37	33	36	17
Appointed 1970–79	50	61	54	67	66	74	58	60	64	83
Appointed After 1979	3	4	2	2	4	4	4	3	0	0
1990 (N)	42,464	10,478	809	454	3,654	1,225	1,276	377	43	17
Under 30	0	1	0	2	0	1	1	2	0	0
30–39	27	42	29	47	26	29	34	43	30	41
40–49	36	35	34	30	40	47	33	33	40	35
50–59	22	14	23	15	26	18	21	17	19	18
60+	15	8	14	7	8	4	12	5	12	6
Total	100	100	100	100	100	100	100	100	100	100
Appointed Before 1970	25	12	20	9	14	7	17	8	16	6
Appointed 1970–79	33	26	27	26	38	37	33	26	47	29
Appointed After 1979	40	60	51	63	45	53	49	63	37	59

Notes: Excludes faculty who declined to identify their race, age, or year of first academic appointment. Percentages for year of appointment may not sum to 100 because of missing cases. Data on age and first academic appointment by race and sex for 1993 are not available.

exception of Asians, 60 percent of women faculty began their careers in the last ten years. There is evidence (Table 9.4) that black and Hispanic females entered academic medicine in great strides in recent years. In 1990, nearly two-thirds of black and Hispanic female faculty were first appointed after 1979. As a result, it may take a while for female faculty, especially underrepresented minorities, to catch up with male faculty in rank attainment.

A possible reason why Asian females, compared to their female counterparts, exhibited a very high rate of increase to higher ranks is their early entry into the profession. A relatively large portion of Asian female faculty was appointed in the 1970s. In 1990, among female faculty, 44 percent of Asians began their careers before 1980, as opposed to 38 percent for whites, 35 percent for blacks and Native Americans, and 34 percent for Hispanics.

The pattern of the first appointment period for male faculty is somewhat different. One of the interesting features in Table 9.4 is that, in 1980, a comparable proportion of white (43 percent) and black (41 percent) male faculty began their careers before 1970. At the same time, as shown in Table 9.2, similar portions of white and black male faculty were tenured (31 percent), yet a higher proportion of whites (34 percent) than blacks (23 percent) were full professors. The black-white male gap became larger in 1990 and 1993.

Careful examination of the age distribution of all groups in 1980 and 1990 suggests that not all female faculty were latecomers. While a large proportion of female faculty was in their thirties, nearly one-half of Asian female faculty was between age forty and forty-nine. This may be one of the factors which underlies the high rate of growth for Asian females at senior ranks and for black females at junior ranks.

Interestingly, although black and white male faculty had fairly similar age distributions in 1990, black males consistently lagged behind white males in rank attainment between 1980 and 1990. Additionally, the age distribution of Hispanic and Native American male faculty in 1990 was somewhat similar. Among male faculty, Hispanics had the highest proportion of young faculty. In 1990, 35 percent of Hispanic male faculty was under forty years of age, compared to 27 percent for Asians. Yet, as shown in Table 9.2, the pattern of rank distribution for Hispanic and Asian males since 1990 has remained fairly comparable. Hence, this Hispanic-Asian convergence in rank attainment should be attributed to the timing of their first appointments rather than to age. Data in Table 9.4 show that approximately one-half of Hispanic and Asian male faculty began their careers after 1980.

However, neither age nor timing of first appointments can fully explain why there is still a race/gender gap in obtaining tenure or why black male faculty are not promoted to higher ranks as fast as other minority faculty. Some have highlighted the problems women and minorities face in academic medicine. As previously noted, a lack of role models and mentors suggests inadequate support and guidance from senior faculty for the career development of minorities. According to the ACP (1991), lack of knowledge about tenure and promotion procedures is not uncommon among women and minority faculty.

Another factor slowing the progress of underrepresented minority faculty in academe is that many of them have to meet the heavy demands of teaching, patient care, and advising. And minority faculty may have to devote more time to meet other service demands, such as counseling students. Because academic promotions tend to be highly associated with productivity, not being able to become involved in research activities as much as their white or male colleagues may be the main reason why black males and women, in general, have slower academic promotion. Dial et al. (1989) have found that female medical faculty are indeed less productive than their male counterparts in terms of publication and other research activities. Fewer resources, such as laboratory space and grant support, may be the contributing factors[15] to lower productivity among female faculty. Nonetheless, the fact that there are more women and minorities at lower ranks suggests more competition for diminishing research resources among them and for those in senior ranks. Indeed, the success in obtaining grants among young faculty is declining (Bickel 1991:256).

Furthermore, medical schools have become more selective in awarding tenures and promotions, largely due to budgetary considerations (Jones 1993:588). Because a large proportion of women and minorities are at junior ranks, any modifications in policies governing tenures and promotions are going to have a greater impact on these groups. On the other hand, many have called for greater efforts to improve the representation of women and minorities in academic medicine and in senior academic ranks (ACP 1991; Petersdorf 1990). This responsibility falls squarely on the shoulders of the deans and department heads of medical schools. The following section examines the involvement of minorities in administration and discusses how administrators can promote the careers of underrepresented minorities.

INVOLVEMENT IN ADMINISTRATION

Moving into leadership positions is a useful indicator of success in a profession. It has been suggested that advancement to administration is associated with a person's academic accomplishment, as well as seniority (Dial et al. 1989:201). Table 9.5 summarizes the distribution of medical school faculty in administration from 1980 to 1993.[16] The number of faculty with administrative responsibilities increased by 31 percent, from 354 in 1980 to 462 in 1990, but subsequently dropped to 320 in 1993. During the same period, minorities gradually increased their representation in administration. In 1980, only 4 percent of medical school administrators were minorities. They comprised 9 percent of those in leadership ranks in 1993. Given that minorities constituted 14 percent of medical school faculties in 1993, they were still underrepresented in authority positions.

Hispanics had the largest increase in administrative participation, but blacks had the highest representation among minorities in administrative ranks. However, as previously mentioned, because a good portion of black faculty was in historically black medical schools, virtually all black faculty administrators might be employed by these institutions as well.[17] Relative to their proportions in academic medicine (9 percent), Asians were the most underrepresented minority group in administration (2 percent) in 1993. Although Asian medical faculty had the fastest rate of growth in the highest rank in the last thirteen years, data in Table 9.5 show they were not making similar progress in entering administration.

Moreover, the data do not sit well with the assumption that entry to administration is necessarily related to higher rank. Although blacks had the lowest representation in higher academic ranks, they were more likely to become involved in administration tasks than were other groups. In 1993, .97 percent of black faculty were administrators, compared with .41 percent for whites, .19 percent for Hispanics, and .11 percent for Asians. One can argue that the unusually high rate of black participation in administration is probably due to blacks' concentration in black medical schools. But how can we account for the exceedingly low rate of Asian involvement in administration? Why are Asians, as a group, the least likely to have administrative responsibilities, although they are overrepresented in academic medicine and have made significant gains at higher ranks? The statistics reflect the presence of a "glass ceiling," which prevents minority faculty from moving to the top. On the other hand, Asians might have a strong preference for teaching and research. The general perception of Asians' excellence in technical tasks may discourage school administrations' assignment of Asian faculty to managerial posts. Absence of Asian medical schools is another reason behind the low rate of Asian involvement in administration. Also, the high turnover of medical school deans in recent decades reflects more stringent criteria for selecting administrators (Banaszak-Holl and Greer 1994). Because of the increasing complexity in the organization of medical schools, an administrator is expected to have

Table 9.5. Distribution of Medical School Faculty in Administration By Race and Sex in 1980, 1990, and 1993

Race / Sex	1980		1990		1993		% Change 1980–90	% Change 1990–93	Total % Change 1980–93
	N	%	N	%	N	%			
White	341	96	436	94	292	91	28	–33	–14
Male	—	—	—	—	239	82			
Female	—	—	—	—	53	18			
Black	12	3	18	4	17	5	50	–6	42
Male	—	—	—	—	12	71			
Female	—	—	—	—	5	29			
Asian	0	0	6	1	7	2	—	17	—
Male	—	—	—	—	3	43			
Female	—	—	—	—	4	57			
Hispanic	0	0	1	—	4	1	—	300	—
Male	—	—	—	—	4	100			
Female	—	—	—	—	0	0			
Native American	1	0	1	0	0	0	0	–100	–100
Male	—	—	—	—	0	0			
Female	—	—	—	—	0	0			
Total	354	100	462	100	320	100	31	–31	–10
Male	—	—	—	—	258	81			
Female	—	—	—	—	62	19			

Notes: Excludes faculty who declined to identify their race. Data on faculty in administration by race and sex for 1980 and 1990 are not available.

excellent managerial skills and extensive professional networks. The development of these skills and ties requires considerable time to be spent in academic medicine. For many minority faculty, making it to the top may take some time, due to their recent entry into the profession. However, an optimistic reading of the trends of minority representation in administration between 1980 and 1993 suggests that leadership in medical schools has become more diversified.

Data in Table 9.5 indicate that women faculty in general are still underrepresented in administration. In 1993, only one out of every five administrators was a woman. However, comparing the representation of women in administration across races reveals huge intra-gender variations. There were no Hispanic or Native American women faculty in administrative posts. Among female faculty, Asians had the highest level of representation in leadership posts. In 1993, 57 percent of Asian medical faculty who had administrative responsibilities were women, compared to 29 percent for blacks and 18 percent for whites. This is an interesting finding, because Asian female faculty were faring better than females and Asian males in terms of representation in administration. Differences in age and period of first faculty appointment might explain in part why Asian females were more likely than their female colleagues to be in administration. Their significant gains at higher ranks since 1980 suggest that more Asian females than other females are in line for top jobs. Although the total number of Asians holding administrative positions is relatively small, the finding that there are more women than men involved in administration implies that different forces might be at work for minority males and females aiming at administrative positions.

Many have argued that top administrators of medical schools should find ways to increase the numbers of underrepresented minority faculty in senior positions (ACP 1991; Bickel 1991; Eisenberg 1991; Jones 1993). In other words, deans of medical schools should play a key role in fostering the professional development of minority faculty in junior ranks. Several measures have been proposed to address racial and gender differences in promotion rates. For example, Bickel (1991) and Eisenberg (1991) underscore the importance of continuing affirmative action in hiring and promotion. The deans should appoint women and/or minorities to advisory groups and faculty search committees to monitor the implementation of affirmative action programs. To achieve the goal of increasing minority representation in medical teaching, Bickel (1991) suggests assigning assistants for minority faculty recruitment to work with department chairs.

To facilitate the advancement of minority faculty to senior ranks, Bickel (1991) also maintains that department chairs should set up committees for minorities for tenures and promotions to monitor their progress and find ways to improve their chances of getting tenures and promotions. The administration should provide more guidance and support to junior faculty. For example, it should make the policies and procedures of tenures and promotions more specific. There are signs of change at the institutional level for making the playing field equal. However, it may not be until the next century that the real impact of these institutional changes on the movement of underrepresented minorities up the academic ladder is seen.

CONCLUSION

This chapter contains the most-asked information about the recent progress of minority males and females in academic medicine. It is a comprehensive update on the trends of representation, as well as the achievements of blacks, Hispanics, Asians, and Native Americans on medical school faculties. Compared with whites and Asians, underrepresented minorities have the fastest rate of growth in academic medicine. One could argue that the large percentage gains simply reflect the small initial number of underrepresented minorities on medical school faculties. The results also provide some support for the "small is valuable" argument, that a small group size enhances the movement of minorities to professional occupations. The fact that black women made the largest gain in entry directly contradicts the "double whammy" thesis. However, blacks as a group do not seem to fare as well as other groups in rank attainment. Black medical school faculty tend to be slower than other groups in moving up the academic ladder. Their proportion in senior academic ranks has decreased. Most of the progress made by blacks in academic medicine between 1980 and 1993 was at the junior ranks. In contrast, Asians and Hispanics tended to perform better than blacks in improving their proportional representation in higher ranks. These results suggest that black faculty may face a set of unique problems that prevent them from moving up the career ladder.

Although, in general, other minorities on medical school faculties fare better than blacks, they have not made much gains in administration. Regardless of their comparative group sizes, blacks, Asians, and Hispanics are underrepresented in leadership ranks. This phenomenon suggests that gaining access to higher-status professions does not necessarily guarantee subsequent entry to decision-making positions. Whether members of a minority group can eventually occupy leadership posts in nonblack medical schools may be independent of their relative group size. High turnover of deans of medicine positions in recent decades implies that, due to financial constraints and organizational complexity, the tasks of running a medical school may become more difficult. On the other hand, these situations may generate relatively more opportunities for minority faculty to participate in the decision-making process.

In sum, if the present trend continues, it would probably take some time to "mainstream"[18] all racial and ethnic minorities into academic medicine. Greater institutional efforts are called for to address racial and gender differences in promotions. Expanding the pool of minority medical school graduates would certainly increase the relative size of minorities on medical school faculties. As more underrepresented minorities move into senior positions, a relatively large proportion of them would be available as mentors and role models for students and junior faculty. Some have suggested more flexibility in hiring and retaining faculty to meet the needs of medical schools in light of the financial situation in higher education. Making the terms for the clinician-educator track more attractive may allow schools to retain more faculty who are interested in patient care and teaching. Meanwhile, because scholarship is one of the most important criteria for obtaining tenures and promotions, underrepresented minority faculty should receive extra institutional support for seeking external research grants and contracts. On the other hand, policies allowing "clock stopping" or parental leave would offer minorities and women sufficient time to develop their research programs (Eisenberg 1991:678; Jones 1991:590–591). Nonetheless, very few would dispute that senior faculty can and should play a key role in fostering the career development of junior minority faculty. In addition to being mentors or role models, senior faculty can provide encouragement and guidance to junior faculty in their research activities. Finally, regardless of subgroup differences, minorities as a whole remain a very small group on medical school faculties. To improve the overall levels of minority representation in academic medicine and senior ranks, perhaps minorities, both male and female, should also actively seek encouragement from and provide support to one another.

ACKNOWLEDGMENTS

I would like to thank Paul Blumberg, Anne E. Figert, and Earl Smith for their comments and suggestions.

NOTES

1. The term "underrepresented minorities" refers to racial groups whose proportion of medical faculty is less than its proportion of the U.S. population. Blacks, Hispanics (especially Mexican Americans and Puerto Ricans), and Native Americans are underrepresented in academic medicine. Asians are not classified as an underrepresented minority because their proportion of medical faculty is higher than that in the U.S. population (AAMC 1993a).

2. According to AAMC (1993b), the proportion of black applicants increased from 7.5 percent to 8.1 percent between 1983 and 1992 while during the same period other underrepresented applicants, such as Indian/Alaskan natives, Mexican American/Chicanos, and mainland Puerto Ricans, increased from 2.6 percent to 3.1 percent. Women accounted for almost 42 percent of the applicant pool in 1992, compared to 34 percent in 1983.

3. AAMC provides an update on the representation of minorities and women in academic medicine every three years. Other medical researchers have analyzed these aggregate statistics to examine retirement patterns as a result of the end of mandatory retirement (Friedman 1992) or gender differences in research activities and academic rank in certain specialties (Dial et al. 1989; Levey et al. 1990). There is a paucity of research focusing on changes in the gender and racial compositions of medical school faculty (Bickel and Whiting 1991; Whiting and Bickel 1990).

4. An overview of recent articles or research reports published in medical journals reveals that a large number of these papers focus on gender, rather than racial, differences in career attainment of medical school faculty (e.g., Bickel and Whiting 1991; Dial et al. 1989; Eastwood 1992; Eisenberg 1991; Levy et al. 1990; Petersdorf et al. 1990; Whiting and Bickel 1990).

5. In 1978, the mandatory retirement age of sixty-five was changed to seventy. The Age Discrimination in Employment Act of 1986 banned this requirement for virtually all workers. However, tenured faculty were exempted before and after the passage of this act. Beginning in 1994, tenured professors can continue to work for as long as they want (Friedman 1992).

6. The aggregate statistics in these two reports are derived from AAMC's Faculty Roster System. AAMC has maintained this data base since 1966 to gather demographic and career information about medical school faculty. It is an ideal data base for studying recent trends of minorities' and womens' participation in academic medicine. AAMC solicits information

from the schools and not from the faculty. The data base contains approximately 85 percent of all active full-time medical school faculty (AAMC 1993). However, it is important to discuss a few of the problems inherent in AAMC's published reports and how they may affect the results. Because of undercounting, we should refrain from generalizing results of the analysis in this chapter to the entire U.S. medical school faculty. Another problem with this data base is that AAMC does not ask schools to report faculty earning levels. As a result, we cannot study how minorities fare economically over the years compared to whites. Finally, inconsistency in the reporting breakdowns by race/sex for (1) tenure status, (2) period of first academic appointment, and (3) participation in administration in the reports (AAMC 1990, 1993) makes long-term comparison difficult. Despite this sampling and nonsampling bias, AAMC's Faculty Roster System constitutes an important—but largely under-utilized—resource for studying the progress of minorities on medical school faculties.

7. Throughout this paper, for brevity, the term *black* will be used to refer to African Americans. This is also the label used by the AAMC to identify African Americans in the data base.

8. Includes Mexican Americans, Puerto Ricans, and other Hispanics.

9. Because of the very small number of Native Americans on medical school faculties, results of this group should be interpreted with caution.

10. This is not to suggest that role models or mentors of the same sex or race are necessarily better than those of the opposite sex or different race in the professional development of women and minorities. However, there is indication that female physicians with female mentors reported having a relatively more satisfying personal relationship. Interestingly, those with senior male mentors said they had more effective career sponsorships (ACP 1991:64). The concept of "homosocial reproduction" also suggests that individuals tend to prefer working with people of the same gender or race. If this is the case, women and minorities may have more difficulty than men or whites in seeking supportive mentors or role models.

11. The index of dissimilarity (*D*) represents the percentage of a group (e.g., minorities or females) who would have to change departments in order for the group to have identical distribution of a comparison group (e.g., whites or males) (Blalock 1967). If two groups have the same departmental distributions, the *D* would be zero. The formula for *D* is:

$$D = \sum_{i=1}^{n} \frac{\left| (B_i/B) - (W_i/W) \right|}{2}$$

where B_i is the number of blacks in department i, B is the total number of black faculty, W_i is the number of whites in department i, W is the total number of white faculty, and n is the total number of departments.

12. The Ds between males and females were 6, 2, and 2, respectively, in 1980, 1990, and 1993; that is, about 6 percent of female medical faculty had to change departments in 1980 to have a distribution identical to that of male faculty. The Ds between whites and minority groups are as follows:

	1980	*1990*	*1993*
Whites and blacks	8	8	8
Whites and Asians	3	2	2
Whites and Hispanics	9	2	2
Whites and Native Americans	18	14	5

13. The nontenure clinician-educator track is different from the regular tenure track in that it is an appointment for physician faculty primarily involved in patient care and teaching. There is less or no emphasis on research activities (Jacobs 1993). Of course, there is also a difference in the reward system for these tracks in terms of title, salaries, and privileges.

14. Most schools award tenure at promotion from assistant professor to associate professor (Bickel 1991; Jones 1993).

15. Dial et al. (1989) found that the number of children and one's marital status were not associated with rank. This is an important observation because of the concern of female medical students about tensions between family commitments and pursuing academic careers (Osborn, Ernster, and Martin 1992).

16. In this chapter, if respondents reported "administration" as their "department" in AAMC's Faculty Roster System, they were assumed to be involved in administration. Unfortunately, there was no information on the position title (e.g., dean, associate dean, assistant dean, department chair).

17. According to Joyner (1988), there were six black departmental chairs but no black deans at nonblack medical schools.

18. This concept is borrowed from the American Medical Association's (1989) Department of Women in Medicine. In this chapter, "fully mainstreamed" is defined as when the proportion of minorities entering academic medicine is the same as their proportion in the U.S. population; or when the proportion of minority medical faculty in higher ranks is proportional to their numbers in academic medicine.

REFERENCES

American College of Physicians [ACP]. 1991. "Promotion and Tenure of Women and Minorities on Medical School Faculties." *Annals of Internal Medicine* 114:63–68.

Association of American Medical Colleges. [AAMC] 1991. *Participation of Women and Minorities on U.S. Medical School Faculties, 1980–1990.* Washington, DC: Association of American Medical Colleges.

———. 1993a. *U.S. Medical School Faculty, 1993.* Washington, DC: Association of American Medical Colleges.

———. 1993b. *Trends in Medical School Applicants and Matriculants: 1983–1992.* Washington, DC: Association of American Medical Colleges.

Banaszak-Holl, Jane and David S. Greer. 1994. "Turnover of Deans of Medicine During the Last Five Decades." *Academic Medicine* 69:1–7.

Bickel, Janet. 1991. "The Changing Faces of Promotion and Tenure at U.S. Medical Schools." *Academic Medicine* 66:249–256.

Bickel, Janet and Brooke Whiting. 1991. "Comparing the Representation and Promotion of Men and Women Faculty at U.S. Medical Schools." *Academic Medicine* 66:497.

Blalock, Hubert M. 1967. *Toward a Theory of Minority-Group Relations.* New York: John Wiley and Sons.

Chamberlain, Mariam K. Ed. 1991. *Women in Academe: Progress and Prospects.* New York: Russell Sage Foundation.

Cunningham, James S. and Nadja Zalokar. 1992. "The Economic Progress of Black Women, 1940–1980: Occupational Distribution and Relative Wages." *Industrial and Labor Relations Review* 45:540–555.

Dial, Thomas H., Janet Bickel, and Ann M. Lewicki. 1989. "Sex Differences in Rank Attainment Among Radiology and Internal Medicine Faculty." *Academic Medicine* 64:198–202.

Eastwood, Gregory L. 1992. "Affirmative Action for Women." *Academic Medicine* 67:253.

Eisenberg, Carola. 1991. "Affirmative Action for Women and Promotion of Academic Excellence." *Academic Medicine* 66:678–679.

Epstein, Cynthia Fuchs. 1973. "Positive Effects of the Multiple Negative: Explaining the Success of Black Professional Women." *American Journal of Sociology* 78:912–935.

Friedman, Paul J. 1992. "Aging of Medical School Faculty and the End of Mandatory Retirement." *Academic Medicine* 67:223–231.

Frisbie, W. Parker and Lisa Neidert. 1977. "Inequality and the Relative Size of Minority Populations: A Comparative Analysis." *American Journal of Sociology* 82:1007–1030.

Haas, Violet B. and Carolyn C. Perrucci. Eds. 1984. *Women in Scientific and Engineering Professions.* Ann Arbor: University of Michigan Press.

Jackson, Kenneth W. 1991. "Black Faculty in Academia." Pp. 135–148 in *The Racial Crisis in American Higher Education,* edited by Philip G. Altbach and Kofi Lomotey. Albany: State University of New York Press.

Jacobs, Michael B. 1993. "Faculty Status for Clinician-Educators: Guidelines for Evaluation and Promotion." *Academic Medicine* 68:126–128.

Jones, Robert F. 1991. "The End of Mandatory Retirement and Its Implications for Academic Medicine." *Academic Medicine* 66:711–718.

———. 1993. "Three Views on Faculty Tenure in Medical Schools." *Academic Medicine* 68:588–593.

Joyner, J. 1988. "Health Manpower Today and Future Implications." *Journal of National Medical Association* 80:717–720.

Kanter, Rosabeth M. 1977. *Men and Women of the Corporation.* New York: Basic Books.

Koelewijin-Strattner, Gijsberta J., Joseph J. Lengermann, and Marina A. Adler. 1991. "Race and Gender in the Chemistry Profession: Double Jeopardy or Double Negative." Paper presented at the 86th Annual Meeting of the American Sociological Association, Cincinnati, Ohio, August.

Kulis, Stephen and Karen A. Miller. 1988. "Are Minority Women Sociologists in Double Jeopardy?" *The American Sociologist* 19:323–339.

Lebra, Takie Sugiyama. 1981. "Japanese Women in Male Dominant Careers: Cultural Barriers and Accommodations for Sex-Role Transcendence." *Ethnology* 20:291–306.

Levey, Barbara A., Nancy O. Gentile, H. Paul Jolly, Harry N. Beaty, and Gerald S. Levey. 1990. "Comparing Research Activities of Women and Men Faculty in Departments of Internal Medicine." *Academic Medicine* 65:102–106.

Lieberson, Stanley. 1980. *A Piece of the Pie: Blacks and White Immigrants Since 1880.* Berkeley: University of California Press.

Loos, Barbara C. 1986. "For Women: Getting Hired is the Easy Part." *Fortune* 114:160.

National Science Foundation. 1992. *Women and Minorities in Science and Engineering: An Update.* Washington, DC: U.S. Government Printing Office.

Osborn, Emilie H.S., Virginia L. Ernster, and Joseph B. Martin. 1992. "Women's Attitudes Toward Careers in Academic Medicine at the University of California, San Francisco." *Academic Medicine* 67:59–62.

Perrucci, Carolyn C. 1970. "Minority Status and the Pursuit of Professional Careers: Women in Science and Engineering." *Social Forces* 49:246–259.

Petersdorf, Robert G. 1989. "The Declining Applicant Pool: An Overview." Pp. 1–3 in *The Declining Applicant Pool: Proceedings—Implications for the Selection of Medical Students*, edited by the Association of American Medical Colleges. Washington, DC: Association of American Medical Colleges.

Petersdorf, Robert G., Kathleen S. Turner, Herbert W. Nickens, and Timothy Ready. 1990. "Minorities in Medicine: Past, Present, and Future." *Academic Medicine* 65:663–670.

Ready, Timothy and Herbert W. Nickens. 1991. "Black Men in the Medical Educational Pipeline: Past, Present, and Future." *Academic Medicine* 66:181–187.

Relman, A.S. 1980. "Here Come the Women." *New England Journal of Medicine* 302:1251–1253.

Smith, Earl and Joyce Tang. 1994. "Trends in Science and Engineering Doctorate Production, 1975–1990." Pp. 96–124 in *Who Will Do Science? Educating the Next Generation*, edited by Willie Pearson, Jr. and Alan Fechter. Baltimore, MD: Johns Hopkins University Press.

———. and Stephanie Witt. 1995. "The Experience of African American Women in the Academic Workplace: Doubly Disadvantaged or Meeting the Challenge of Greater Opportunity." *Review of Public Personnel Administration* 15:24–40.

Sokoloff, Natalie J. 1992. *Black Women and White Women in the Professions: Occupational Segregation by Race and Gender, 1960–1980.* New York: Routledge.

Whiting, Brooke E. and Janet Bickel. 1990. "Women on Faculties of U.S. Medical Schools, 1978–1989." *Academic Medicine* 65:277–278.

Whitley, N.O. et al. 1987. "Advancement of Women in Academic Radiology." *Investigating Radiology* 22:431–435.

Yamanaka, Keiko and Kent McClelland. 1994. "Earning the Model-Minority Image: Diverse Strategies of Economic Adaptation by Asian-American Women." *Ethnic and Racial Studies* 17:79–114.

10

Conclusion

EARL SMITH AND JOYCE TANG

We fear some of the readers of our book may have come to it with a priori assumptions of what represents the conclusions—work, occupations, and possibly professions—of the chapters contained in it. Based on the work we did with each chapter contributor, we feel that without having read the book, no one could have predicted what is found in all of the chapters.

Sex and race segregation of the American labor force is one of the more perplexing social problems facing our society today. Because of the seriousness of this problem, sociologists and other social-behavioral scientists are beginning to pay serious attention to sex and race segregation in the workplace (Aronowitz and DiFazio 1994; Smith and Witt 1995; Tomaskovic-Devey 1993). We would rate this problem as being number one among a myriad of social problems facing the nation.

Our book, which addresses the workplace concerns of both women and ethnic minorities pursuing and/or already involved in professional careers, takes as its subject matter several professional career tracts that have been identified as being critically important as we move closer to the twenty-first century.

Having a successful professional career is important in American society, and this is especially true today as individuals strive for better training in a widely growing arena of professional fields. Because of the growth of professional fields of employment, it is important to define the term *professions* employed throughout the book. Some of the earliest discussions of professionalism in the United States used the term in ways that would differ from its generic meaning today. In defining professions today, we almost universally mean those occupations that individuals engage in—after adequate training and the awarding of credentials—to earn their annual incomes. More formally, we believe that Freidson (1970, 1973, 1983, 1986) has provided us with a definition that still remains effective. He says (1986:xii):

> Professions are those occupations that have in common credentials testifying to some degree of higher education and that are prerequisites for holding jobs. Higher education presupposes exposure to a body of formal knowledge, a professional discipline.

Freidson's contributions to the study of professions set the stage for a more systematic study of the world of professional occupations. Because of these advances, since the middle to late 1970s, we begin to see a deeper concentration on the contributions women have made within professions and, since the late 1980s, minorities (Freeman 1990).

Many professions exist in the United States today. The exact number of professions is not known to us. What we do know, however, is that to reproduce social relations and enhance life chances, we will need many highly trained people (Reich 1992). Many of the fields of work that hold such importance are analyzed herein. What would our society, homes, and the workplace be like without computer specialists, social workers, dentists, doctors, military personnel, educators, and lawyers? It is a frightening scenario.

Several questions have been used to guide this conclusion. The first question is, "What accounts for the over- and under-representation of women and minorities in the professions analyzed in this book?" The easiest and most straightforward answer is that we are only approaching explanations for questions as difficult as this one, evidenced by the chapters compiled herein. The legislation that freed women and minorities from the restraints imposed upon them, oftentimes in the form of barriers, including the "glass ceiling," was a first step that came with the many Great Society Programs of the 1960s (Murray 1984). In spite of the many criticisms of these programs, they made it possible for women and minority group members to take their rightful place as citizens, gaining access, over time, to the occupational structures operative in the United States (Blau and Duncan 1967; Jaynes and Williams 1989).

Overrepresentation is the result of ghettorization. Underrepresentation is the result of discrimination. Based on the analysis contained in the chapters by Liska, Tang, Scott, Leighninger, Wright, DiTomaso and colleagues, how else, then, do we explain these findings? If either overrepresentation and/or underrepresentation were not problematic, we would not have the "pipeline" problems in science and engineering education which impact national and international educational standings (NSF 1994) and/or sex-segregated workplaces (Jacobs 1995; Reskin and Padavic 1994). These are real issues that continue to plague our society today.

A second question that guides the discussion in this conclusion is, "How do women and minorities fare in earnings, career opportunities, and promotions?" Chapters in this book address the larger ramifications of this question. For example, in the chapter by Wright, "Women in Computer Work," we learn that women have narrowed the gap in earnings when compared to men in computer work. The greatest advances came between 1971 and 1990. Wright argues that as more and more women are employed in the computer business, the more likely their earnings gap with men will lessen. Although inconclusive, Wright's work is important for its empirical base as well as its results of the analysis. In 1982, women earned 83.4 percent of what men earned annually, and by 1990, this gap narrowed to 90 percent.

Another example, in the chapter by DiTomaso and Smith, "Race and Ethnic Minorities and White Women in Management," shows an almost opposite effect. The authors found that major disparities still exist for women and minorities in management. Even though the business organization was one of the first to grapple with social change—the result of the modern Civil Rights movement and the demand for jobs and freedom, this chapter's disturbing conclusions send shock waves of reality. Even with the claims corporate America makes for itself on diversity, equal opportunity, and affirmative action, DiTomaso and Smith have uncovered information pointing to the exact opposite. This helps them demonstrate that career opportunities are not that attractive when looked at empirically. In an analysis of primary data, some of it from the Equal Employment Opportunity Commission, the authors examined inequalities via the performance appraisal system. They found that prior to the advent of progressive civil rights legislation, women and minorities were rated lower than were whites on their job appraisal ratings in the managerial labor force. Puzzling, though, is their other finding—that after civil rights legislation was passed, women and minorities' job ratings improved and, in some instances, they were rated above white males. The complexities of this type of research are clear and the call for further research along these lines is well-founded.

The concerns regarding job promotions were directly addressed by Smith. When looking at officer career mobility of African Americans in the U.S. military, Smith found that African American officers were promoted less often than their white counterparts. As he put it:

> Yet, when one understands mobility in the U.S. armed forces, we are more likely to understand that advancement up the ranks as officers is critical to where one begins this process.

That is to say, if African Americans are to ever gain parity with their white male and female officers in military service, then they must obtain a good number of the coveted seats in Officer Candidate School classrooms as opposed to Reserve Officer Training Corps programs. The answers, by different authors, to the second question are not very encouraging.

The third question examined is, "Is there any evidence of segregation by sex and/or race in specialties and in work settings?" Tang zeros in on this question in "Medical School Faculty Then and Now." She shows in her chapter that gaps still exist between male and female medical school faculty, beginning with the fact that scientists pay little attention to the composition of medical school faculties—which remain predominantly white and male. Tang's chapter also shows that 10 percent of the medical schools in America employ 40 percent of the minority faculty. This is so because it is the minority-oriented medical school that employs minority faculty. However we decide to examine this issue, it is spelled *discrimination*. Tang points out that sixty percent of the Puerto Rican faculty were employed by Ponce, Puerto Rico, and Central Del Caribe. A clear pattern of segregation exists. And, while these same patterns are not wholly tolerated in the United States at this point in time, they still exist.

In her analysis, Tang also found that among Hispanic, African American, and Asian medical school faculty, no group, except Asians, approach parity on medical school faculties as per their representation among the U.S. population. Asians comprise 3 percent of the population and 9 percent of medical school faculty. Tang notes that women have increased their representation among medical school faculty, from 16 percent in 1980 to 23 percent in 1993. And, while the distinct reason for such a jump over thirteen years is less apparent, it is significant as college and university faculty still rank very high among those occupations which carry above-average prestige rankings.

French sociologist Pierre Bourdieu, who understands the importance of prestige ranking systems of social stratification within advanced postindustrial societies, has written an entire book which examines distinctiveness, or what he calls *tastes*. The prestige factor, says Bourdieu, is a kind of cultural capital (see also Coleman 1988) allowing individuals in certain selected professions to accumulate wealth and power as well. The college/university professor is ranked only behind the well-respected physician, accruing a score of 78 out of 100 (physicians have a score of 82).

Unlike any other book, we deliberately compiled a volume of contributors who would direct their concerns to women and minorities in mainly white-collar professions. Our fourth question addresses the issue of discrimination, which remains a barrier to career advancement, in a most direct manner. This argument was most forcefully made by Joan Norman

Scott in, "Watching the Changes: Women in Law." Analyzing data on private practice law firms, Scott demonstrates that, prior to the early 1960s, very few, if any, lawyers were women. Currently, women represent approximately 20 percent of the legal profession. Using data from telephone interviews, Scott argues that the mark of success in a private law practice is obtaining a partnership. Controlling for other extraneous irrelevant factors, Scott shows that female partnerships are only half the rate of men's:

> The findings from the survey by the Women Lawyers Association of Los Angeles . . . suggest that women have a lot to learn. . . . A woman lawyer in her mid-30s whom I interviewed in the study learned the hard way what it is all about. For four months, "Laura" commuted thirty miles daily, from her West Side office to a new East Side branch office. She had volunteered to open the new office fully expecting her effort to be rewarded with the position of managing partner. In addition to attending to the myriad details involving the opening of a new branch office, Laura maintained her general practice and supervised the care of her invalid mother. Because her hours were extraordinary, Laura missed those critical informal and formal settings where networking takes place, that is, the lunches and golf games with senior partners and potential clients in which her male counterpart participated. Her male counterpart became the managing partner of the branch office Laura built, without ever setting foot on the premises.

The chapters which make up this book are impressive. The larger arguments for inclusion and the destruction of barriers resonates throughout the book and collectively challenges conventional wisdom regarding the lack of concentration and abilities that women and minorities bring to the workplace.

These chapters demonstrate that women and minorities are still fighting for (and securing, in some instances) equal employment/professional rights that have not been granted to them in the past. This fact alone makes our research of great value, both theoretically and practically, and rings in the call to further explore the topics addressed in this book.

REFERENCES

Aronowitz, Stanley and William DiFazio. 1994. *The Jobless Future: Sci-Tech and the Dogma of Work.* Minneapolis, MN: University of Minnesota Press.

Blau, Peter and Otis D. Duncan. 1967. *The American Occupational Structure.* New York: John Wiley and Sons.

Bourdieu, Pierre. 1984. *Distinction: A Social Critique of the Judgement of Taste.* R. Nice (Trans.). Cambridge, MA: Harvard University Press.

Coleman, James. 1988. "Social Capital in the Creation of Human Capital." *American Journal of Sociology* 94:s95–s120.

Freeman, Sue. 1990. *Managing Lives: Corporate Women and Social Change.* Amherst, MA: University of Massachusetts Press.

Freidson, Eliot. 1970. *Profession of Medicine.* New York: Dodd, Mead.

———. 1973. "Professionalism and the Organization of Middle-Class Labor in Postindustrial Society." *Sociological Review Monograph* 20:47–59.

———. 1983. "The Reorganization of the Professions By Regulation." *Law and Human Behavior* 7:279–290

———. 1986. *Professional Power.* Chicago: University of Chicago Press.

Jacobs, Jerry A. Ed. 1995. *Gender Inequality at Work.* Thousand Oaks, CA: Sage.

Jaynes, Gerald and Robin Williams, Jr. 1989. *A Common Destiny: Blacks and American Society.* Washington, DC: National Academy Press.

Murray, Charles. 1984. *Losing Ground: American Social Policy, 1950–1980.* New York: Basic Books.

National Science Foundation. 1994. *Women, Minorities, and Persons with Disabilities in Science and Engineering.* Arlington, VA: National Science Foundation (NSF 94–333).

Reich, Robert. 1994. *The Work of Nations: Preparing Ourselves for 21st Century Capitalism.* New York: Random House.

Reskin, Barbara and Irene Padavic. 1994. *Women and Men at Work.* Thousand Oaks, CA: Pine Forge Press.

Smith, Earl and Stephanie Witt. 1995. "The Experience of African American Women in the Academic Workplace: Doubly Disadvantaged or Meeting the Challenge of Greater Opportunity." *Review of Public Personnel Administration* 15:24–40.

Tomaskovic–Devey, Donald. 1993. *Gender and Racial Inequality at Work: The Sources and Consequences of Job Segregation.* Ithaca, NY: ILR Press.

Contributors

Boris W. Becker is a professor and coordinator of the marketing program in the College of Business at Oregon State University. Becker's previous research has appeared in *Journal of Organizational Behavior, Public Opinion Quarterly, Journal of Marketing, Journal of Marketing Research, Journal of Advertising,* and *Journal of Advertising Research.* He has an ongoing interest in management and the marketing of services, particularly professional services, and in the influence of personal values on consumer and organizational phenomena. He recently published "Personal Values and Management: What Do We Know and Why Don't We Know More" (with Patrick E. Connor) in *Management Inquiry* and "Positioning Health Care Services: Yellow Pages Advertising and Dental Practice Performance" (with Dennis O. Kaldenberg and James H. McAlexander) in *Journal of Health Care Marketing.*

Nancy DiTomaso is a professor and chair of the Department of Organization and Management at Rutgers, the State University of New Jersey. She received her Ph.D. from the University of Wisconsin, Madison. Her research interests include the management of diversity and change in organizations. Her recent research includes a multi-company survey of diversity among scientists and engineers.

Dennis O. Kaldenberg is a research associate and director of the professional services program of the Marketing Department in the College of Business at Oregon State University. Kaldenberg's previous research has appeared in *Journal of Organizational Behavior, Journal of Advertising, Journal of the American College of Dentists,* and *Journal of Advertising Research.* His research interests include the professions, research methodology, and marketing of services. Current work includes a study of the personal values of dentists. Some recent publications include "Work and Commitment

Among Young Professionals: A Comparison of Male and Female Dentists" in *Human Relations* (with Boris W. Becker and Anisa Zvonkovic) and "Mail Survey Response Rates in a Population of Elderly" in *Public Opinion Quarterly* (with Harold Koenig and Boris W. Becker).

Leslie Leighninger, M.S.W. (Syracuse University) and D.S.W. (University of California, Berkeley) is a professor and associate dean at the School of Social Work, Louisiana State University. Her major research interests are social policy, sociology of professions, and the history of social work and social welfare. Her dissertation on social work history since 1930 led to the publication of *Social Work: Search for Identity* in 1987. Recent publications include "Historiography," an entry in the *Encyclopedia of Social Work*, 19th ed., 1995, and *Social Work, Social Welfare and American Society*, with Philip R. Popple, 3rd ed., 1996.

Allan Liska is currently with the University of Maryland. His main interest is studying culture. In particular, he is interested in Native American cultures and the developing culture of the Internet. His most recent works include "Ghost Dancers Rise," published in *Humanity and Society*, and "The Internet As a Post-Model Culture," available in the *Progressive Sociologists Network* Gopher Site.

Joan Norman Scott, Ph.D., has applied her sociological training from the University of Southern California to watching the changes in the law profession from the vantage point of spouse to a senior partner of a major law firm. Her research efforts present, from a historical prospective, the contemporary picture of men and women lawyers in a large metropolitan city. Other publications include topics about the courtroom experience of senior citizens as victims and witnesses of crime, the relevance of age and social roles to women professionals, and children's attitudes toward aging. Her research interests continue to track the ongoing changes in the law profession as men and women work together as peers.

Earl Smith is a professor and dean of the Division of Social Sciences at Pacific Lutheran University in Tacoma, Washington. He received his Ph.D. from the University of Connecticut at Storrs. His major research interests are in the areas of race relations, the sociology of sport, urban sociology, and the sociology of science.

Steven A. Smith is currently a doctoral candidate at Rutgers University's Graduate School of Management, where he also teaches the course "Managing Diversity in Organizations." His research interests are in the fields of organizational and institutional theory, labor market economics, and the management of scientists and engineers. He received both his B.S. in chemical engineering and his M.B.A. from Rutgers University.

Joyce Tang is an assistant professor of sociology at Queens College of the City University of New York. Her research focuses on the careers of scientists and engineers. She is conducting a study on the career experiences of academic and nonacademic engineers in the United States.

Rosemary Wright is an assistant professor of sociology at the Florham-Madison campus of Fairleigh Dickinson University, where she teaches courses on computers and society, gender, inequality, and work. She does research on women in computing, management, and traditionally male occupations in general. For over a decade, prior to becoming a sociologist, she was a computer professional, manager, and consultant. Her current projects expand on the research described in this volume.

Anisa M. Zvonkovic is an associate professor of human development and family sciences at Oregon State University. Her area of primary research interest is work and family. Zvonkovic's previous research has appeared in *Journal of Social and Personal Relationships, Marriage and Family Review, Human Relations*, and *Journal of Family and Economic Issues*. Her recent work includes "The Marital Construction of Gender Through Work and Family Decisions: A Qualitative Analysis" (with Kathleen M. Greaves, Cynthia J. Schmiege, and Leslie D. Hall) in *Journal of Marriage and the Family* and "Influence Strategies Used When Couples Make Work/Family Decisions and Their Importance for Marital Satisfaction" (with Cynthia J. Schmiege and Leslie D. Hall) in *Family Relations*. Her newest grant concerns how families involved in the fishing occupation manage their family lives and businesses around the extended absences and dangers that are part of the fishing industry.

Index